D0213772

Preventing Early
School Failure

Related Titles of Interest

Bechtol and Sorenson, *Restructuring Schooling for Individual Students*

Choate, *Successful Mainstreaming: Proven Ways to Detect and Correct Special Needs*

Crawford, *Language and Literacy Learning in Multicultural Classrooms*

Mann, Suiter, and McClung, *A Guide to Educating Mainstreamed Students, Fourth Edition*

Radencich, Beers, and Schumm, *A Handbook for the K–12 Reading Resource Specialist*

Slavin, Karweit, and Madden, *Effective Programs for Students at Risk*

Preventing Early School Failure

Research, Policy, and Practice

Robert E. Slavin

Nancy L. Karweit

Barbara A. Wasik

EDITORS

The Johns Hopkins University

Allyn and Bacon
Boston • London • Toronto • Sydney • Tokyo • Singapore

LB1139.25
.P76
1994

Copyright © 1994 by Allyn and Bacon
A Division of Simon & Schuster, Inc.
160 Gould Street
Needham Heights, Massachusetts 02194

All rights reserved. No part of the material protected by this copyright
notice may be reproduced or utilized in any form or by any means, electronic
or mechanical, including photocopying, recording, or by any information
storage and retrieval system, without written permission from the
copyright owner.

Library of Congress Cataloging-in-Publication Data

Preventing early school failure : research, policy, and practice/
  Robert E. Slavin, Nancy L. Karweit, Barbara A. Wasik, editors.
      p.   cm.
  Includes bibliographical references and index.
  ISBN 0-205-13991-4 (casebound)
  ISBN 0-205-15684-3 (paperback)
  1. Early childhood education—United States. 2. School failure—
United States. 3. School management and organization—United
States. I. Slavin, Robert E. II. Karweit, Nancy L. III. Wasik,
Barbara A.
LB1139.25.P76 1993
372.21'0973—dc20   93-16546
                                                           CIP

Printed in the United States of America
10 9 8 7 6 5 4 3   97 96 95

For our children—
Jacob, Benjamin, Rebecca, Jennifer, Alex, and Julia

PUR 4/26/96 DBCN ACY-3828

MAY 14 1996

Contents

Preface

Once upon a time there was a town that happened to have a playground located at the edge of a cliff. Every so often a child would fall off this cliff and be seriously injured. At last the town council decided to take action but was immediately deadlocked on what to do. Should they put a fence at the top of the cliff or an ambulance at the bottom?

In education, we have long been in the business of putting "ambulances at the bottom of the cliff" to help children who fall behind their peers in academic performance. We wait until children fail in the early grades and then provide remedial or special education. These services are extremely expensive and not very effective. Wouldn't it be better to keep at-risk children from falling behind in the first place?

Over the past decade, there has been a growing consensus among researchers and policy makers that prevention of learning problems makes much more sense than remediation. One of President Clinton's key education policies is to support a dramatic expansion of Head Start. Educators can readily accept the idea that an ounce of prevention is worth a pound of cure, but an ounce of *what*? Is preschool enough, or is intervention before or after age 4 necessary to prevent school failure? What about tutoring first-graders, or changing school organization, or reducing class size, or changing curriculum?

The purpose of this book is to review research on the most widely proposed alternatives intended to keep at-risk students from failing in the early grades. We have reviewed research on each of many programs and strategies and have used a common set of standards and procedures so that educators and policy makers can compare the likely effectiveness of each. Our conclusions based on our reviews of hundreds of studies are both optimistic and cautionary. Our optimism is based on clear evidence that early school failure can be prevented for almost all at-risk children, and research and development now under way is continuing to provide means of expanding the number of children who can be guaranteed success in the early grades. Our caution, however, is based on a growing consensus that in itself preschool for 4-year-olds is not enough to ensure success for at-risk children. Expanding Head Start is a good idea, but it will not solve the serious educational problems of so many children headed for failure, special education, or long-term remediation.

Preventing Early School Failure: Research, Policy, and Practice is intended to be read by researchers, educators, policy makers, and students interested in prevention of early learning failure. It provides no sure-fire formulas for success, but instead offers the reader an intelligent, thoroughly documented discussion of the state of the art in prevention and early intervention. We know that a fence at the top of the cliff is better than an ambulance at the bottom. This book is a fencemaker's guide to early education.

ACKNOWLEDGMENTS

This book was written under funding from the Office of Educational Research and Improvement (OERI), U.S. Department of Education (No. OERI-R-117-R90002). Research conducted by the authors and summarized in this book was supported by grants from OERI and from the Carnegie Corporation of New York, the Pew Charitable Trusts, the Abell Foundation, and France and Merrick Foundations. However, any opinions expressed are those of the authors.

We would like to thank Nancy A. Anderson of the University of South Florida, Carol Anne Pierson of the University of Central Arkansas, and Gloria Albanese of the John F. Kennedy School in Somerville, Massachusetts, for their helpful comments on an earlier draft. We would also like to thank Alta Shaw, K. Lynne Mainzer, Robert Petza, Mary Alice Bond, Elizabeth Lowry, Verian Dunbar, Barbara Haxby, Gretta Gordy, Irene Waclawiw, and Cherie Jones of the Johns Hopkins University for their help.

About the Editors

Robert E. Slavin is currently Director of the Early and Elementary School Program at the Center for Research on Effective Schooling for Disadvantaged Students at Johns Hopkins University. He received his B.A. in Psychology from Reed College in 1972 and his Ph.D. in Social Relations in 1975. Dr. Slavin has authored or coauthored more than 120 articles and 11 books, including *Educational Psychology: Theory into Practice* (Allyn and Bacon, 1986, 1988, 1991, 1994), *School and Classroom Organization* (Erlbaum, 1989), *Effective Programs for Students at Risk* (Allyn and Bacon, 1989), and *Cooperative Learning: Theory, Research, and Practice* (Prentice Hall, 1990). He has received the American Educational Research Association's Raymond B. Cattell Early Career Award for Programmatic Research in 1986 and the Palmer O. Johnson Award for the best article in an American Education Research Association journal in 1988.

Nancy L. Karweit is currently a principal research scientist at the Johns Hopkins University's Center for Research on Effective Schooling for Disadvantaged Students. She received her Ph.D. in Sociology from the Johns Hopkins University in 1976. She is a coauthor of *Effective Programs for Students at Risk* (Allyn and Bacon, 1989) and *Friends in School* (Academic Press, 1983). Her work has focused on school organization, time and learning, disadvantaged students, and development of integrated curriculum for prekindergarten and kindergarten classrooms.

Barbara A. Wasik is a research scientist at the Center for Effective Schooling for Disadvantaged Students at Johns Hopkins University. She received her B.A. and M.A. from Rutgers University and her Ph.D. in developmental psychology from Temple University. Dr. Wasik has written on metacognition, early intervention, and tutoring. She directs the development and implementation of the tutoring component of Success for All. Currently, she is developing an early learning program that will focus on developmentally appropriate curriculum for children from birth to kindergarten.

Preventing Early School Failure

► 1

Preventing Early School Failure

The Challenge and the Opportunity

ROBERT E. SLAVIN

We live in a remarkable period in the history of American education. Reform is in the air; from the White House to the schoolhouse, there is a broad consensus that a major restructuring of our education system is needed.

While most of the restructuring proposals now being discussed are still at the rhetorical or pilot stage, there is one area in which actual reform is proceeding at a remarkable rate. This is the area of early childhood education. There is a growing consensus among policy makers and educators that effective interventions in preschool, kindergarten, and/or first grade will pay off in later achievement, reduced need for remedial and special education, and other outcomes. More remarkably, legislatures, school districts, and other funding agencies have actually devoted substantial funds to strengthening early childhood education. This investment has gone into quite varied programs. National Head Start funding has steadily increased, and many states and districts are expanding preschool opportunities for 4-year-olds and full-day kindergartens for 5-year-olds. Others have implemented IBM's Writing to Read program in kindergarten and first grades. The state of Mississippi has expanded this program statewide. Tennessee, Indiana, Nevada, and school districts

1

elsewhere have implemented substantial reductions in class size in the early grades. Reading Recovery, a first-grade tutoring program, is now widely used in Ohio and is expanding rapidly across the country. All of these interventions, plus others that are less widely used or less publicized, begin with the same rationale: Start students off with success, and they will build on this success throughout their school careers. Much of the interest in early childhood interventions focuses on disadvantaged students who are believed to be likely to fall behind in basic skills in the early grades and then never catch up.

PREVENTING SCHOOL FAILURE: THE CHALLENGE

The many changes now occurring in early childhood education are taking place against a backdrop of growing concern about the effectiveness of our nation's schools, particularly for the children of the poor. This concern is certainly warranted. The National Assessment of Educational Progress (NAEP) (Mullis & Jenkins, 1990) has found steadily increasing reading scores for African-American and Hispanic students, but these students still fall far behind nonminority students. On the 1988 assessment, 62 percent of all 9-year-olds could read at what is called the basic level, but only 39 percent of African-American 9-year-olds could do so. Yet the basic level is hardly considered stellar performance for *any* 9-year-old. To illustrate this, a sample item indicating basic performance is as follows (Mullis & Jenkins, 1990, p. 27):

> Read the story below so that you can answer a question without looking back at the story.
>
> Timothy wasn't big enough to play ball. In the summer he sat on the steps of his brownstone building and watched things. People washing cars. Children playing games. Teenagers standing in circles talking about how hot it was. Workers tearing down the building across the street.
>
> DO NOT LOOK BACK!

Without looking back at the story, answer the following question:

What were the teenagers talking about?

A. Timothy
B. Music

C. How hot it was
D. The people washing cars
E. The building across the street

In schools serving large numbers of disadvantaged students, the situation is, of course, much worse. In our own research on our Success for All program (Slavin, Madden, Karweit, Dolan, & Wasik, 1992) the lowest-performing quarter of students could hardly read at all at the end of first grade. They averaged a grade equivalent of 1.2 (first grade, second month) on individually administered measures. This means, for example, that these students were unable to read and comprehend the following simple passage from the Durrell Silent Reading scale (Durrell & Catterson, 1980):

I have a little black dog. He has a pink nose. He has a little tail. He can jump and run.

One outcome of widespread reading failure is a high rate of retentions in urban districts. In many, 20 percent or more of the children repeat first grade, and more than half of all students have repeated at least one grade by the time they leave elementary school. In the early grades, performing below grade-level expectations in reading is the primary reason for retention.

The consequences of failing to learn to read in the early grades are severe. Longitudinal studies find that disadvantaged third-graders who have failed one or more grades and are reading below grade level are extremely unlikely to complete high school (Lloyd, 1978; Kelly, Veldman, & McGuire, 1964). Remedial programs, such as Chapter 1, have few, if any, effects on students beyond the third grade (see Kennedy, Birman, & Demaline, 1986). Many children are referred to special education programs largely on the basis of reading failure, and then remain in special education for many years, often for their entire school careers.

Almost all children, regardless of social class or other factors, enter first grade full of enthusiasm, motivation, and self-confidence, fully expecting to succeed in school (see, for example, Entwistle & Hayduk, 1981). By the end of first grade, many of these students have already discovered that their initial high expectations are not coming true, and they have begun to see school as punishing and demeaning. Trying to remediate reading failure later on is very difficult because by then students who have failed are likely to be unmotivated, to have poor self-concepts as learners, to be anxious about reading, and to hate it. Reform is needed at all levels of education, but no goal of reform is as important as seeing that all children start their school careers with success, confidence, and a firm foundation in basic skills. Success in the early grades does not guarantee success throughout the school years and beyond, but failure in the early grades does virtually guarantee failure in later schooling. This is one problem that must be solved.

PREVENTING SCHOOL FAILURE: THE OPPORTUNITY

Looking at the long-standing and seemingly intractable problems of education, it is easy to be pessimistic. The litanies of problems constantly seen in the popular press and elsewhere make the situation sound hopeless: Increasing drug use, disintegration of families, lack of respect for teachers, television watching, and increasing numbers of minority students are common culprits (see, for example, Natriello, McDill, & Pallas, 1990). These problems are indeed serious, although by this point they are hardly new. It is interesting to note that the very groups presumed to suffer most from these trends, African Americans and Hispanics, are the only groups who are increasing in achievement over the years. In contrast, the reading achievement of white students aged 9, 13, and 17 has increased only slightly since 1971, and not at all since 1975 (Mullis & Jenkins, 1990).

The main reason for optimism lies not so much in the continuing (though slow) improvement in the performance of minority students as in other developments on the horizon. There are two things that must happen if there is to be a marked improvement in the academic performance of young students. First, there must be a strong commitment of resources and support from policy makers. Solving the problem of school failure is going to take money over the long haul, and it is going to take sustained interest by legislators, political leaders, and the public at large in doing so. Second, there must be proven, reliable, and replicable means of turning money into success for young children. That is, there must be programs far more effective than those in general use today capable of ensuring reading success for virtually all children.

On the first criterion there are several promising signs. The 1988 Hawkins-Stafford Act allowed schools, especially those serving large numbers of disadvantaged students, to use their Chapter 1 resources more flexibly, and in recent years the U.S. Congress increased Chapter 1 funds by more than $2 billion, to about $6.7 billion per year in 1992. As mentioned earlier, states and districts throughout the United States are investing heavily in programs for young children, such as preschool, extended-day kindergarten, reduced class size in first grades, and IBM's Writing to Read program. Several states have been forced by legislative and political pressures to reduce funding inequalities between wealthy and less wealthy districts. In general this means major increases in funding for poor districts. In New Jersey, one of the states moving toward funding equalization at this writing, districts about to receive additional funding must submit plans showing how they will use these funds on proven programs to increase student achievement. Kentucky has also linked funding equalization to use of effective practices, including expanded preschool opportunities.

Increased funding in itself is no guarantee of enhanced outcomes. The new monies must be spent on reliably effective programs. On this front there is also major progress on the horizon. The principal purpose of this book is to review the evidence on programs capable of preventing reading failure on a broad scale. The conclusion we draw from this evidence is unequivocal: *Virtually every child can be successful in the early grades.* The success of every child can be ensured by using programs that are now available and that can (with care) be replicated on a wide scale. "Virtually every child" means all children who are not mentally retarded or do not have extreme learning disabilities; there is evidence to suggest that even most students currently identified as having a learning disability on the basis of reading problems can also be successful if they are given appropriate instruction and other services from the beginning of their school experience (or earlier). Evidence that virtually every child can learn to read comes from studies of one-to-one tutoring (Chapter 7); of the Success for All program, which also uses one-to-one tutoring (Chapter 8); and of many other programs and practices that contribute to reading success in the early grades and could therefore be part of a comprehensive reorganization of the elementary grades.

The knowledge that school failure is preventable could (and should) fundamentally change the political calculus surrounding the education of students at risk of school failure. Many policy makers and even many educators believe that adding significant resources to schools, particularly inner-city schools, is money down a rat hole, that any additional money would simply be misspent or mismanaged. Many others have serious doubts about whether the problems of urban schools are solvable under any circumstances until "underclass" parents begin to behave like middle-class parents. A clear understanding that at least one key problem, early school failure, is essentially solvable would go a long way toward dispelling these myths and the related belief that money doesn't matter.

There is a profound and unique opportunity presented by the confluence of the two trends currently on the horizon—a growing recognition that school failure can be prevented and a political willingness to spend money on programs that are known to work. Sooner or later, a school district or state is going to be in a position to eliminate failure among its students, and will decide to do so. If this district or state is successful, others will surely follow. Early school failure could be perceived as being like a preventable disease such as typhoid or polio. No one begrudges funding to fight such diseases because money spent on preventing them is known to pay off in enhanced public health. With continued research, continued development, continued dissemination of effective strategies, and a political will to do what it takes to eradicate it, early failure for nonretarded children could someday become as rare as typhoid or polio— scourges of an earlier age.

THE PURPOSE OF THIS BOOK

The purpose of this book is to explore the impacts of the most widely discussed, widely implemented, and plausible early intervention programs on success in early schooling, especially in early reading. We have chosen to focus on early reading for several reasons. First, there is widespread acceptance of the conclusion that students who fail to learn to read in the first grade are seriously at risk. If a child fails to read, he or she is in deep trouble. Reading performance can be readily measured in the early grades by using individually administered measures (although there is serious debate about the meaning of standardized reading test results for young children). Perhaps most importantly, there is little question that success in first grade is essentially synonymous with success in reading. Few first-graders who are reading adequately are retained or assigned to special education programs. It cannot be said that students who are good and enthusiastic readers in the early grades are always assured success throughout their school careers. There are many other subjects to be mastered and pitfalls to be avoided on the journey to high school and college graduation. Yet it can assuredly be said that students who fail to read well in the early grades will almost always have difficulties in school.

In addition to reading, there are other indicators of early school success or failure emphasized in this book. One is retention in grade, and another is assignment to special education for learning problems. These are, of course, highly correlated with reading failure, but are by no means identical; several programs have effects on reading but not on retentions or special education placements, and others have effects on retentions or special education but not on reading.

Several studies, especially of early childhood (birth to age 5) programs, have used IQ or IQ-related language measures as outcomes. These are important predictors of school success, but it is less valid to see them as indicators of success in themselves. Because they are often the only mea- sures available for young children, IQ-related measures are emphasized in studies of young children. However, once students enter first grade, read- ing performance, retention, and special education placement become more valid indicators of success and failure than IQ. If a third-grader is reading well, keeping up with her class, and staying out of special education, she is succeeding, regardless of her IQ. If she is far behind in reading, failing her grade, or in a special education program for learning disabilities, she is failing, no matter how high her IQ. Unfortunately, an overemphasis on IQ (rather than achievement) in U.S. psychology and education has created a situation in which many otherwise excellent longitudinal studies of early intervention programs have failed to measure students' actual achievement, but have focused primarily or entirely on IQ (see Chapters 2 and 3).

The types of approaches to early childhood education discussed in this book vary widely. One category includes provision of programs before formal reading instruction begins, such as preschool, kindergarten, and such intensive early intervention programs as the Milwaukee Project (Garber, 1988) and Abecedarian Project (Ramey & Campbell, 1984). Within this category are studies both of provision of services (e.g., preschool vs. no preschool, full-day vs. half-day kindergarten) and of particular instructional approaches within a given type of early childhood service (e.g., IBM's Writing to Read program and other kindergarten models).

A second category of approaches to at-risk youngsters involves a variety of means of giving young students additional time if they appear to need it, allowing further development to take place before full-scale reading instruction begins. Examples of such "extra-time" policies range from retaining students in kindergarten or first grade to providing "developmental kindergarten" or "transitional first grade" programs that add a specially designed year of instruction between kindergarten and first grade for students who do not appear ready for first grade. The idea behind such programs is that there are students who have late birthdays or who are slow to develop but just need a little more time in a supportive environment and will then be more likely to start their formal schooling (in first grade) with success.

Other approaches to ensuring success in the early grades involve interventions in first grade and beyond, when students have entered the formal curriculum. One issue at this level has to do with such features of school and classroom organization as class size, instruction aides, reading groups, and the nongraded primary. An old intervention program experiencing a considerable revival is one-to-one tutoring for first-graders who are at risk for reading failure. Success for All—a program that combines one-to-one tutoring with many other changes in curriculum, instruction, and school and classroom organization—incorporates much of what is currently known about preventing reading failure.

This book reviews research on all these strategies and uses a common set of standards of evidence in synthesizing outcomes. Whenever possible, long-term effects, as well as immediate effects, of the programs are considered. No simplistic ranking of programs is provided, but the chapters do attempt to identify the types of early childhood programs that have the strongest evidence of effectiveness, as well as those that have little promise or that have not been adequately researched. The book is not intended to provide educators with a cookbook (take one unit of preschool, two units of tutoring . . .), but it does try to provide the information needed for educators and policy makers to intelligently design school programs that are likely to prevent failure for the largest possible number of children.

WHY MONEY MATTERS

One important feature common to most of the programs and policies discussed in this book is that they are expensive, and most fall within similar orders of magnitude of cost. For example, reducing class size by half (e.g., from 30 to 15) requires hiring an additional certified teacher for each class. This same teacher could teach a preschool class, could be added to the kindergarten staff to enable a school to have full-day kindergarten, or could tutor about 15 low-achieving first-graders 20 minutes per day. Retention or provision of extra-year programs for kindergartners or first-graders adds one year's per-pupil cost per child—about $5,000 in round numbers. The implementation of Writing to Read and other integrated computer-assisted instruction programs requires at least one additional aide per school plus initial and continuing costs roughly comparable to the cost of additional certified teachers. Only such policies as changing elements of curriculum and school organization are relatively cost free, and few would expect such changes by themselves to lead to a major reduction in school failures. The growing investment in such expensive interventions as preschool, extended-day kindergarten, Writing to Read, and tutoring for young children is heartening in that it indicates our society's increasing concern for the success of all children, and an understanding that effective uses of increased monies in the early grades can pay off in economic terms in the long run (see Barnett & Escobar, 1987).

However, the costly nature of many of the innovations proposed for the early grades also creates a need for rigorous research and evaluation. For large numbers of school districts or states to invest heavily in a particular approach and then have that approach turn out to be ineffective would not only waste a great deal of taxpayers' money but would, more importantly, undermine policy makers' faith in educators' abilities to solve important educational problems, a disaster of the first order. The perceived failure of the Follow Through Planned Variation study of the 1970s (see, for example, Kennedy, 1978; Rhine, 1981), which compared several promising approaches to instruction in grades 1 through 3, set back government support for research-based innovation by more than a decade. The problem was that most of the methods evaluated in the Planned Variation study had never been evaluated before. They were subjected to a high-profile, high-stakes evaluation involving implementations in many geographically and demographically diverse sites before anyone knew whether they worked anywhere and certainly before anyone knew the conditions necessary for them to work. As a result, the evaluations found that most of the methods did not produce better outcomes than control groups.

In the new cycle of reform, educators and administrators must avoid repeating the mistakes of Planned Variation. This time rigorous standards must be applied to evaluations of programs so that when schools and districts begin to replicate and evaluate programs they will know what they must do to see that the programs will succeed, and if they do those things, they will see their children succeeding.

SCOPE AND METHODS OF REVIEWS

The chapters in this book review research on the effects of various early childhood interventions on the performance of young children, particularly those who are at risk for reading failure. The reviews presented in each chapter use a review method called "best-evidence synthesis" (Slavin, 1986)—a technique combining elements of meta-analytic and traditional narrative reviews. In each area, a broad literature search is conducted to identify a set of studies that meet preestablished criteria in terms of internal and external validity.

The major outcome of interest in all the chapters is reading in the early elementary grades (grades 1 through 3). Whenever possible, individually administered reading measures are emphasized. The inadequacies of group-administered standardized tests are well known, but in recent years, as schools have learned to teach narrowly to standardized tests, first-grade tests have become particularly susceptible to "teaching-to-the-test" effects (see Koretz, Linn, Dunbar, & Shepard, 1991). However, when group-administered standardized tests are the only measures available, effects on these measures are reported (with appropriate qualifications).

In most cases, effects of various programs are characterized as effect sizes. These are computed as the difference in performance between students who received a given program and those who did not, divided by the comparison group's standard deviation (Glass, McGaw, & Smith, 1981). When means or standard deviations are not reported, effects sizes are estimated from Fs, ts or other statistics (see Glass, McGaw, & Smith, 1981). The numerator of the effect size formula may be adjusted for pretests or covariates by computation of gain scores or use of ANCOVA, but the denominator is always the unadjusted individual level standard deviation of the control group, or (if necessary) a pooled standard deviation. If effect sizes cannot be computed, then program effects are simply characterized as significantly positive or negative, or as not significantly different from the comparison group (see Slavin, 1986).

INCLUSION CRITERIA

In order to be considered germane to the scope of this book, studies had to meet the following criteria:

1. The programs evaluated had to be directed toward increasing the success of students in the early grades, in particular success in reading and in avoiding retention and special education placement.
2. Special education programs were excluded, although programs primarily intended to prevent special education placements were included.
3. Programs involving instruction in languages other than English (e.g., bilingual education) were not included.
4. Studies included had to compare students in the program to students receiving instruction typical for their age level. For example, students in preschool programs might be compared to those out of school (a typical arrangement for 4-year-olds), while at-risk first-graders in a tutoring program might be compared to similar students receiving traditional Chapter 1 services.
5. Evidence had to be presented to indicate that the comparison group was initially similar to the experimental group on achievement level, measures of intelligence, socioeconomic status, and/or other variables, either through measurement of these variables or random assignment of individual students to treatments.

These criteria excluded very few studies that assessed programs for young children designed to prevent school failure, as the great majority of studies of such programs include control groups and present evidence of initial equality. Additional inclusion criteria and descriptions of types of studies included appear in several of the chapters in this book, but every attempt was made to use similar selection procedures and other methods in the different chapters so that comparisons across chapters (and therefore across program types) can legitimately be made.

A FINAL WORD OF INTRODUCTION

This book represents the state of the art regarding programs and practices designed to prevent early school failure. It should go without saying that the conclusions drawn can only be interim ones, as later evidence may change them. On the other hand, it is clear that a great deal is known about preventing school failure. This book reviews hundreds of studies. Although evidence concerning some of the programs reviewed is too limited in quantity or quality for solid conclusions, that concerning others is relatively clear and consistent. There is more than enough evidence in this book to support the idea that school failure can be prevented, but the *most* effective or cost-effective ways of doing so can certainly be disputed. We have tried to avoid oversimplified presentations of summative effect sizes; rather, we have tried to provide "order of magnitude" estimates of program effects and informed discussions of the substantive and methodological issues characteristic of each type of research we reviewed. We have tried to be no more technical than necessary, yet still be complete enough and clear enough about our procedures so that later researchers could replicate our methods and findings.

The evidence presented in this book has profound implications for educational policy and practice, but we are not revolutionaries. Rather, we are researchers who believe that through a painstaking process of research and development and clear presentation of findings (and their limitations), we can move forward the practice of education. The reader who is looking for quick fixes or easy answers will not find them in these pages, but the reader who is looking for intelligent discussion of practical means of preventing school failure among our nation's children will, we hope, find it in this volume.

REFERENCES

Barnett, W. S., & Escobar, C. M. (1987). The economics of early educational intervention: A review. *Review of Educational Research, 57,* 387–414.

Durrell, D., & Catterson, J. (1980). *Durrell Analysis of Reading Difficulty.* New York: The Psychological Corporation.

Entwistle, D., & Hayduk, L. (1981). Academic expectations and the school achievement of young children. *Sociology of Education, 54,* 34–50.

Garber, H. L. (1988). *The Milwaukee Project: Preventing mental retardation in children at risk.* Washington, DC: American Association on Mental Retardation.

Glass, G. V., McGaw, B., & Smith, M. L. (1981). *Meta-analysis in social research.* Beverly Hills, CA: Sage.

Kelly, F. J., Veldman, D.J., & McGuire, C. (1964). Multiple discriminant prediction of delinquency and school dropouts. *Educational and Psychological Measurement, 24,* 535–544.

Kennedy, M. M. (1978). Findings from the Follow Through Planned Variation study. *Educational Researcher, 7,* 3–11.

Kennedy, M. M., Birman, B.F., & Demaline, R. (1986). *The effectiveness of Chapter 1 services.* Washington, DC: U.S. Department of Education.

Koretz, D. M., Linn, R. L., Dunbar, S. B., & Shepard, L. A. (1991, April). *The effects* of high-stakes testing on achievement: Preliminary findings about generalization across tests. Paper presented at the annual meeting of the Education Research Association, Chicago.

Lloyd, D. N. (1978). Prediction of school failure from third-grade data. *Educational and Psychological Measurement, 38,* 1193–1200.

Mullis, I. V. S., & Jenkins, L. B. (1990). *The reading report card, 1971–88.* Washington, DC: U.S. Department of Education.

Natriello, G., McDill, E. L., & Pallas, A. M. (1990). *Schooling disadvantaged children: Racing against catastrophe.* New York: Teachers College Press.

Ramey, C. T., Bryant, D., & Suarez, T. (1985). Preschool compensatory education and the modifiability of intelligence: A critical review. In D. Detterman (Ed.), *Current topics in human intelligence* (pp. 247–296). Norwood, NJ: Ablex.

Ramey, C. T., & Campbell, F. A. (1984). Preventive education for high-risk children: Cognitive consequences of the Carolina Abecedarian Project. *American Journal of Mental Deficiency, 88,* 515–523.

Rhine, W. R. (Ed.). (1981). *Making schools more effective: New directions from Follow Through.* New York: Academic Press.

Slavin, R. E. (1986). Best-evidence synthesis: An alternative to meta-analytic and traditional reviews. *Educational Researcher, 15*(9), 5–11.

Slavin, R. E., Madden, N. A., Karweit, N. L., Dolan, L., & Wasik, B. A. (1992). *Success for All: A relentless approach to prevention and early intervention in elementary schools.* Arlington, VA: Educational Research Service.

Off to a Good Start

Effects of Birth to Three Interventions on Early School Success

BARBARA A. WASIK   NANCY L. KARWEIT

Children who get off to a good start in the early years stand a better chance of being successful in school. Experiences in the years from birth to age 3 set a foundation for language and cognitive skills that prepare children for formal schooling and help prevent school failure. These early experiences are especially important for disadvantaged students who may have limited early experiences and come to school on a very unequal footing with their nondisadvantaged peers.

Over the past 10 years, there has been an increasing emphasis on early intervention. An important milestone in this area has been the passing of the Education for All Handicapped Children Act (Public Law 99–497), which calls for "a statewide, comprehensive, coordinated, multidisciplinary, interagency program of early intervention services for handicapped children and their families" (P.L. 99–457, Sec. 671). Although the law only suggested that discretionary programs for children from birth to age 3 be developed (Part H of the statute), all states elected to begin planning activities for children in this age group. One limitation of P.L. 99–457, however, is that it specifically focuses on children with developmental delays or handicapping conditions. Unfortunately, most children born into poverty do not show early obvious signs of delay. For example, it is easier to identify at an early age a child who has cerebral palsy because of significant delays in motor activities than to identify a child who is not talked to or read to or who lives in a deprived environment. The concern is that many disadvantaged children will not be identified for services from which they could benefit and will continue to enter school poorly prepared to learn.

Research consistently supports the effectiveness of early intervention programs (Casto & White, 1985; Farran, 1990). However, there are still many unanswered questions about these intervention programs. How intensive does an early intervention need to be? Can programs for infants and toddlers have lasting effects on children as they enter first grade, or does intervention need to continue throughout the preschool and early elementary years? At what age does the intervention need to occur in order for it to be beneficial? Are parental intervention or child-focused programs alone as effective as working with both the parent and the child?

The answers to these questions are important because they will help shape policy about early intervention programs. In order for disadvantaged children to be successful in school, they need to enter school with the same skills as nondisadvantaged students. In attempting to provide answers to the questions that have been raised, this chapter reviews research on early intervention programs. Our purpose is to identify key aspects of what makes programs effective and to attempt to determine what components are necessary and sufficient for an effective early intervention program.

SCOPE OF THE REVIEW

Since the issue of program intensity is central to the question of early intervention, we have grouped programs according to the intensity of the intervention: high, moderate, and low intensity. For our purposes, intensity takes into account the extent of intervention, including persons and resources involved, and the duration of the intervention. A high-intensity program is one in which parents and/or children spend an extended period of time and in which there are considerable resources such as special day-care curricula, highly qualified staff, and low staff-to-child ratios. Low-intensity programs, on the other hand, are ones in which the total duration of the program or the weekly contact with the program is relatively short and the resources and staffing are minimal. Moderate-intensity programs are those that fall between these two levels of duration and resource intensity.

Only programs that were evaluated in comparison to equivalent control groups were included in this review. In addition, we included only those programs whose primary focus was on programs for children from birth to age 3, so programs such as Head Start and the Perry Preschool Project, which included 3-year-olds, were not discussed here, but are discussed in Chapter 3 with preschool programs.

Finally, because they are the best data available, we rely primarily on IQ and language proficiency scores, special education referrals, and retention data as measures of children's success in each program. Although we acknowledge that there is controversy regarding the relationship between IQ scores and achievement (Ceci, 1991), IQ and related language assessments are the best measures typically used when assessing children at a young age and following them longitudinally. In long-term follow-ups in the elementary years, we would much prefer measures of achievement (e.g., reading tests), but only one study provided such data.

HIGH-INTENSITY PROGRAMS

The Milwaukee Project

The Milwaukee Project (Garber, 1988) focused on enriching the early experiences of children born to retarded and impoverished mothers. The purpose of this project was to determine if the cognitive development of children born in seriously disadvantaged environments can be altered by providing optimum environments, regardless of the cost or intensity of intervention. In other words, the Milwaukee Project was designed not to test a model that could be easily and cheaply replicated but to test the practical limits of high-quality, early, and continuous intervention. If long-term changes could result from early, intensive intervention, this would be evidence that, in principle, environmental changes could positively affect the outcomes of extremely disadvantaged children.

Families began the Milwaukee Project when their children were as young as 3 months old and continued until entry into first grade. Follow-up data on reading, school achievement, and special education referrals were collected on these children through the fourth grade.

Mothers were selected from one of the poorest neighborhoods in Milwaukee, identified by 1960 census data, to be representative of the general disadvantaged population. Screening for families was done through well-baby clinics by researchers from the University of Wisconsin. Mothers who had healthy deliveries and a standard score of 6 or less on the vocabulary subtest of the Wechsler Adult Intelligence Scale (WAIS) were selected to participate. (This score would typically indicate mild to moderate retardation). Since it was not possible to identify enough infants meeting this criterion who were between 3 and 6 months old at a single point, the selection process occurred over a period of 24 months. When eligible mothers and their children were selected to participate, they were assigned on an alternating basis to either the experimental intervention group or the no-intervention control group. A low-risk comparison group of mothers with average IQs was also selected in order to compare children in the same disadvantaged neighborhoods to children of mothers without cognitive limitations.

A total of 82 infants meeting the criteria were identified during the 24-month screening period. However, 27 could not be assigned for several reasons, including family mobility, refusal to participate, limited English proficiency, or inability of the mother to be administered the WAIS because she was too young. A total of 28 experimental and 28 control families with infants younger than 6 months was assigned over the 24-month period. Even before the study began, 8 families from the experimental group and 7 from the control group dropped out. At the beginning of the study, there were 20 families in the experimental condition and 20 in the control condition. At the end of this longitudinal study, there were 17 experimental families, 18 control families, and 8 low-risk control families. No families were added to the study after the initial selection and placement.

The Milwaukee intervention had two components: a child intervention component that had several phases, and a family/maternal rehabilitation component. The children attended the intervention program seven hours a day, five days a week. The first phase of the child intervention, an infant stimulation program, began when the children were 3 months old. Children were provided with one-on-one care by paraprofessionals who worked on sensory stimulation and social and emotional development. The paraprofessional caregiver spent considerable time playing, talking, touching, and interacting with the children. At approximately 12 months, children began the toddler phase of the program and two caregivers worked with two infants. During this phase, there was increasing emphasis on language skills, including vocabulary development, expressive language skills, and gross and fine motor skills. At about 2 years of age, children entered the early childhood phase of the program. At this point the program was similar to a preschool program and each caregiver worked with a group of three children. Language, problem solving, and motor skills were initially emphasized, but as the children grew, there was increasing emphasis on more academic material, such as alphabet recognition and reading and math readiness skills. There was also an emphasis on the development of social skills.

The parent education component of the Milwaukee Project focused on home management skills as well as basic caregiving skills. Parents were taught such skills as managing household budgets, caring for a sick child, and handling emergencies. However, most of the emphasis was on providing the mothers with vocational skills so they could obtain jobs and support their families. Job counseling, education, and on-the-job training were provided. Mothers were assisted in finding jobs. Even after formal job training was complete (within about one year), a liaison from the day-care center kept in touch with the mothers and worked with them on issues concerning their children and the family.

The results of the Milwaukee Project are quite impressive (see Table 2.1). The children in the Milwaukee Project showed consistently higher IQ scores than the control group, with the lowest effect size* of +.23 documented at the very beginning of the program and the highest effect size of +3.19 found when the children were 3 years old. At the end of the program, when children were age 6, the experimental group scored 2.6 standard deviations higher than the control group, with mean IQs of 119.24 as opposed to 86.89. When compared to the low-risk control group, the children in the Milwaukee Project also performed consistently better. These findings suggest that the intensive intervention helped these disadvantaged students do better than children whose mothers were not retarded.

The intensive intervention ended when the children entered first grade. Additional follow-up data were collected on the children to indicate the long-term effects of the early intervention. However, there are several design issues that influence the usefulness of the data. In Milwaukee in the early 1970s, there was an open enrollment policy in the city schools. Garber (1988), attempting to provide the best possible resources for the children in the program, identified schools that had the highest achievement scores for the city (scores in the 60th percentile for national norms based on the Iowa Test of Basic Skills) and arranged for the children to attend these schools. The seven neighborhood schools that the children would have attended, and consequently that the control children did attend, had average achievement scores at the 36th percentile. In addition to this differential school placement for experimental children compared to the control group, the Milwaukee Project conducted a summer school program that provided the children with additional help in reading and math. Therefore, the children in the Milwaukee Project had an intensive early intervention followed by a minimal intervention as the children continued through school.

School readiness data were collected on all children entering the first grade, and IQ scores, achievement data, and special education information were collected for all children from the first to the fourth grades.

In the spring of the year before the children entered first grade, the
(Text continues on page 27.)

---

*ES = Effect size. Effect size is the difference between experimental and control means divided by the control group standard duration. See Chapter 1 for a complete explanation.

TABLE 2.1 Early Intervention Programs

Project Name	Description of Intervention	Comparison Group	Age of Intervention	Duration	Measures	Effect Sizes Exp. vs. Control	Exp. vs. Low-Risk Control	n Exp.	Control	Low-Risk Control
Milwaukee Project	Intensive day-care developmental program until kindergarten. Minimal intervention from 1st grade. Minimal parent education intervention.	No treatment control. Subjects were alternately assigned to experimental or control groups as they became eligible for the program. Also, comparison of low-risk control group.	3 to 6 months	Intensive intervention, infancy through K; minimal intervention, 1st through 4th grades.	Gesell DQ					
					10 mo.	+.23	+.46	17	11	6
					14 mo.	+.45	+.50	12	13	7
					18 mo.	+1.60	-.03	15	12	7
					22 mo.	+2.01	+.34	16	14	6
					Standford-Binet					
					24 mo.	+2.78	+.80	15	17	7
					30 mo.	+3.11	+.50	17	18	8
					36 mo.	+3.25	+.71	17	18	8
					42 mo.	+3.19	+.66	17	18	8
					48 mo.	+2.72	+.28	17	18	7
					54 mo.	+2.78	+1.11	17	18	6
					60 mo.	+2.14	+.62	17	18	8
					66 mo.	+2.64	+.53	17	18	7
					72 mo.	+2.56	+.70	17	18	8
					WISC Full Scale (Follow-Up)					
					84 mo.	+2.54	+.03	17	17	8
					96 mo.	+2.14	+.30	17	15	6
					108 mo.	+1.69	+.02	17	15	6
					120 mo.	+1.77	+.24	17	17	6

Project Name	Description of Intervention	Age of Intervention	Duration	Comparison Group	Measures		Effect Sizes — Exp. vs. Control	n — Exp.	n — Control
Abecedarian Project	Early intervention focused on language and communication skills.	3 months	5 yrs. plus 2 yrs. for some children.	Randomly assigned to experimental or control. Control group received nutrition and medical treatment.	Bayley Scale				
					MDI	6 mo.	+.39	53	53
					PDI	6 mo.	+.28	53	53
					MDI	12 mo.	+.39	51	53
					PDI	12 mo.	+.39	51	53
					MDI	18 mo.	+1.61	51	49
					PDI	18 mo.	+.03	51	49
					Standford-Binet	24 mo.	+1.23	51	48
					McCarthy	30 mo.	+.83	50	48
					Standford-Binet	36 mo.	+1.22	50	48
					McCarthy	42 mo.	+.79	50	47
					Standford-Binet	48 mo.	+.93	50	47
					McCarthy	54 mo.	+.73	49	46
					WPPSI	60 mo.	+.47	49	47
					WISC-R	70 mo.		EE 25 / EC 24	CE 21 / CC 22
						EEvCC	+.40		
						ECvCC	+.47		
						EEvEC	+.06		
						ECvCE	+.53		
						EEvCE	+.46		
						CEvCC	+.07		

Continued

TABLE 2.1 *Continued*

Project Name	Description of Intervention	Comparison Group	Age of Intervention	Duration	Measures	Effect Sizes			*n*		
						CEC vs. C	FE vs. C	CEC vs. FE	CCEC	FE	C
Project CARE	Daycare plus family education, compared to family education alone.	Randomly assigned children to experimental or control.	3 months	5 yrs.	Bayley MDI						
					6 mo.	+.06	−.06	+.13	15	26	23
					12 mo.	+.72	−.04	+.77			
					18 mo.	+1.06	−.58	+1.60			
					Stanford-Binet						
					24 mo.	+.69	−.38	+1.06			
					36 mo.	+.73	−.28	+1.00			
					48 mo.	+.19	−.38	+.56			
					McCarthy						
					30 mo.	+.47	−.67	+1.13			
					42 mo.	+.53	−.27	+.80	12	13	8
					54 mo.	+.53	−.33	+.86			

Project Name	Description of Intervention	Comparison Group	Age of Intervention	Duration	Measures	Effect Sizes
						Exp. vs. Control
Family Development Research Program	Structured day-care program continued with preschool program. Included home visit and parent education component.	No random assignment. Two comparison groups: one selected from other day-care centers from 3 months to 3 years; the other group selected at 36 months from other preschool program.	Parent intervention began at 3rd trimister. Child intervention began at 6 months.	5 yrs.	Catell	
					36 mo.	+1.32
					48 mo.	+.61
					Stanford-Binet (1 yr. Follow-Up)	
					72 mo.	+.28

					Effect Sizes									n							
Project Name	Description of Intervention	Comparison Group	Age of Intervention	Duration	Measures	EEE vs. C	EEC vs. C	CEE vs. C	ECE vs. C	ECC vs. C	CEC vs. C	CCE vs. C	C	EEE	EEC	CEE	ECE	ECC	CEC	CCE
Gordon Parent Education Program	Parent and child intervention through home visit parent education program.	Random assignment to experimental or controls; 8 groups varying in duration of services.	3 months	Ended at 3rd birthday	Griffith 1 yr.	+.43	+.44	+.47	+.25	+.86	+.28	–	58	49	28	19	18	11	24	–
					Bayley 2 yrs.	–.15	–.39	–.18	–.66	–.21	–.18	–.12	41	20	10	8	7	9	10	37
					Binet 3 yrs.	+.69	+.43	+.71	+.09	+.06	–.10	+.35	45	21	12	9	9	9	13	52
					Binet 4 yrs.	+.70	+.77	+.74	+.14	+.59	–.43	+.40	43	21	9	9	8	9	12	42
					Binet 5 yrs.	+.53	+.63	+.49	+.23	+.49	–.21	+.01	52	25	11	9	11	11	15	48
					Binet 6 yrs.	+.67	+.89	+.57	+.12	+.21	+.13	+.57	49	26	11	8	9	11	13	49
					WISC-R 10 yrs.	+.99	+.69	+1.69	+.04	+.20	+.19	+.35	24	21	11	1	5	8	4	32

Continued

TABLE 2.1 *Continued*

Project Name	Description of Intervention	Comparison Group	Age of Intervention	Duration	Effect Sizes		n	
					Measures	Exp. vs. Control	E	C
Parent-Child Development Center	*Birmingham:* Full-time infant and toddler program plus parent education.	Random assignment of mother to experimental or no-treatment control.	3–5 months	3 yrs.	Bayley		Entry 162	89
					4 mo.	+.50		
					10 mo.	+.23		
					22 mo.	+.75		
					Stanford-Binet		71	65
					36 mo.	+.72		
					48 mo.	+.40		
	Houston: Home visit parent education during the first year and center-based parent education the second year. Child program the second year.	Random assignment of families to experimental or no-treatment control.	1 year	2 yrs.	Bayley		Entry 97	119
					12 mo.	+.03		
					24 mo.	+.75		
					Stanford-Binet		44	58
					36 mo.	+.32		
	New Orleans: Full-time infant and toddler program with parent part-time education.	Random assignment of mothers to experimental or no-treatment control.	2 months	3 yrs.	Bayley		Entry 67	59
					7 mo.	–.17		
					13 mo.	+.25		
					19 mo.	–.09		
					25 mo.	+.06		
					Stanford-Binet (Follow-Up)			
					36 mo.	+.50		
					48 mo.	+.83	19	15

						Effect Sizes		n		
Project Name	Description of Intervention	Comparison Group	Age of Intervention	Duration	Measures	E vs. C_1	E vs. C_2	E	C_1	C_2
Verbal Interaction Project's Mother-Child Home Program	Home-based parent education program. Parents were modeled activities emphasizing verbal interaction with their children.	1967-1972 data, housing projects, not individual subjects, were randomly assigned to experimental or control. 1973-1975, a true randomly design was conducted. Random assignment of subjects to experimental or control.	2 and 3 years	7 months	**1967-1972 Data** Levenstein (1970)					
					Pretest					
					Catell or Stanford-Binet	-.22	-.74	33	9	11
					PPVT	-.73	-.57	29	9	11
					Posttest					
					Catell or Stanford Binet	+1.42	+.89	33	9	11
					PPVT	+.85	+.02	29	9	10

Measures	E vs. C	E	C
Levenstein (1976)			
Pretest			
Catell 2 yr. olds	-.95	3	10
Stanford-Binet (Follow-Up) 3 yrs. old	+.60	4	5
Posttest			
Stanford-Binet 4½ & 5½ yrs. old	+.69	8	15
WISC 3rd & 4th grades	+.79	7	14

1973-1975 Data

Measures	E vs. C			n					
	1973 Cohort	1975 Cohort	1976 Cohort	1973		1975		1976	
				E	C	E	C	E	C
Posttest Stanford-Binet	+.10	-.43	-.36	18	16	17	12	29	26

Continued

TABLE 2.1 *Continued*

Project Name	Description of Intervention	Comparison Group	Age of Intervention	Duration	Measures	Effect Sizes			n		
						TD vs. C	MD vs. C	TD vs. MD	TD	MD	C
Chicago Housing Project	Compared two parent education models: Levenstein's VIP model (TD) vs. a mother's discussion (MD) group based on Auerbach and Badger's parent education programs.	Sites, not subjects, were randomly assigned to experimental or control sites.	18 months	2 years	Catell						
					22 mo.	+.40	+.10	+.35	21	15	21
					31 mo.	+.69	+.18	+.52	21	15	21
					McCarthy						
					3 yrs old	+.63	+.75	−.10	21	15	21
					PPVT						
					22 mo.	+.65	+.64	+.01	20	15	20
					31 mo.	+.88	+.92	−.02	20	15	20
					3 yrs	+.21	+.30	−.08	20	15	20

Project Name	Description of Intervention	Comparison Group	Age of Intervention	Duration	Measures	Effect Sizes	n	
						Home Visit vs. Control	H	C
Family-Oriented Home Visiting Program	Home visiting program vs. minimal contact control group.	Random assignment of families to 3 groups. Home visit vs. materials only vs. control.	At least 6 months of age	9 months	Bayley			
					Pretest (6–24 mo.)	+.25	−*	−*
					Stanford-Binet			
					Post 1 (immediately following intervention)	+.20	20	17
					Post 2 (10 mos. after intervention)	+.36	20	17
					Post 3 (1½ yrs. after intervention)	+.10	20	17

Project Name	Description of Intervention	Comparison Group	Age of Intervention	Duration	Measures	Effect Sizes			n		
						Nursery vs. Control	Home vs. Control	Nursery vs. Control	N	H	C
Mailman Center Project	A home-visit parent training program was compared to a nursery program plus parent training.	Random assignment to 3 groups: home visit, nursery, or control.	Up to 6 months	6 months	Bayley						
					MDI 8 mo.	+.26	+.20	+.06	38	35	37
					PDI 8 mo. (follow-up)	+1.13	+.80	+.33	38	35	37
					MDI 1 yr.	+.93	+.46	+.46	36	34	35
					PDI 1 yr.	+1.13	+.46	+.66	36	34	35
					MDI 2 yrs.	+1.26	+.40	+.86	33	31	30
					PDI 2 yrs.	+1.26	+.53	+.73	33	31	30

Continued

TABLE 2.1 *Continued*

Project Name	Description of Intervention	Age of Intervention	Duration	Comparison Group	Measures	CT vs. C	DT vs. C	CT vs. DT	CT	DC	C
							Effect Sizes			*n*	
Harlem Study	A concept training (CT) curriculum was compared to a self-discovery condition (DT). Age of intervention was tested as a variable.	Some children entered when they were 2 yrs. old; some entered when they were 3 yrs. old.	7 months	Random assignment to groups: two experimental groups and one no-treatment control.	*2-Yr.-Old Group*						
					Stanford-Binet						
					2 yrs. 8 mo.	+.46	+.74	+.38	51	44	57
					3 yrs. 8 mo.	+.22			64**		52
					(1 yr. Follow-up)						
					4 yrs. 8 mo.	+.20			70**		44
					PPVT						
					2 yrs. 8 mo.	+.15	+.40	+.28	51	44	57
					3 yrs. 8 mo.	+.09			64**		52
					4 yrs. 8 mo.	-.006			70**		44
					3-Yr.-Old Group		CT vs. Control		CT		C
					Stanford-Binet						
					3 yrs. 8 mo.		+.42		97		52
					4 yrs. 8 mo.		+.62		96		44
					PPVT						
					3 yrs. 8 mo.		+.15		97		52
					4 yrs. 8 mo.		+.24		96		44
					Two- and Three-Yr.-Old Groups Combined (Follow-up)						
					WISC 7th grade		+.22		104		28

*No data reported.

**N's for CT and DT combined.

Metropolitan Readiness Battery was administered to the experimental and control children. The Metropolitan assesses students' knowledge of skills, including letter-symbol matching, letter identification, and picture-word correspondence. This test was administered when the experimental children were completing their last semester of the intensive early childhood program and the control children were in their final semester of kindergarten in the public schools. For the children in the Milwaukee Project, 100 percent of the children scored average or better on the Metropolitan Readiness Test. Seventy-seven percent of the experimental children scored in the high-normal or superior range. In contrast, only 26 percent of the children in the control group scored in the average or better range for children their age and 73 percent scored in either the low-normal or low range. By this measure, the children in the Milwaukee Project entered school far better prepared to learn than did the control children.

The IQ data collected on all the experimental, control, and low-risk control children also strongly favored the intervention group. The Wechsler Intelligence Scale for Children (WISC) was administered to children at the end of the first, second, third, and fourth grades. At the end of the first grade, children in the experimental group had significantly higher IQ scores (ES = +2.54). Although the effect decreased from the first to the fourth grade, the effects were still very large (ES = +2.14, +1.69, and +1.77, respectively, for the second, third, and fourth grades). There were, however, no significant differences between the experimental and the low-risk control group on IQ scores for first through fourth grades. The effect sizes were +.03, +.30, +.02, and +.24, respectively, for first, second, third, and fourth grades.

Metropolitan Achievement Tests were administered to the experimental and control children as they progressed through the first to fourth grades. In the first grade in reading, children in the experimental group scored at the 1.8 grade level and the control group scored at 1.6. Compared to the IQ data, these differences are not large. In second and third grades, the experimental children scored at the 2.35 and 2.69 grade levels for reading, respectively, while the control group scored at the 1.95 and 2.33 grade levels. The differences between the two groups in reading became greater as they continued in school. By the fourth grade, the experimental group was reading a half year ahead of the control group (3.19 vs. 2.51, respectively). It is important to note, however, that the experimental group was still reading below grade level.

In the 1970s, the Milwaukee public schools implemented a policy of not retaining any students in grades 1 to 3, so early program effects on retention could not be determined. However, at the end of the fourth grade, 5 of the 17 children in the experimental group (29 percent) were retained, in comparison to 10 of the 18 control children (59 percent).

Data on the number of children receiving special education assistance were also collected for both the experimental and control groups. In the first grade, 1 child in the experimental group was receiving special education services, compared to 7 in the control group. By the third grade, 8 children in the experimental group were receiving some type of special education services, compared to 7 children in the control group. At the end of fourth grade, 7 (41 percent) of the 17 experimental children were receiving special education service and 16 (89 percent) of the 18 control children were receiving some special education services.

Was the Milwaukee Project successful? The children in the Milwaukee Project entered the first grade with the necessary skills to successfully meet the demands of school. All the experimental children had IQ scores within the average range, compared to the control children who were primarily in the low-average range. Of the 17 children in the Milwaukee Project born to retarded and impoverished mothers, fewer than half were receiving special education services (in comparison to 89 percent in the control group). These students were reading about 6 months below grade level at the end of the fourth grade, but this was 7 months ahead of the control group.

The Carolina Abecedarian Project

The Abecedarian Project (Ramey & Campbell, 1984; Ramey, Bryant, & Suarez, 1895) was developed at the Frank Porter Graham Child Development Center of the University of North Carolina at Chapel Hill. The project was a center-based program intended to provide early systematic education to children who were identified as being at risk for cognitive deficits. Although families did receive some social work services, the primary emphasis was on directly affecting the children, not the parents.

Screening for families was done either before or after children were born at local prenatal clinics and social service agencies. Once a family was identified as a possible participant, each family was visited by a member of the staff and was administered a High-Risk Screening Index (Ramey & Smith, 1977), which contained information on parents such as mother's and father's education, income level, family history of school failure, and a history of family cognitive functioning. The final decision to admit families to the program was made after the mother was administered an IQ test and was interviewed. The average IQ of the mothers was approximately 85.

Selection of families for the study took place over a 5-year period with four cohorts of children. As the families were brought into the study, children and families were matched on their scores on the High-Risk Screening Index (Ramey & Smith, 1977) and mother's IQ and then randomly assigned to either the intervention group or control group. Children born with biological risks, such as mental retardation, were not included in the study.

Of 122 families selected to participate, 121 agreed and 109 families accepted their assignment to the experimental or control group and actually took part in the study. The 109 families had 111 children, including one set of twins and two siblings. Of the total, 57 children were randomly assigned to the preschool experimental group and 54 were assigned to the control group. Early attrition resulted in 53 in the experimental group and 53 in the control group.

There were two components to the Abecedarian Project: a preschool program that served children from 6 weeks old to kindergarten, and a school program that began at kindergarten and ended at the completion of second grade. When it was time for the Abecedarian children to enter kindergarten, half of the experimental children continued on into the school-age program (EE) and half continued into traditional kindergarten programs (EC). At this time half of the control children were placed in the school-age program (CE) and the remaining half of the control children continued with no intervention (CC). Having these four groups allowed comparisons to be made on the effectiveness of the preschool program alone, the school program alone, and the combination of the preschool and school program.

The birth to age 3 program was very early and intense. Children entered the Abecedarian program as young as 6 weeks of age, and 95 percent of all the children were attending by 3 months of age. Children attended the program five days a week for a minimum of seven hours a day.

The infant stimulation part of the preschool program was designed to support optimal development in the preschool years. In the nursery, there was one adult to three infants. An infant curriculum, *Learning Games for the First Three Years*, which was developed by Sparling and Lewis (1981), was used in the program. It emphasized language, motor, social, and cognitive skills. At about 3 years of age, the children cycled into the preschool program. In the preschool, more standard preschool curricula, such as the Peabody Early Experience Kit (Dunn et al., 1976) and Bridges to Reading (Greenberg & Epstein, 1973), were used. There was a strong emphasis on language and communication skills. Daily activities consisted of conversing with the students and included both individual and group oral reading.

Children in the control group were primarily in day-care settings that did not emphasize these linguistic or academic activities. All children in the study did receive other services such as nutritional services, social support services, and medical care.

The school program began when the children entered kindergarten. A resource teacher who was an experienced certified teacher made both home and school visits. Resource teachers filled a variety of functions. They developed individualized activities to supplement the basic school curriculum in reading and math; they met with the classroom teacher to make sure that home activities coordinated with the school curriculum; they taught parents how to use the activities with their children; they consulted with the classroom teacher when problems arose; and they were advocates for the children, making sure that any school or home problems did not interfere with their work at school. A resource teacher visited each child's home approximately 15 times and visited the school about 17 times during the school year. In addition, the resource teachers tutored children who were doing poorly in reading and math for six weeks during the summer.

Parents were taught how to use the materials that the resource teachers developed, and they were encouraged to work with their children every day after school. Parents reported that they spent an average of 15 minutes after school working with their children.

The results for the Abecedarian Project are presented in Table 2.1. Children in the Abecedarian Project consistently scored higher on IQ tests than the control children. At 12 months of age, the children in the Abecedarian Project had higher IQs than the children in the other settings (ES = +.39) on the Bayley Mental Development Index. At 36 months of age, IQs were still higher for the experimental group on the Stanford-Binet (ES = +1.22).

At the end of kindergarten, children from all four groups—preschool and school-age program (EE), preschool only (EC), school-age program only (CE), and the no-treatment control (CC)—were administered the Wechsler Intelligence Scale for Children-Revised (WISC-R). The data showed that children in the preschool-only program (EC) had higher IQs than children in the school-age program only (CE) (ES = +.53) and the no-treatment control group (ES = +.47). There was little difference between the children in the preschool-only program, compared to children who received both the preschool program plus the school-age program (ES = +.06). In other words, the two-year school-age program added little to the effectiveness of the five-year program, at least in terms of IQ gains.

Retention data were also collected for the children in these different comparison groups. Only 12 percent of the children who were in both the preschool and in the school-age (EE) program were retained by the time they reached the second grade. However, 25 percent of the children who were in the preschool-only (EC) program and 38 percent of the children who were in the school-age only (CE) program were retained by the second grade. Thirty-two percent of the children in the no-treatment control were retained by the second grade. These data suggest that although early intervention alone may be enough to increase student IQs, school-age interventions are also needed to carry children through the demands of early schooling.

Peabody Individual Achievement Tests were administered to the children at the end of kindergarten and first grade (Ramey & Campbell, 1984).

The data were presented only graphically and effect sizes could not be calculated based on the information from the graph. However, the children who received the preschool and school-age programs performed at the 50th percentile without a decrement from kindergarten to first grade. Children who attended preschool but did not receive school-age services declined slightly from kindergarten to first grade, from the 50th to the 48th percentile. However, children who received only the school-age intervention beginning at kindergarten were performing at the 38th percentile at kindergarten and improved only slightly after the intervention (from the 38th to the 40th percentile). Children who received no intervention were at the 38th percentile in kindergarten and then declined at the first grade to the 36th percentile. Thus, there is a clear difference between the children in the early intervention group and those who did not receive any intervention.

The results from the Abecedarian Project suggest that early intervention is effective, yet continued intervention as the children progress in school can help maintain the positive effects of the early intervention. Early intervention without continued support may result in a downward spiral of the child's performance in school.

Follow-up data were collected when the children in the Abecedarian Project were 12 years old (Ramey, 1992; Ramey & Ramey, in press). Results from the Wechsler IQ test showed that children in the Abecedarian Project had, on average, higher IQ scores than children in the control group: IQ = 94 and 85, respectively (ES = +.40). On the Woodcock-Johnson Reading Test, children in the treatment group also scored better than children in the control group (ES = +.60). Small differences were found on the Woodcock-Johnson Mathematics Test (ES = +.20). These findings suggest that early intervention does have long-term positive effects.

Project CARE

Project CARE was an extension of the Abecedarian Project. One of the goals of Project CARE was to assess the effects of different levels of intervention on children's development. Ramey and colleagues (Ramey, Bryant, Sparling, & Wasik,* 1985; Wasik, Ramey, Bryant, & Sparling, 1990) added a parent education component to the Abecedarian model to determine if the two components together affected the disadvantaged children's development more than parent education alone.

Sixty-five families living below the poverty level were screened and selected on the High-Risk Screening Index (Ramey & Smith, 1977) over an

---

*The Barbara H. Wasik involved in the Project CARE research is unrelated to the first author of this chapter.

18-month period. Families were randomly assigned to three conditions: Child Development Center plus family education (CEC plus), family education only (FE), and a no-treatment control group. Because of limited space in the Child Development Center, only 17 children were placed in this group. There were 25 families in the family education only and 23 in the control group. At the end of three years, 82 percent, 92 percent, and 96 percent of the families remained in the CEC plus, FE, and control group, respectively, and all of these families continued in the project until the children were 54 months of age.

The program used in the CEC plus condition was the same program used in the Abecedarian Project. This included the *Learning Games for the First Three Years* (Sparling & Lewis, 1981) curriculum as well as an emphasis on language development and exposure to books. As in the Abecedarian Project, children entered day care as young as 3 months of age and attended the program five days a week for three years.

The FE component consisted of home visits approximately every 10 days (Ramey, Sparling, & Wasik, 1981). A basic part of the family education program was a curriculum designed to teach parents problem-solving skills to use when faced with the day-to-day rearing of children, such as discipline skills, home management, and financial issues. Parents were also instructed in ways to interact with their children to facilitate cognitive and social growth. Family educators were paraprofessionals who met weekly with the professional staff for supervision and guidance. In addition to home visits, parent meetings were held once a month to discuss information on nutrition, health, and safety.

Home visits continued for both groups for two years after the children left the CEC. The frequency of the visits during this time was designed to fit the individual needs of the families. Home visits averaged 1.4 per month for the FE group and 1.1 per month for the CEC plus group. The visits averaged between 30 and 60 minutes per meeting.

IQ data were collected on children in all three groups at 6-month intervals for the first 36 months and then at 48 and 54 months (see Table 2.1). By 12 months, the children in the day care plus family education had significantly higher scores on the Bayley than the family education only group (ES = +.77) and the control group (ES = +.72). However, there was no difference between the family education group and the control group. At 18 and 24 months, differences for both the CEC plus and FE groups were large. However, the effects for the FE group decreased at 36 months. The results from the Stanford-Binet showed an effect size for the day care plus family education of +.73, and for the family education alone, an effect size of −.28. At 48 months, which is one year after the CEC plus group ended day care, the CEC plus group still had higher scores on the

Stanford-Binet than FE and the control group. Follow-up at 54 months showed a similar pattern.

Because Project CARE can be considered a replication of the Abecedarian Project with a family education component, we compared the data from the two projects to determine if day care alone compared to day care with family education made a difference in the IQ scores. This comparison is only exploratory, as the two types of treatment were compared to different control groups at different times. When comparisons are made at 12 months, the effect size for day care alone was +.38 and day care with family education was +.72. However, at 36 months the effect sizes for day care only and day care with family education were +1.22 and +.72, respectively. The data suggest that in the long run, developmental day care with or without family education significantly increases at-risk children's cognitive development. However, since no longitudinal data were collected, it is premature to say that family education had no impact on the children's development.

The Family Development Research Program

The Family Development Research Program (FDRP) was primarily a center-based program started by J. R. Lally with the intention of helping economically disadvantaged parents and their children. Children were provided with enriched day care and preschool experiences that were intended to facilitate cognitive development. There was also a home visit component to the program in which families were taught child development skills and were provided with opportunities to complete or continue school and obtain job-training skills.

It is not specifically stated how families were recruited for the FDRP. The families who participated in the study are described as predominantly unwed mothers, with a mean age of 18 and an income of under $5,000 a year (Honig & Lally, 1982). In addition, families were not randomly assigned to either the treatment or control groups. There were two different comparison groups used in the evaluation. The comparison group for the day-care program children was selected from among children who participated in other community programs such as traditional nurseries and day-care settings. When the program children entered preschool, a group of control children was recruited based on specific demographic variables and matched to the children in the FDRP. In addition, a contrast group of children from middle-class, two-parent families was matched on age and sex to the experimental group in order to have a low-risk comparison group.

Infants participated in a half-day infant program until they were 15 months old. Four infants were assigned to one caregiver. During this time, the infants engaged in sensory-motor and language activities. Game activities were used to help develop cognitive skills (Lally & Gordon, 1977). From 15 months until 5 years of age, children attended a full-day multi-age-group experience, which was called the family style model. The curriculum was modeled after the British Infant Schools and emphasized four main areas: fine motor coordination, gross motor coordination, sensory experiences, and creative expression (which included playing with clay, play dough, and painting). A significant emphasis was placed on positive social and emotional development.

The day-care providers were certified teachers. They were trained for two weeks before the program began in the teaching techniques and philosophy of the program.

Home visits were also a part of the FDRP. Once a week, paraprofessionals visited families and taught them ways of effectively interacting with their children. This included instruction in playing with toys, reading books, and applying effective discipline measures. The home visitors also helped families make contact with social agencies for medical or other needs and helped transport parents to the weekly and monthly parent workshops that were held at the Center.

The home visitors, who were called Child Development Trainers (CDTs), were also involved in an initial two-week training along with the teachers and other staff members. Throughout the year, the CDTs met weekly with the project coordinators for case conferences about the families they visited. Each CDT visited approximately 15 families a week during this five-year period.

Honig and Lally (1982) reported that services were provided to 108 families. Unfortunately, there are no data on how many families began the program, if any dropped out after a period of time, or how many children were administered IQ tests as well as other measures.

Language, cognitive, and social interaction data were collected on the children while they were in the program and as they continued into kindergarten and first grade. In addition, extensive parent interviews were conducted. For the purpose of this chapter, however, only IQ data are reported.

The results from the FDRP were initially very impressive, but did not maintain when the children left the program (see Table 2.1). At age 36 months, children in the FDRP performed significantly better than their comparison group on the Catell Intelligence Test (ES = +1.32). (The effect size was computed using the standard deviation of the test since the standard deviation for the sample was not available.) At age 48 months, the children in the FDRP continued to have higher scores on the Catell than the control children. However, these effects did not maintain after the children were out of the program for one year. At age 72 months, the children in the FDRP did not differ from children who were in alternative programs (ES = +.28).

MODERATE-INTENSITY PROGRAMS

The Gordon Parent Education Program

The Gordon Parent Education Program (GPEP) (Jester & Guinagh, 1983) was a home-based program designed to enhance the cognitive and linguistic development of children by working directly with their parents, not the children themselves. The program was based on the assumption that parents have the most significant impact on children, especially in the early years. Therefore, providing parents with ways of instructing their children was expected to help the children do well in school.

Mothers with newborns were identified by the obstetric staff of the University of Florida hospital, which serviced 12 counties in northern Florida. Families included in the study were classified as "indigent" on the hospital records, had no history of mental illness or mental retardation, and had no complications in delivery. A total of 397 mothers and their children were recruited between June 1966 and September 1967 and were randomly assigned to the treatment or control groups. Of the 397 families, 60 refused to be a part of the study. By the end of the first year, 90 families were in the treatment group and 67 were in the control group. This high attrition is the result of many families moving away and others refusing to continue the program. By the time the children were 11 years old, the total number of families had dropped to 99.

Beginning in November 1968, new families with 2-year-olds were recruited to be a part of the Home Learning Approach to Early Stimulation (HLC). One hundred and eighty-six families who had children born during the same time period as the babies in the original sample were contacted. Families were found by searching hospital records, visiting neighborhood churches, and tracking down family members through neighborhood contacts. Of the 186, 121 were assigned to the treatment condition, 51 to the existing control group, and 14 were not assigned because they refused to participate. By the time the project began, 82 families were in the treatment group and 51 in the control group.

The GPEP was a three-year intervention project. There were three phases to the GPEP: Infant Stimulation Through Parent Education (PEP), Early Child Stimulation Through Parent Education (PEP2), and a Home Learning Approach to Early Stimulation (HLC). All interventions ended when the children were age 3, but the children and their mothers were followed on a yearly basis to age 6, then at 10.4 years, and again at 11 years of age.

The PEP program was designed for infants from 3 months to 1 year of age. The core of this program was a weekly home visit with the mother and her infant from a paraprofessional parent educator. During the visit, the parent was taught an activity that the mother could do with the child during the week. The activities were based on Piaget's theory of cognitive development and were intended to facilitate cognitive growth and interaction between the mother and child. For example, mothers were instructed to make a game of the object permanence task and repeat this activity with their children. PEP2 was basically an extension of PEP for 1 to 2–year-olds and the activities matched the developmental level of the children. The children entered the HLC part of the program at age 2. The HLC phase had an organized curriculum that could be followed in step-by-step procedures. The activities are published in *Child Learning Through Child Play* (Gordon, Guinagh, & Jester, 1972). Paraprofessionals continued to visit the home once a week during the HCL phase and to teach these activities to mothers.

The GPEP study was designed so that the longitudinal effects of the program as well as different levels of participation in the program could be evaluated. As Table 2.1 indicates, there are IQ data for children who were systematically assigned to the program for all three years, and children in for one and two years with all possible combination of levels of participation—for example, only the first year (ECC), only the second year (CEC), and the first two years (EEC).

This design helps answer many questions about the effectiveness of each phase and intensity of the program. Table 2.1 contains the IQ data for children with different levels of participation for ages 1 through 4, 6, and 10. When the children were tested at 4 years of age, those who had at least two consecutive years of intervention had higher IQ scores than the control group (ES = +.70, +.77, and +.74 for the EEE, EEC, and the CEE groups, respectively). Also at age 4, children with one year of intervention (either their first year or their third year) had large gains in IQ (ES = +.59 and +.40 for the ECC and CCE groups, respectively). At age 6, the positive effects remained for the three groups with two consecutive years of intervention and for the CCE group. All the other groups that had either just one year of intervention or did not have intervention for consecutive years (i.e., ECE) did not have positive effects for IQ at age 6.

As part of the Consortium for Longitudinal Studies, follow-up data on IQ, special education referrals, and retention were collected for the children at 10 years of age. (For a complete review, see Lazar, Darlington, Murray, Royce, & Snipper, 1982.) At 10 years of age, children who had been in the program for all three years had higher IQ scores than children who were in the control group (ES = +.99). The large differences were also found for children who were in the program for second and third years, compared to the control group (ES = +1.69). Very small effects were found for children who were in the program for only one year (ES = +.20, +.19, and +.35 for children in the ECC, CEC, and CCE, respectively). However, as of age 6, no differences were found for children who were in the program for their first year, left their second year, and returned their third year (ES = +.04). The lack of continuity in the intervention could explain these results.

Special education data were also collected for children who had been in the GPEP and the control group when they were 10 years old. Unfortunately, the data are not broken down to show the percent of children at the different intervention levels who received special education services. For all the children in the GPEP, 23.2 percent were referred for some special education services, compared to 53.8 percent in the control group (Lazar et al., 1982).

Retention data were also reported. Essentially, there are no differences in retention for the two groups. Twenty-seven percent of the children in the GPEP were retained, compared to 28 percent of the control children, by the time they reached the fifth grade. However, since data are not available for retention rates for children who received different levels of the intervention, it is not possible to tell if children with more intervention were retained less.

An overall summary of the data indicates that children who were in the program for all three years or at least for the second and third years had the largest effects, compared to the no-treatment control at age 10. Long-term effects were not found for children who were in the program for only one year, regardless of which year the intervention was administered. Also, when children were not in the program for two consecutive years, the intervention did not have long-lasting effects. From these data, it appears that the intervention must be administered for at least two consecutive years for the effects to be long lasting.

The Parent-Child Development Center Model

The Parent-Child Development Center (PCDC) programs (Andrews et al., 1982) were designed to promote the development of children from low-income families by providing extensive education and supportive services to their mothers. The PCDC programs were the largest government parent education programs aimed at early prevention and intervention.

Three PCDC programs in different regions of the country were evaluated: Birmingham, Alabama; Houston, Texas; and New Orleans,

Louisiana. The three PCDCs adopted common strategies for educating parents. All PCDC programs targeted families living in poverty, and the programs focused on children between the ages of birth to 3 years. The programs were directed at the broad range of problems that confront poor families, and all three centers included programs for both mother and children. Other families members were included to varying degrees across the different sites.

Although there were common elements among the three PCDC programs, there were many important differences. These differences are important because they allow us to evaluate the effectiveness of the PCDC programs at different levels of participation, intensity, and timing of intervention. From this study, we can try to determine how much of a similar intervention is required to obtain long-lasting effects.

The Birmingham model was a center-based program that served African-American and white families. Mothers entered the program when their children were 3 to 5 months old and remained until they were 3 years old. Half the mother-child pairs were recruited through door-to-door canvassing of low-income neighborhoods; the other half were referred from community agencies or were volunteers who had heard about the program from friends or family. Mothers and children with severe abnormalities were not accepted. Participants were then randomly assigned to treatment or control groups. A total of 162 mother-child dyads were in the program; 89 were in the control groups. Mother-child pairs that remained in the program and control groups for at least 28 months totaled 71 and 65, respectively. The fact that control mothers could continue to work or attend school while the program mothers could not may account for the high attrition rate in the program group.

The PCDC was structured in three phases, with each phase emphasizing increasing responsibility for the mothers. During the first year, mothers spent three half-days per week at the center learning about child development while caring for their own children. Mothers were involved in semi-structured seminars taught by experienced "teaching" mothers and included hands-on learning, demonstrations, and videotapes. Mothers were taught how to care for their children's physical needs and to develop their cognitive abilities. During the second phase of the program, mothers spent four half-days per week as understudies to the teaching mothers. On the fifth day, they were in training classes in child development, social services, and health-related issues. When the children were between 18 and 30 months, mothers entered the third phase of the program. Four mornings were spent conducting the children's programs and teaching other mothers child-development skills. The remaining time was spent in training sessions and workshops that focused on parenting skills and job skills such as interviewing techniques and job-preparation skills.

By itself, this model might be considered a high-intensity parent program. However, since it was combined with the less intensive children's program, it is grouped under the moderate-intensity programs. The entire focus of the program was to educate mothers so they could provide for and teach their own children.

Another variation of the PCDC, the Houston model, was developed in response to the special needs of the Mexican-American community that it served. This included incorporating a home visit component and a heavy emphasis on bilingual education. Families were recruited by door-to-door canvassing of homes in low-income areas. Families were then randomly assigned to either the control or the treatment group and asked if they wanted to participate in the project. Ninety-seven mother-child pairs were enrolled in the program group and 119 pairs in the control group. Of these, 44 program families and 58 control families remained in the study for two years. Most of the drop in both groups was due to the high mobility of Mexican-American families in this community.

The two-year Houston program was home based for the first year and center based for the second year. Mothers entered the program when their children were 1 year old. During the first year of the program, there were 30 90-minute home visits made by paraprofessionals who trained the parents in child development and parenting skills. During these home visits, parents were taught how to do a variety of activities with their children, such as reading and playing with toys. In addition, English courses were offered to the parents free of charge. During the second year, mothers spent half of their time at the Center on home-management skills and the other half of their time in child-development classes.

The third evaluation of the PCDC was done in New Orleans. The participants in the New Orleans program were low-income, African-American families living in the inner city. This model was center based and emphasized health prevention and education. Potential participants for this project were identified by birth records of a state-supported charity hospital in New Orleans. Birth records were screened for any abnormalities, including problems in delivery and birth weight, and then mother-child pairs were recruited from this list of children who did not have such problems. Participants were randomly assigned to the treatment or control group. A total of 67 mother-child dyads enrolled in the program group and 59 in the control group; 19 dyads in the program group and 20 dyads in the control group completed the project. This high attrition was attributed to the high commitment demands of the program.

Mothers entered the program when their children were 2 months old and ended when they were 3 years old. Mothers attended the program two mornings a week for three hours; one session addressed specific child-developmental issues and the other focused on the mothers' relationships to their families and community. No home visits were made and, unlike the Birmingham model, no emphasis was placed on career counseling or job placement for the mothers.

Each of the PCDC models varied in the intensity of the intervention. The most intensive, the Birmingham model, targeted the children at an early age, and the mothers attended the program five days a week for three years. The Houston program's intervention began when the children were already 1 year old. Although the New Orleans program began when the children were 2 months old, the intensity of the intervention was significantly less.

The data show interesting effects. At various points from 3 months to 3 years of age, all children from the three models were assessed on the Bayley Test of Infant Development and the Stanford-Binet. Between 22 and 25 months, children in the Birmingham and Houston models performed significantly better than children in the control group (ES = +.75). The similarity in these models is important because it appears that similar effects are found for children who were in the Birmingham model for two years and in the Houston model for only one year. Also, the Houston model was clearly less intense than the Birmingham model. Children in the New Orleans model after two years, however, showed no difference from their controls.

Children in all models were given the Stanford-Binet at 3 years of age; again, the results show different patterns. The Birmingham program had the largest effects (ES = +.72) followed by the New Orleans program (ES = +.50) and finally the Houston program (ES = +.32).

Only the Birmingham and the New Orleans models have follow-up data one year after the intervention. The New Orleans model in which the children entered as early as the Birmingham model but did not receive such intensive services maintained significant, positive effects one year after the program ended. The Birmingham program showed a slight decline in the effect size one year after the intervention (ES = +.40). The interesting finding is that the New Orleans program showed no effects until the children were 3 years old, and, despite having the least intervention, this program had larger effects at 4 years of age than the Birmingham program.

LOW-INTENSITY PROGRAMS

The Verbal Interaction Project's Mother-Child Home Program

The Mother-Child Home Program was an outgrowth of the Verbal Interaction Project, developed by Phyllis Levenstein and colleagues (Levenstein, 1970, 1977; Levenstein, O'Hara, & Madden, 1983; Madden, Levenstein, &

Levenstein, 1976). The program was designed as an inexpensive intervention for low-income parents to enhance the early cognitive and emotional
development of their children. The program was a home-based intervention program for children 2 and 3 years old that emphasized instructing the
primary caregiver in ways to interact effectively with their children.

Families who were eligible for public housing, did not have more than
a high school education, were English speaking, and had no major disabilities were selected to participate in the project. Two waves of data were
collected on the Mother-Child Home Program. Between 1967 and 1972,
families were recruited by letter and then door-to-door canvassing in low-
income housing projects. Assignment to treatment conditions was not
random. Housing projects, not individual families, were assigned to either
the treatment or control groups. The data collected from 1973 to 1975 were
from subjects who were randomly assigned to either the treatment or
control group. Because different results were found from the quasi-experi-
ment and true experiment, the results are presented separately.

The program utilized paraprofessionals who were trained as Toy Demonstrators (TDs). The TDs made weekly or semi-weekly visits to families.
They brought books and toys to the home visit and followed a guide sheet
on how to use the materials. Although there was a specific curriculum, it
was not rigidly followed and was adapted for the individual needs of each
family. An example of teaching concepts through toy demonstration
would be to play with a container with child and mother and during the
activity talk about concepts such as "in the container, out of the container,
and beside the container." Levenstein pointed out that the goal was not to
directly instruct parents in methods of working with their children but
instead to model techniques that were designed to encourage verbal interaction between the mother and her child.

A portion of the data collected from 1967 to 1972 is reported in Levenstein (1970). Thirty-three 2- and 3-year-olds were in the treatment group.
There were two control groups; one group (C1) had a visitor who visited
homes over a period of seven months but did not demonstrate anything to
the mother ($n = 9$), and the other control group (C2) received no treatment
($n = 10$). At the end of the seven-month intervention, all children were
administered the Catell or Stanford-Binet and Peabody Picture Vocabulary
Test (PPVT). (Some children were administered the Stanford-Binet and
some the Catell. Since those tests are highly correlated, effect sizes were
computed for pooled scores.)

The results are presented in Table 2.1. There were pretest differences on
the Catell/Stanford-Binet and the PPVT favoring the control groups but the
differences were not significant. After the intervention, children in the
treatment group had higher IQ scores than children in both control groups
(ES = +.1.42 and +.89, respectively, for C1 and C2). On the PPVT, children
in the treatment group did better than children in the control group who

had a visitor but no program. However, there were no differences between children in the treatment group and the no-treatment control group.

Additional data collected from 1967 to 1972 are reported in Madden, Levenstein, and Levenstein (1976). This study included follow-up data on the different groups. There were a total of six treatment groups that received variations in the duration of treatment. Of the six treatment groups and three control groups, only one treatment and one control group had subjects of the same age (both had 2- and 3-year-olds), and therefore are the only two groups that can be compared. This treatment group was initially intended to be a placebo group that had a TD who came to the mothers' homes but were instructed not to interact with the mothers or children. The TD merely observed the mother and her child. The second year, this group was given one year of the intervention. The control group received no treatment.

The Catell was administered to the 2-year-olds and the Stanford-Binet was administered to the 3-year-olds as pretest measures. Since the sample size is very small for the treatment group ($n = 3$ in the 2-year-old group and $n = 4$ in the 3-year-old group), effect sizes do not accurately represent the data, although the scores do suggest there are pretest differences. These differences favored the control group for the 2-year-olds and the treatment group for the 3-year-olds. Posttests were not given immediately following the intervention. Instead, posttesting was done 28 months after the intervention ended when the children were 4½ and 5½ years old. Instead of reporting the data separately for each age group, the scores for all the children were pooled. Pooling IQ data for children at this age does not provide an accurate assessment of children's performance. In addition, the small sample size makes it difficult to interpret the results. The same is true for the follow-up IQ data collected when the children were in the third and fourth grades.

Additional data on retention and special education referrals are presented in Lazar and associates (1982). When the data for all of the children are pooled, 24.1 percent of the children in all the treatment groups had been retained by the time they reached the third grade. This is compared to 44.7 percent of the children in the control group. However, looking only at the comparable treatment and control groups, the data look different; 50 percent of the children in the treatment group were retained ($n = 6$) and 15 percent of the children in the control group were retained ($n = 13$).

Regarding special education referrals, 13.7 percent of the children in the pooled treatment groups were referred for some type of special education services, compared to the 39.1 percent of the children in the control group. Again, looking at the comparable treatment and control group, 17 percent of the children in the treatment ($n = 6$) and 38 percent of the controls were referred for services ($n = 13$).

Far less promising outcomes were found in the true experiment groups that were tested from 1973 to 1975. Stanford-Binet scores were reported for three cohorts of children who were in the program. In the 1973 cohort, no differences were found between children in the treatment group and those in the control group. For the two other cohorts, it appears that the children who did not receive any services performed slightly better than the program children. Levenstein, O'Hara, and Madden (1983) did argue that the data from a randomized sample included a large number of families who were not motivated to be in the program and did not follow through. However, the data were collected on families that did stay on long enough to have their children assessed. There are no follow-up data from these children nor is there any information on special education referral or retention.

It appears from the data that the best that can be said is that the Verbal Interaction Project had effects immediately after the intervention for the group of children whose parents were committed to completing the program. The long-term effects of the program can not be determined because of insufficient data.

The Chicago Housing Project Program

The Chicago Housing Project program compared the effectiveness of two parent education models: the Levenstein toy demonstration model (TD) and the Auerbach-Badger mother's discussion group (MD) model. Slaughter and colleagues (1983) wanted to determine if emphasizing different roles for mothers in the parent education programs had different effects on the children's cognitive growth.

The program was a two-year intervention project with low-income mothers and their children (ages 18 to 44 months). Mothers were recruited from three Chicago housing projects. All were African Americans. Sites (not individual subjects) were randomly assigned to either the treatment or the control group. Social workers went door to door to solicit volunteers to participate in the study. A total of 132 mothers was selected to participate in the study—41, 53, and 38 in the TD, MD, and control group, respectively. After attrition due to families moving and refusing to continue in the program, the program started with 26 in the toy demonstration (TD) model, 26 in the mother discussion (MD) group, and 31 in the control group. Children with severe health problems or handicaps were not included in the sample.

The TD model was explained in detail in the previous section. The Toy Demonstrators were trained by Levenstein and her staff.

The MD group was based on the elements of Auerbach's (1968, 1971) and Badger's (1968, 1971, 1973) approaches to parent education. Mothers and the group leader met for two hours a week for two years. Each of the three group leaders had his or her own group with approximately seven mothers in the group. During the meeting, parents would discuss any concerns or problems that they might have regarding their children. Mothers were encouraged to share their own experiences and to learn from one another. The group leaders were social workers who were trained in parent education techniques.

If children were brought to the session, they would play in an adjoining room during the meeting. Unlike the TD group, the mothers were given no special instruction on how to play with or use toys with their children. Some discussion of infant curriculum activities did take place in the first year and Badger, who had developed an infant program, provided consultation services to the program. However, there was no formal training in any techniques used with the children.

A variety of mother-child interaction observation and maternal child-rearing attitudes data were collected from both the TD and MD groups (Slaughter, 1983). However, for this chapter only IQ data and PPVT scores will be presented.

Children were administered the Catell test at 22 and 31 months of age and the McCarthy scales at 44 months of age. At age 22 months (which was four months into the program), the children in the TD group performed better on the Catell than the children in the MD group (ES = +.40) or the control group (ES = +.10). At age 31 months, the differences between the groups were larger (ES = +.69 and +.18, respectively). By the end of the two-year program, both the TD and the MD groups scored better than the control group, but there were no differences between the two interventions. The Peabody Picture Vocabulary Test was administered at the same time as the Catell and McCarthy tests. At ages 22 and 31 months, children in the TD and MD performed better than the control group but there were no differences between the two interventions. At 44 months of age, no differences were found among the TD, MD, or the control group.

The results from this study of two parent interventions suggest that working with the parent alone (the MD group) or working with the parent as the parent worked with the child (the TD group) is equally effective. However, since there are no follow-up data on this project, there is no way of knowing if this parent education intervention had lasting effects on the children.

The Family-Oriented Home Visiting Program

The Family-Oriented Home Visiting Program (FOHV) (Gray & Ruttle, 1980) targeted low-income families who had at least two children younger than 5 years old. The focus of this home-based program was on teaching mothers how to interact effectively with their children and to work on developing skills that would enhance their children's cognitive development.

Families were selected from the area surrounding Nashville, Tennessee, based on the following criteria: (1) low income, defined as a family of four living on $4,137 in 1980; (2) one child between 17 and 24 months and another child under 5 years old; (3) children had no organic problems; and (4) mother had to be nonworking to be available for the program. Families were then randomly assigned to one of three groups: extensive home visiting group, materials only group (this group was eventually dropped because of high attrition), and a minimal contact control group. Control families were visited four times during the intervention and were compensated with small toys. There were 20 families in the program group and 17 families in the control group.

Families in the FOHV were visited weekly by experienced professional social workers or trained paraprofessionals for a period of nine months. What the home visitors did is described in detail in the manual, *Helping Families Learn* (Hargde & Gray, 1975). Parents were instructed in managing behavior, in organizing the environment to enhance their child's learning, and in increasing the amount of verbal interaction between parent and child. Home visitors adapted each program to fit the needs of each family. To keep program costs at a minimum, materials were either inexpensive or homemade so parents could continue to do the activities with the children after the program ended.

Children were initially pretested on the Bayley and then posttested at three different intervals on the Stanford-Binet: immediately after the intervention, 10 months after the intervention, and 18 months after the intervention. The goal was to determine if limited, early intervention could sustain long-term effects. There were small pretest differences on the Bayley between the intervention group and the control group (ES = +.25). To control for this, this difference was factored out of the posttest effect sizes. Immediately after intervention, there were small residual differences on the Stanford-Binet between the children who received the intervention and those who did not (ES = +.20). At 10 months after the intervention, the results were more positive for the intervention group (ES = +.36). At 18 months after the intervention, the Stanford-Binet scores were still slightly higher for the intervention group than the controls, but the difference was not meaningful (ES = +.10).

The FOHV project was very similar to the Mother-Child Home Program except that the MCHP lasted longer and intervened with children at an earlier age. However, it appears that the limited intervention of parent education without directly impacting the child does not have long-term effects.

The Mailman Center Project

The Mailman Center Project was developed by Tiffany Field and colleagues (Field, Widmayer, Greenberg, & Stoller, 1982) to help teenage mothers and their infants. This project compared a home-based parent-training program to a nursery parent-training program. Field and colleagues wanted to see if intervening with both the teen mother and her children could have positive long-term effects on both mother and child.

Mothers were recruited from a large university hospital in Miami, Florida. All mothers were between 13 and 19 years old; were from low-income, African-American families; and, in almost every case, lived with some family member. Infants who had prenatal complications or who were born with obvious birth defects were not included in the study. Of the 120 mothers who were selected, 40 were randomly assigned to one of three groups: home visit intervention, nursery intervention, and a control group. Attrition was low; at one year, 34, 36, and 35 mothers remained in the home, nursery, and control group, respectively.

The intervention lasted six months. Mothers and their children began the program within one month of the child's birth. Two-year follow-up data were collected on the children to determine if the intervention had lasting effects.

The home visit intervention consisted of six months of biweekly visits to train the teen mothers in child-care skills, sensorimotor activities, and basic techniques for interacting with a young child. Many of the activities were adapted from the Brazelton Neonatal Assessment scale and the Bayley Scale of Infant Development. Home visits were made by psychology graduate students who demonstrated the activities to the mother. Mothers were taught six exercises per session and materials were provided that outlined the exercises. They were asked to demonstrate each activity they were taught and were instructed to practice each activity daily for five minutes with their child. A Comprehensive Employment Training Act (CETA) aide accompanied each graduate student and watched the other children in the family while the mother was receiving instruction. At each subsequent visit, the home visitor followed up on activities presented the previous week and then presented new activities.

The nursery intervention included parent training, job training, and full-time care for the infants. The mothers served as aide trainees in the medical school day-care center that their children attended. The job was intended to provide the mothers with job skills and an income. Mothers in this program were not only taught infant stimulation exercises but, because they worked in the day-care center, they saw examples provided by other child-care workers who spent considerable time with their own children. Therefore, mothers had daily ongoing training experience in caring for their infants.

Bayley tests were obtained at age 8 months, at 1 year old, and again on each child's second birthday. The findings are presented in Table 2.1. With the exception of the scores on the Bayley (MDI & PDI) at age 8 months, children in the nursery group outperformed children in the home group. Six months after the intervention ended, children in the nursery and home group had higher MDI scores (ES = +.93 and +.46, respectively) and PDI scores (ES = +1.13 and +.46, respectively) than children in the control group. This pattern continued 18 months after the intervention when the children were tested on their second birthday. One explanation for the nursery group's higher performance could be that because those children were in a structured day-care setting they received more stimulation, and their mothers had more ongoing training experiences in effective ways of care for young children.

The Harlem Study

The Harlem Study was designed by Francis Palmer (1983) and colleagues to test the effects of a concept training program on disadvantaged boys. The Harlem Study was based on the assumption there are certain basic concepts that children need to know that set a foundation for future learning, and that children could best learn these concepts in a one-to-one situation. The Harlem Study was a center-based project that focused on the child, not on the parent.

Screening for potential participants was done through birth records at Harlem and Sydenham Hospitals and the Bureau of Vital Statistics. Nine-hundred and fifty-three children were identified as potential participants. The following criteria were used for selecting participants: male (because Palmer argued that boys had more difficulty in school than girls); both parents African American; birth weight over 5 pounds; no multiple births; mother's ages between 15 and 45; no history of drug abuse or other complication; and residence at birth in Harlem.

There were three groups: the Concept Training (CT) group, which was the intervention group; a Discovery Training (DT) group, which was intended to have the same experience as the Concept Training group at the Center without the Concept Training curriculum; and a no-treatment control group. There were two waves of program implementation—one for children who began the program when they were 2 years old and one for another group of children who began the program when they were 3 years old. The purpose of this was to determine whether the age of intervention was a factor in the effectiveness of the program.

Children who were in both waves of the project were recruited at the same time. Children born in the months of August to October 1964 were randomly assigned to either the CT or DT group. In these groups, children were then randomly assigned to the 2-year-old group, which began the program immediately, or to the three-year-old group, which would begin the program the following year. Children born in November to December 1964 were recruited specifically as controls. The same control group was used for both the 2- and 3-year-old groups.

Of the initial 1,474 families identified for the study, a total of 440 met the criteria and agreed to participate. In the 2-year-old group, 119 children were in the two treatment groups combined and 68 were in the control group. Half of the children in each group were from low social economic status (SES) homes and half were from middle SES homes. At the end of the intervention, 51, 44, and 57 families remained in the CT, DT, and control groups, respectively. In the 3-year-old group, 115 of the children were in either the CT or DT group and 57 in the control group. At the end of the intervention, 97 children were either in the CT or DT group and 52 in the control group.

The intervention was not intensive; children attended the Center for two hours a week for seven months. In the CT group, children were taught basic concepts (e.g., big and little) using a structured, curriculum (Palmer, 1978). The children were given toys to play with and activities were designed to give hands-on experience to the basic concepts and to provide opportunities to explore these concepts. In the Discovery condition, children were given the same toys to play with as the children in the Concept training condition, but they received no instructions on how to use the toys. The control children did not receive instruction, nor did they have access to the toys.

The 2- and 3-year-old groups were assessed on the Stanford-Binet and the Peabody Picture Vocabulary Test (PPVT) after the seven-month intervention and then on follow-up at various points. The results are presented in Table 2.1. No differences were found for children of high versus low SES, so the groups were combined. For the group that began the program when they were 2 years old, both the Concept Training and the Discovery groups performed better than the control group (ES = +.46 and +.74, respectively) on the Stanford-Binet. When the Concept Training group is compared to the Discovery group, the Concept Training children did perform better (ES = +.38). On the PPVT, the Discovery group did better than the control group (ES = +.40) but the Concept group did not perform significantly better than the control group (ES = +.15). Small differences were found between the Concept Training and Discovery groups. Because Palmer (1983) found no differences between the Concept Training and Discovery group when he did an ANOVA on the data, he combined the two groups in subsequent analyses and did not have the Discovery group in the 3-year-old cohort.

At one year after the intervention, the combined Concept Training and Discovery group performed only slightly better than the control group on the Stanford-Binet (ES = +.22) but not on the PPVT (ES = +.09). Two years after the intervention, the same pattern of results was found.

For the group that began the program when they were 3 years old, the Concept Training group performed better on the Stanford-Binet than the control group did (ES = +.41) but not on the PPVT (ES = +.15). At one year after the intervention, the differences between the Concept Training and the control group were larger on the Stanford-Binet (ES = +.62) and the PPVT (ES = +.24).

A follow-up was done when the children from the 2- and 3-year-old groups were 12 years old. (This was 10 years after the 2-year-old group was in the program and 9 years after the 3-year-old group was in the program.) The program children and the control group were administered the WISC. The data for the two treatment cohorts were combined. The program children performed slightly better than the control group (ES = +.22).

Retention data were also reported on the program children (n = 104) and the control group (n = 28). Of the program children, 24 percent were retained by the seventh grade. This is compared to 44.7 percent of the control children who were retained by the seventh grade. Since there were a disproportionately large number of program children reported in the follow-up, these data could favor the program children and should be interpreted with caution.

It is difficult from these results to determine whether entering this program at 2 years old was more beneficial than entering the program at age 3. One reason is that the program changed from the 2- to a 3-year-old cohort when the Concept Training and Discovery groups were combined.

CONCLUSION

There are several conclusions that can be drawn from these early intervention programs. However, before they are presented, some methodical limitations of these programs need to be addressed. Longitudinal field tests of programs have great value and contribute significantly to understanding the impact of an intervention over time. However, this research also is accompanied by methodical limitations that should be acknowledged when the data are being interpreted. In the programs presented, there are two principal limitations—bias in subject selection and differential attrition—that should be considered when interpreting these findings.

There is always the danger of selection bias in any study, especially in long-term, intensive programs where subject participation is demanding. In 8 of the 11 programs reviewed, subjects were randomly assigned to either the treatment or control group, which reduces selection bias. However, in Levenstein's Verbal Interaction Project (1967–1972) study and the

Family Development Research Program, sites, not individual subjects, were assigned as treatment or control group. For example, one housing project was designated as the treatment site, and anyone from this site who agreed to participate in the study was a part of the experimental group. In the Chicago Housing Project study, there was no random assignment of subjects, and willing participants were selected into the treatment group. In these three programs, selection bias could influence the outcome of the study. For example, parents who chose to participate in the intervention may have been more motivated or better at parenting skills than those in the control group.

Also, with any longitudinal study, differential attrition is a problem. As Table 2.1 indicates, the sample size for all the groups decreased over time. This is especially true for the subject attrition in the Birmingham and Houston PCDC (almost half of the subjects dropped out), which suggests that there is a differential attrition bias for the subject who remained in the study. Subjects who remained in the study may have been a select, highly motivated group of participants. When attrition is significantly higher in the experimental group than the control group, the possibility of bias is especially high. Another problem with attrition is that when the effects for retention and special education are computed, the sample size does not reflect the number of original subjects in the group, and in some instances, the follow-up sample is significantly smaller. For example, at follow-up in the Harlem Study, there were 104 subjects from the treatment group and only 28 from the control group. This disproportionate representation of subjects from the treatment group may not present a true comparison of the treatment and control group. Therefore, these data need to be interpreted with particular caution.

Do Early Intervention Programs Work?   Early intervention programs do help children get off to a good start. Of the 11 programs that were reviewed, 8 programs showed positive results immediately after intervention. However, although early intervention programs with continued follow-up do appear to have long-term benefits for children, those without continued follow-up are not generally sufficient to help children maintain their success in school. The results from the Abecedarian and Milwaukee Projects support this conclusions. The Abecedarian Project clearly showed that children who received early intervention did better than children who received their first intervention in kindergarten. However, when the intervention did not continue as the children entered kindergarten, their achievement scores declined as they continued through first grade. Children who continued in the Abecedarian Project in kindergarten and first grade maintained their high performance in school. Similarly, children in the Milwaukee Project were given follow-up intervention by being placed in schools where the achievement scores were higher than in the schools attended by the control children and by attending summer programs. At follow-up, children in the Milwaukee Project performed substantially better than the control group. Early intervention with continued follow-up in elementary school can clearly help disadvantaged children to be successful in school.

What Components Are Necessary for a Program to be Effective? Table 2.2 shows a matrix of the programs categorized based on the intensity of parent and child involvement in the programs and pooled effect sizes for programs in each category. Programs with intensive child interventions were programs that have a center-based day-care program for the children; minimal child intervention programs were those that did not have any organized day-care experience and, instead, parents demonstrated activities to their children. Intensive parent programs were programs in which parents met with program staff for more than one year on a weekly or semiweekly basis and were taught how to interact effectively with their children. The minimal parent intervention programs met parents for less than one year and also taught mothers strategies for working with and caring for their children.

It is clear from Table 2.2 that intensive child and intensive parent programs are the most effective interventions, not only immediately but for at least one year following the intervention. (Data on long-term effects were available for only one program.) Programs such as the Milwaukee Project and Project CARE had an extensive day-care and preschool program for the children. These programs also included an extensive parent education component. In the Milwaukee Project, the mothers were provided with job-training skills and specific parenting education. In Project CARE, mothers were taught decision-making skills to be used in a variety of situations that arose around such topics as child rearing and home management.

It also appears that intensive parent programs with minimal child intervention and intensive child programs with minimal parent intervention are equally effective. However, the pooled effects from the programs with intensive parent and minimal child intervention need to be interpreted with caution. Of the four programs grouped in this category, the results from Project CARE show different results from the other three programs. The data from Project CARE are especially important because the effects of child day care plus family education compared to family education alone were systematically tested. The results show that children whose mothers received parent education did not differ on IQ tests, compared to children in a no-treatment control group. These data suggest that parent education alone is not sufficient as an effective intervention. This is

TABLE 2.2

No Parent

	Immed.	1 yr.	LT
Minimal Child			
Harlem Project (7 months)	+.15	+.22	+.22 (10 yrs.)

Minimal Parent

	Immed.	1 yr.	LT
Minimal Child			
Verbal Interaction Project (Levenstein, 1970) (7 months)	+0*	–	+.79 (3rd & 4th grade)
Family-Oriented Home Visit (9 months)	+.20	+.36[1]	+.10
Mailman Ctr. #2 (6 months)	+.20	+.40[2]	–
x̄ ES	+.13	+.38	+.44
Intensive Care			
Abecedarian (5 years)	+.47	+.47	–
Mailman #2 (6 months)	+.26	+1.26[2]	–
Houston–PCDC (2 years)	+.32	–	–
New Orleans–PCDC (3 years)	+.50	+.83	–
x̄ ES	+.38	+.84	

Intensive Parent

	Immed.	1 yr.	LT
Minimal Child			
Care #2 (Parent Ed) (5 yrs.)	–.33	–	–
Gordon Project (3 yr. data)	+.69	+.70	+.99 (10 yrs)
Chicago Housing Project #1 (TD) 2 yrs.	+.63	–	–
Chicago Housing Project #2 (MD) 2 yrs.	+.75	–	–
x̄ ES	+.43	+.70	
Intensive Care			
Milwaukee (5 years)	+2.56	+2.54	+.24
Care #1 (CEC) (5 years)	+.53	–	–
Family Development R.P.	+.61	+.28	–
Birmingham–PCDC	+.72	+.40	–
x̄ ES	+1.11	+1.07	+.24

[1] 10 months.

[2] 16 months.

*Average across studies.

52

further supported by the review by White, Taylor, and Moss (1992), which concluded that parent involvement was not necessary for early intervention programs to be effective. The other programs in the intensive parent and minimal child interventions category did not systematically test this comparison between parent education, only programs and child and parent programs.

The data also consistently support the effectiveness of programs with intensive child and minimal parent intervention. Programs such as the Abecedarian Project, the Mailman Center Project, and the New Orleans PCDC program show moderate effects immediately after the intervention. One year after the intervention, the effects not only maintained but the differences were larger in favor of the program children. Given that intensive child programs are effective and it appears that parent involvement may not add significantly to the intervention, programs that focus primarily on the child may be an effective model for early intervention.

Minimal parent and minimal child intervention programs show small immediate effects on children's cognitive development. The data suggest that when parent involvement is limited and the child is not in any organized setting, the effects on the children's IQ are minimal. The effects one year after the intervention are greater than immediately following the intervention, but they are still modest. It appears that short-term programs have a small impact on children's long-term development.

Are Center-Based Programs More Effective than Home-Based Programs?
The answer to this question is confounded with the level of intensity of the program. However, it does appear that center-based programs can provide more effective experiences for the child than home-based programs. The most intensive models, the Milwaukee and Abecedarian Projects, were center based and also placed a great emphasis on direct services to the child. Project CARE and the Mailman Center Project, which compared home and center programs, showed that the center programs were more effective. This difference was primarily attributed to the day-care intervention that the children received as part of their Center experience. In Project CARE, the mothers who received home visits were only instructed in child-care skills, but the mothers who took their children to the Center had their children in an enriched environment and also received parent education. The experience was the same for the mothers in the Mailman Project. Mothers in the nursery group were given job-training and parenting skills and their children were in day care. The enriching experience of the day-care environment could have provided stimulation for the child as well as an opportunity for the parents to observe and model effective parenting skills.

The quality of individual programs is also an important factor in evaluating the effectiveness of a program. The Abecedarian Project and the

Family Development Research Program appear on the surface to be comparable programs. Both programs had an intensive day-care and a family education component and both were five-year interventions. However, the Abecedarian Project maintained greater effects one year after the intervention. One explanation for this difference could be that the two programs emphasized different areas of development. The Abecedarian program emphasized language development, and the FDRP emphasized sensorimotor activities. These program differences could explain the differences in the long-term effectiveness of programs that appear to be otherwise very similar. This reinforces the conclusion that although programs can be grouped together, each program has unique aspects that contribute to its success. It would be an important contribution to systematically study individual program components to learn what are the essential pieces to a successful early intervention program. For example, is an emphasis on oral language as important as early sensorimotor stimulation? These are empirical questions that can contribute to understanding what makes an effective early intervention program.

How Early Does Intervention Need to Occur?   Again, this is a difficult question to answer because most of the programs began when the children were in their first year of life. However, data from the Gordon Parent Education Program can address some issues. The findings from this study suggest that the intervention needs to be longer than one year. In the Gordon project, children who were in the program for only one year, regardless of how old they were at that year, did not perform as well as children who were in the program longer. Again, Gordon's work showed that when children were not in the program for consecutive years, the program was not as effective. Finally, the earlier the intervention, the better the results appear to be. Gordon's project showed that when children entered the program early, they performed better. The findings from the Abecedarian Project also support this claim. Children who were involved in the early intervention program did better than children who were given additional help only upon school entry.

Early intervention for disadvantaged children will get them off to a good start. The findings from all of the programs reviewed suggest that early, intensive intervention, along with continued follow-up as children enter school, can keep disadvantaged children from falling behind. Programs that provide intensive intervention directly to the child appear to be the most effective and have the longest lasting results. Educators need to invest in children at an early age so that they can have the opportunity to enter school on an equal footing with other children and learn from the start that they can be successful.

REFERENCES

Andrews, S. R., Blumenthal, J. B., Johnson, D. L., Kahn, A. J., Ferguson, C. J., Lasater, T. M., Malone, P. E., and Wallace, D. B. (1982). *The skills of mothering: A study of parent child development centers.* Monographs of the Society for Research in Child Development Series, no. 198, Vol. 74 (6).

Auerbach, A. (1968). *Parents learn through discussion: Principles and practices of parent group education.* New York: Wiley.

Auerbach, A. (1971). *Creating a preschool center: Parent development in an integrated neighborhood project.* New York: Wiley.

Badger, E. (1968). *Mothers training program in educational intervention by mothers of disadvantaged infants.* Washington, DC: National Institute of Education. (Eric Document Reproduction Services, No. ED 043 378).

Badger, E. (1971). A mother's training program—The road to a purposeful existence. *Children, 18,* 168–173.

Badger, E. (1973). *Mother's guide to early learning.* Paole, PA: McGraw-Hill.

Casto, G., & White, K. (1985). The efficacy of early intervention programs with environmentally at-risk infants. In M. Frank (Ed.), *Infant intervention programs: Truths and untruths* (pp. 37–50). Binghampton, NY: Harworth Press.

Ceci, S. J. (1991). How much does schooling influence general intelligence and its cognitive components? A reassessment of the evidence. *Developmental Psychology, 27* (5), 703–722.

Dunn, L. M., Chun, L. T., Crowell, D. C., Dunn, L. M., Alexy, L. G., & Yachel, E. R. (1976). *Peabody Early Experience Kit.* Circle Pines, MN: American Guidance Services.

Farran, D. C. (1990). Effects of intervention with disadvantaged and disabled children: A decade review. In S. J. Meisels & J. P. Shonkoff (Eds.), *Handbook of early childhood intervention* (pp. 501–539). New York: Cambridge University Press.

Field, T., Widmayer, S., Greenberg, R., & Stoller, S. (1982). *Pediatrics, 66* (6), 703–707.

Garber, H. L. (1988). *The Milwaukee Project: Preventing mental retardation in children at risk.* Washington, DC: American Association on Mental Retardation.

Gordon, I. J., Guinagh, B. J., & Jester, R. E. (1972). *Child learning through child play.* New York: St. Martin's Press.

Gray, S. W., & Ruttle, K. (1980). The family-oriented home visiting program: A longitudinal study. *Genetic Psychology Monographs, 102,* 299–316.

Greenberg, P., & Epstein, B. (1973). *Bridges to Reading.* Morristown, NJ: General Learning Corp.

Hargde, B., & Gray, S. (1975). *Helping families learn: A home-based program.* Demonstration and Research Center for Early Education. Peabody College, Nashville, TN.

Honig, A. S., & Lally, J. R. (1982). The family development research program: Retrospective review. *Early Child Development and Care, 10,* 41–62.

Honig, A. S., Lally, J. R., & Mathieson, D. H. (1982). Personal-social adjustment of school children after five years of family enrichment program. *Child Care Quarterly, 11* (2), 138–146.

Jester, E. R., & Guinagh, B. J. (1983). The Gordon Parent Education Infant and Toddler Program. From *As the twig is bent . . . Lasting effects of preschool programs* (pp. 103–132). Hillsdale, NJ: Erlbaum.

Lally, J. R., & Gordon, U. J. (1977). *Learning games for infants and toddlers.* Syracuse, NY: New Readers Press.

Lazar, I., Darlington, R., Murray, H., Royce, J., & Snipper, A. (1982). *Lasting effects of early education: A report from the consortium for longitudinal studies.* Monographs of the Society for Research and Child Development Series, no. 195, Vol. 47 (2–3).

Levenstein, P. (1970). Cognitive growth in preschoolers through verbal interaction with mothers. *American Journal of Orthopsychiatry, 40* (3), 426–432.

Levenstein, P. (1977). The mother-child home program. In M. C. Day & R. R. Parker (Eds.), *The preschool in action* (2nd ed.). Boston: Allyn and Bacon.

Levenstein, P., O'Hara, J., & Madden, J. (1983). The mother-child home program of the Verbal Interaction Project. From *As the twig is bent . . . Lasting effects of preschool programs* (pp. 237–263). Hillsdale, NJ: Erlbaum.

Madden, J., Levenstein, P., & Levenstein, S. (1976). Longitudinal IQ outcomes of the mother-child home program. *Child Development, 47* (4), 1015–1025.

Palmer, F. H. (1970). Socioeconomic status and intelligence among negro preschool boys. *Developmental Psychology, 3* (1), 1–9.

Palmer, F. H. (1978). *One to one: A concept training curriculum for children ages two to five.* Stony Brook, NY: Early Intellective Development.

Palmer, F. H. (1983). The Harlem Study: Effects by type of training, age of training, and social class. From *As the twig is bent . . . Lasting effects of preschool programs* (pp. 201–236). Hillsdale, NJ: Erlbaum.

Ramey, C. T. (1992). High risk children and IQ: Altering intergenerational patterns. *Intelligence, 16,* 239–256.

Ramey, C. T., Bryant, D. M., Sparling, J. J., & Wasik, B. H. (1985). Project CARE: A comparison of two early intervention strategies to prevent retarded development. *Topics in Early Childhood Special Education, 5* (2), 12–25.

Ramey, C. T., Bryant, D. M., & Suarez, T. M. (1985). Preschool compensatory education and the modifiability of intelligence: A critical review. In D. Ditterman (Ed.), *Current topics in human intelligence.* Norwood, NJ: Ablex.

Ramey, C. T., & Campbell, F. A. (1984). Preventive education for high-risk children: Cognitive consequences of the Carolina Abecedarian Project. *American Journal of Mental Deficiency, 88* (5), 515–523.

Ramey, C. T., & Campbell, F. A. (1987). The Carolina Abecedarian Project: An educational experiment concerning human malleability. In J. J. Gallagher & C. T. Ramey (Eds.), *The malleability of children* (pp. 127–139). Baltimore: Paul H. Brookes.

Ramey, C. T., & Ramey, S. L. (in press). Which children benefit most from early intervention. *American Journal of Public Health.*

Ramey, C. T., & Smith, B. (1977). Assessing the intellectual consequences of early intervention with high-risk infants. *American Journal of Mental Deficiency, 81,* 318–324.

Slaughter, D. T. (1983). Early intervention and its effects on material and child development. *Monographs of the Society for Research in Child Development* Series, no. 202, Vol. 48 (4).

Sparling, J., & Lewis, I. (1981). *Learning games for the first three years: A program for parent/center partnership.* New York: Walker Educational Book Corp.

Wasik, B. H., Ramey, C. T., Bryant, D. M., & Sparling, J. J. (1990). A longitudinal study of two early intervention strategies: Project CARE. *Child Development, 61,* 1682–1896.

White, K. R., Taylor, M. J., & Moss, V. D. (1992). Does research support claims about the benefits of involving parents in early intervention programs? *Review of Educational Research, 62,* 91–125.

▶ 3

Can Preschool Alone Prevent Early Learning Failure?

NANCY L. KARWEIT

There is a strong belief among educators and the general public that early childhood education is a good investment, especially for promoting later school success for disadvantaged students. Support for public investment of preschool programs continues to be high and includes endorsements from such organizations as the Committee for Economic Development, the National Governors' Association, the Council of Chief State School Officers, and the National Association of State Boards of Education.

Many factors have helped create and maintain support for public preschool programs. Demands for public preschool have been fueled by the growing number of children under the age of 5 who are living in poverty, the increasing number of children from diverse cultures and language backgrounds, and a dramatic increase in need for child-care arrangements. One superintendent recently summarized this conventional wisdom by the following statement: "The effect of early intervention on school success is well documented. I believe that early intervention therapy, language stimulation and rich experiences at ages three and four will do more to increase the achievement of at-risk children and to reduce dropouts than any amount of money spent at grades seven through twelve" (Lubeck & Garrett, 1989, p. 8).

Clearly, one source of the well-documented effects of which Lubeck and Garrett speak is the Perry Preschool Project. Perhaps the best-known study of the effects of preschool, the Perry Preschool Project has now followed its initial sample of preschoolers for over two decades after their enrollment in preschool as 3 and 4 year olds. This study documented that quality preschool programs benefit those attending them in several important ways, including short-term cognitive gains as well as longer-term positive effects on such outcomes as higher rates of school completion, lower unemployment rates, and lower teenage pregnancy rates.

The results from the Perry Preschool study, as well as other studies from the Consortium of Longitudinal Studies, have helped shape a belief in the efficacy of preschool as an intervention strategy for disadvantaged children. As Haskins (1989) observes, "It seems clear that the nation has been left with the impression that preschool programs for poor children have been proved effective and that they produce large benefits that in the long run will more than repay the public's investment. These claims have been repeated in testimony before legislative committees . . . and by national columnists" (p. 4). Haskins cites the frequently quoted estimate that $1.00 invested in preschool education saves $4.75 in subsequent spending, and he cautions about limits to the generalizability of the cost-benefit analyses to ordinary preschool or Head Start programs.

Other critics suggest that it is overly optimistic to expect that a one or two-year school program at age 3 or 4 could have sufficient impact to permanently affect the education and occupational achievements of a child brought up in poverty. For example, Fuerst and Fuerst (1991) argue that preschool by itself is not enough to alter the life chances of children born and reared in poverty. They document that sustained intervention over a period of years—not just a brief shot in the arm—is needed to make a difference for disadvantaged children. The Fuersts base their claim on a long-term study of children enrolled in Chicago's Parent Child Center and in subsequent Follow Through programs. In the case of the children studied in Chicago, Fuerst and Fuerst found that it took four to six years of sustained intervention for the girls and seven to nine years for the boys for a detectable achievement difference to be sustained. They argue that a one- or even two-year preschool program may be of value, but that it is not the kind of response that makes a significant contribution to the school success of those born into poverty. There is no simple short-term solution for long-term complex problems, they argue.

The policy implications the Fuersts draw from their research is that we should "use what funds are available for early childhood education for a smaller number of students, but for more years, rather than spending the money on a maximum number of children for only one year" (Fuerst, 1992).

The role of preschool, then, in promoting the long-term school success of disadvantaged children is currently the topic of some debate. While few would argue that preschool is without merit, the widely held view that

high-quality preschool can ameliorate the effects of poverty is being challenged. Instead, it is suggested, preschool should be seen as only one
strategy, not a miracle cure.

It is of some importance from a policy and practical point of view to be
clear about the effects of preschool on the chances for school success for
disadvantaged children. Fuerst (1992) argues that preschool by itself is not
enough and that the results demonstrated in the Chicago study are more
likely to be representative of preschool in general than are the results
demonstrated by the Perry Preschool study. The High/Scope Foundation
(developers of the Perry Preschool), on the other hand, argues that quality
preschool programs, in and of themselves, can have lasting effects on
young children.

This question of whether preschool in and of itself is effective is
actually part of a larger question about the effectiveness of differing arrangements of early childhood interventions. Intervention programs for 3-
and 4-year-old children can originate from a variety of directions and
philosophies. In some cases, such as the Perry Preschool, intervention is
designed as a stand-alone program. In other cases, the preschool is designed as a follow through for infancy programs or as a first step in a
school-based program. What can be learned from existing variations in
preschool arrangements about their effectiveness under different circumstances? Does the continuity of preschool, either with infant programs that
precede it or with elementary programs that follow it, make a difference?
Does participation in these programs significantly improve the chances for
poor children's school success, not just in comparison to a control group
but in comparison to average children? This chapter addresses these issues
by looking at studies that have used contrasting arrangements of services
for 4-year-old children.

ARRANGEMENT OF SERVICES
FOR FOUR-YEAR-OLDS

The primary question of interest in this chapter is whether there are
differences in effectiveness of preschool programs that are related to the
arrangement of services. To explore this issue, we contrast the effects from
studies that have utilized differing arrangements of programs for 4-year-
olds. Three classifications of programs for 4-year-olds are examined. *Preschool only* consists of those studies that examined the effect of a stand-
alone preschool. *Preschool and elementary* interventions focus on the preschool as the first step in the start of the child's school career and attempt to
link the experiences in the preschool to that of the elementary school in a
coherent way. These interventions also differ from the preschool-alone

interventions in duration of exposure. Finally, we look at the effect of those interventions that provide *infant, preschool, and/or elementary intervention.* The purpose of this chapter is to examine the relationship between these arrangements and short-term, mid-term, and long-term cognitive effects. For the purposes of this chapter, we are interested only in studies that can provide high-quality evidence on the effectiveness of the different arrangements. Unfortunately, although there are thousands of studies of preschool, there are very few studies that are methodologically rigorous enough to shed light on this topic.

We located six studies that provided programs for 4-year-olds, that employed randomized designs or utilized appropriate controls for existing entering differences, that followed the children for an adequate period of time, and that had contrasting service delivery models. These studies are the Early Training Project, the Perry Preschool Project, the Institute for Developmental Studies, the Philadelphia study, the Milwaukee Project, and the Carolina Abecedarian Project. The basic characteristics of these projects are listed in Table 3.1.

The programs vary in focus, intensity, and ages of children served. Some programs focus on children and parents, some operate as summer schools, some operate as regular school programs, and still others are extensions of infant programs. The programs are thus diverse and were begun with different intentions and different philosophies. On the other hand, all programs do serve preschool-age children and all are designed to help alleviate the effects of disadvantage, especially with respect to school functioning. How well do the differing approaches accomplish these school-oriented objectives? And are there particular arrangements of programs that seem related to effectiveness?

The Early Training Project (Gray)

Gray's Early Training Project (Gray, Ramsey, & Klaus, 1983) consisted of a 10-week summer program in which students met for four hours daily, five days per week. Students participated in a class of 20, served by one teacher and four assistants. During the school year, home visitors also worked with each family once a week for a period of one hour. The Early Training Project focused on perceptual/cognitive and language development using a traditional nursery school format, but with activities sequenced to become increasingly complex and carefully focused on increasing language use. The first entry in Table 3.1 summarizes the major features of Gray's study.

Some 61 students were randomly assigned to one of three groups: two groups that entered the program just described at different ages and one untreated control group. An additional control group in another city was also used. The two different treatment conditions differed only in the age

TABLE 3.1 Characteristics of Preschool Programs

Program	Focus	Ages Served and Amount of Time	Parent Component and Intensity	Intervention Before Age 3	Intervention After Age 4
Early Training Project (Gray)	Summer program (traditional nursery school program)	3½ to 6½ years old, 10 weeks, 4 hours/day	Yes; weekly home visits. **Low**	No	No
Perry Preschool Project (Weikart)	Curricular intervention, Piagetian preschool program	3 and 4 years old, mid-Oct. to June, half-day program	Yes; weekly home visits. **Low**	No	No
Institute for Developmental Studies (Deutsch)	Curricular intervention, focus on language	4 to 8 years old, regular school year	No	No	Yes K–3
Philadelphia Study (Beller)	Duration of participation in preschool	4 and 5 years old, regular academic year, half-day program	No	No	Yes PK, K, 1
Milwaukee Project	Intensive intervention, birth to kindergarten	0 to 5 years old, 7 hrs/day, 5 days/week	Yes **Low**	Yes	Yes K
Abecedarian Project	Educational day care; health, welfare services	0 to 8 years 0ld, 7 hours/day, 5 days/week	Yes **High**	Yes	Yes K & 1

at which the children started the program. The pretest IQ scores for the treatment and control groups were 89.4 and 87.3, respectively. At age 5, after participation in the program, the IQ scores were 96.05 and 86.3. By age 17, the IQs were once again very similar: 78.7 and 76.4.

Gray determined that 2.4 percent of the program children were placed in special education and 23.8 percent of the control children were so placed. The program children also showed a greater likelihood of not being retained in grade. Nearly 56 percent of the program children were retained in grade, whereas the figure was closer to 69 percent for the control children. About 22 percent of the program children dropped out of high school prior to completion; the corresponding figure for control children was about 43 percent. Thus the program had significant effects on important variables of grade repetition, special education placement, and high school completion.

Concerning the effects on reading and mathematics achievement in elementary schools, Gray's Early Training Project provides little reason to expect continued effects of program participation. The performance of students in the program was not significantly different from that of control students in math or reading at grades 4 and 6. Thus the study does not lend support to long-term effects of this type of early intervention effort on achievement. Table 3.2 summarizes the cognitive effects of this study (first entry in the table).

When the effects are analyzed separately by gender, a somewhat different picture emerges. There are pronounced differences. In particular, the Gray program appears to have been beneficial for girls but not for boys. It is not clear what factors or processes created these differences in the Gray study.

The Perry Preschool Project (Weikart)

Perhaps the most influential study of the effects of preschool has been the study of the Perry Preschool. There are really two parts to the Perry Preschool data: the documentation of the effects of preschool in general and the documentation of the effect of participation in particular preschool curricula. Here we are primarily interested in the demonstration of the effects of preschool.

The sample consisted of 123 disadvantaged, low-IQ children from Ypsilanti, Michigan. The subjects were recruited by locating all families with 3-year-old children and interviewing the parents to determine occupation, education, and household density. Children from low-SES families were administered an IQ test, and those who scored in the 70–85 range were selected. Students were randomly assigned to treatment and control groups.

TABLE 3.2 Summary of Cognitive Effects

Program	Exp/Ctl	IQ End PS	IQ End Gr. 3	Sp Ed %	Retain %	HS Grad %	Academic Achievement
Early Training Project (Gray)	E	96	94	2.4	56	78.0	No significant differences E/C grades 4 or 6. No IQ effects age 17. Gender interactions favor females.
	C	86	86	23.8	69	57.0	
	ES	.81	.51				
Perry Preschool Project (Weikart)	E	94	88	31	15	67	CAT percent correct ages 7–14 have effect sizes .05 to .17. NS still below normal.
	C	83	87	45	13	49	
	ES	1.01	.11				
Institute for Developmental Studies (Deutsch)	E	100	97	–	–	–	PPVT end of PK, K, and 3 favor EXP. Significant effect sizes approx. 50 at all 3 points.
	C	93	93	–	–	–	
	ES	.57	.27				
Philadelphia Study (Beller)	E	–	98	–	19	–	Effects on school grades, other achievement through grade 5 more consistent for girls than boys.
	C	–	92	–	24	–	
	ES	–	.40				
Milwaukee Project	E	126	103	41	29	–	On Metropolitan at grades K, 1, 2, 3, 4, E>C, but still below grade level.
	C	96	83	89	59	–	
	ES	2.15	1.46				
Abecedarian Project	E	102	–	–	12	–	K–1 for EE, EC, CE, CC: 50–50 (EE), 50–48 (EC), 38–40 (CE), 38–36 (CC).
	C	89	–	–	32	–	
	ES	.93	–				

E = Experimental

C = Control

ES = Effect Size

There were five waves of this study, beginning in 1962 and continuing through 1967. Across the five waves, 58 students were assigned to the preschool condition and 65 to the no preschool condition.

In contrast to the Early Training Project, the Perry Preschool Project took place during the academic year as a regular school program. The curricular approach was based on the developmental theories of Jean Piaget. The theoretical framework emphasized the interplay of content (e.g., classification and spatial relationship), three levels of representation (e.g., index, symbol, and sign), and two levels of operation (motor and verbal) (Lazar & Darlington, 1982). The approach emphasized developmentally appropriate activities and stressed the role of students' planning and initiation in their own learning.

Children entered the program at age 3 and attended the program for two years, from mid-October to May. The sessions were half-day, five days per week. In addition, the teachers visited the home of the students for 90 minutes weekly.

The short-term benefit of the Perry Preschool program was most pronounced in an average difference of 11 points in IQ scores between program and control groups. The percent enrolled in special education was also appreciably lower for the preschool enrollees (45 vs. 31 percent). The difference between those repeating a grade in the treatment (15 percent) and the control group (13 percent) was not significant. The largest differences were in the percent who graduated from high school, with 67 percent of the experimental students completing high school and only 49 percent of the students in control classes. Similar differences in the percent employed and arrested were found, favoring the Perry Preschool Project.

The differences in the percent correct on the Children's Apperception Test (CAT), measured at ages 7, 8, 9, 10, 11, and 14, favored the Perry Preschool children but were not statistically significant. The differences ranged from 2 to 8 percent. Both the Perry Preschool group and the control group were still well below grade level.

Both the Early Training Project and the Perry Preschool Project support the conclusion that preschool programs can have strong immediate effects on cognitive functioning, as measured by IQ tests. These effects are apparent at the onset of treatment and continue several years afterward. In the case of Perry Preschool, the experimental group is 44 percent of a standard deviation above the control at age 7. In the case of Gray's Early Training Project, the effects are still detectable six years after the initial treatment (effect size about .5) at age 10. Table 3.3 contains the effect sizes for the differences in IQ scores for the various programs.

Both studies also showed similar patterns of effects on reduced referral to special education and lower rates of dropping out of high school. In the case of the Early Training Project, the effect was greater for girls than

TABLE 3.3 Effect Sizes for Differences Between Control and Experimental Groups on IQ Scores

Program	E/C	12 Mos.	24 Mos.	36 Mos.	4 Yrs. Pretest	4 Yrs. Post	5 Yrs. Kinder.	6 Yrs. G1	7 Yrs. G2	8 Yrs. G3	10 Yrs. G5
Early Training Project (Gray)	E				90	96	95	98	94		88
	C				87	86	82	90	86		81
	ES				.15	.81	1.09	.63	.51		.54
Perry Preschool Project (Weikert)	E				79		95	91	92	88	85
	C				79		83	86	87	87	85
	ES				0		1.01	.45	.44	.11	.03
Institute for Developmental Studies (Deutsch)	E				92	99	100		97		
	C				92	92	94		93		
	ES				0	.57	.46		.27		
Milwaukee Project	E	117	125	125		126	118	119	103	103	104
	C	113	96	94		96	93	87	81	83	86
	ES	.26	1.9	2.0		2.0	1.7	2.1	1.5	1.3	1.2
Abecedarian Project	E	111	96	91		102	101				
	C	105	85	84		89	94				
	ES	.40	.73	.46		.86	.46				

Note: An effect size that is underlined indicates that the intervention was in effect when that comparison was made between the control group and the experimental group.

for boys. Both studies showed minimal long-term effects on achievement as measured by standardized tests. Gray's study measured achievement at grades 4 and 6 and showed no significant effect on achievement scores at either grade. By age 17, the IQ scores were equivalent. Weikart's study also shows only modest and nonsignificant achievement effects (effect sizes of 0.05 to 0.17).

The Institute for Developmental Studies (Deutsch)

The Institute for Developmental Studies (IDS) implemented an early enrichment program that was to become the forerunner of Head Start. The program brought 4-year-olds into special classes in the neighborhood school and continued to work with these children until the third-grade year. This study is of interest here because it coupled preschool with an elementary school intervention.

The study utilized random assignment to treatment and control conditions from a sample recruited to participate. The experimental group received an enriched program from prekindergarten through third grade. The control group began attendance at either kindergarten or first grade. A new wave of children attending prekindergarten classes began each year from 1963 to 1969. In total, there were 1,293 participants across the seven waves of this study.

The comparison groups consisted of the experimental groups, which received continuing treatment from prekindergarten through the third grade, and four control groups. The Css control group were those students who had volunteered for participation but who did not participate due to lack of space. Another control group, Ck, was the group of children who entered without prekindergarten experience directly into kindergarten. The C1 group entered at first grade without any kindergarten experience. Another control group, C123, entered at first grade with irregular amounts of prekindergarten or kindergarten experience.

The educational intervention was carefully structured to provide experiences for the children in prekindergarten through third grade who were seen as needed to remediate their learning difficulties. For example, there was a large emphasis on language development and the formation of positive self-concepts since these were areas in which previous research had shown striking differences between more and less advantaged youngsters.

In the initial study, significant differences were found between control (Css) and experimental children on the Stanford-Binet and on the Peabody Picture Vocabulary Test (PPVT) at the end of prekindergarten and at the end of kindergarten. At the end of the prekindergarten year, across four waves of data analysis, the average IQ difference was about seven points.

The average difference between the group that had not volunteered and the experimental group was slightly larger, about eight points. At the end of the kindergarten year, after the control group had entered school, this difference of seven points was maintained. The average IQ for the experimental group was about 100 and the average IQ for the original control group was 93.

At the end of the third grade, there were still differences between the groups in terms of IQ. The experimental group had an average IQ of 97, whereas the control group that did not attend preschool had an IQ of 93. Those entering at kindergarten had an IQ of 92 and those entering at first grade had an IQ of 89. Similar results were obtained with the PPVT. The results of this study are summarized in Table 3.1.

The Philadelphia Study (Beller)

Beller's Philadelphia Study examined the role that duration of preschool experience had on the disadvantaged children's socioemotional and cognitive growth and development. A quasi-experimental design was implemented in which three groups of Philadelphia children were compared; those with prekindergarten and kindergarten experience prior to first grade, those with kindergarten experience only prior to first grade, and those with no preschool experience prior to first grade. We include this study because of its relevance for the question of the effects of preschool as a single intervention in contrast to preschool as a part of a longer-term intervention. The students were initially studied from preschool through fourth grade. Follow-up data were obtained for the students in tenth and eleventh grades.

There were no statistically meaningful differences at pretest among the three groups on demographic measures, such as sex, race, presence of father in the home, and mother's educational level. The children, however, were not randomly assigned to the initial conditions. The children in the nursery school group (preschool) were recruited to attend the new program, so that factors affecting selection into the program are uncontrolled in the following analyses.

The nursery school program was a child-centered model that focused on the development of the child's creativity and need for discovery. The program provided a balance between structured and child-initiated activities. The classes operated for four days each week. The fifth day was used by the teacher for in-service training or for home visits. The kindergarten and first-grade program followed the educational philosophy of the preschool program. However, the staff-to-child ratio changed from 1:15 to 1:25. The students were assessed along a number of demographic, intellectual, and socioemotional dimensions. Three tests were utilized to assess intellectual functioning (Stanford-Binet, PPVT, and Draw-A-Person). In addition, the extent of success of the student as he or she progressed through the school was tapped by measures of grade retention, completion of high school, and college attendance. The Piers-Harris self-esteem scale was used to measure the child's self-esteem. Attitudes toward work and occupation were measured by the Career Maturity Inventory attitude scale.

Beller (1983) concluded that all three groups received a boost in IQ upon entry to school but that the boost was greatest among the group entering first (i.e., the nursery school group). He concluded that "the first year impact on the level of intellectual functioning is greater the earlier an economically disadvantaged child is exposed to an organized program of education." The same pattern held true for the scores on the PPVT, but not on the Draw-A-Person test.

The study also examined the effects of variations in preschool attendance on grades, general academic performance, and retentions. The researchers found that the participation in preschool positively affected grades for girls but did not consistently do so for boys. We note that these results may be consistent with the sex differences found in the Gray study and that done by the Fuersts. In terms of teacher evaluations of student progress as gleaned from report cards, Beller found that there was a significantly positive relationship with the duration of preschool. The relationship of retention and preschool experience did not reach statistical significance for the entire sample, but separate analyses by family background did show significance in the predicted direction.

Intellectual aptitude, measured from preschool through fourth grade, was significantly affected by the duration of preschool experience. The effects of preschool experience were substantially greater on girls than they were on boys. The credibility of the conclusions of the Beller Philadelphia Study rests on the belief that the groups were in fact equivalent at the outset. However, since the groups were not randomly assigned to the different conditions, it is not possible to separate the effects of continued selection bias from treatment effects.

The Milwaukee Project

The Milwaukee Project intervened for up to six years in the lives of children born to retarded and poor mothers. (See Chapter 2 for a detailed discussion of this project.) At about 2 years of age, the children went from the toddler and infant program into the early childhood program. A caregiver worked with these children in the early education program that emphasized language and problem solving and academic readiness. The mothers were also a part of the intervention.

The comparisons of the IQ scores of the control and experimental groups indicate that the Milwaukee Project was very effective. Moreover, the comparisons with the low-risk control group indicate that the experimental group was close to this group in terms of IQ scores at first through fourth grades. This finding of comparability with the low-risk control group is very important. Few studies have examined how the treatment group did in comparison to a normally progressing group. Information on performance relative to an equated control group as well as in comparison to a low-risk group is needed to provide a complete picture of the children's progress.

Fewer than half of the children in the experimental group received special education services, in contrast to about 90 percent of the control group. In terms of reading performance, the experimental group was seven months ahead of the control group at the end of the fourth grade (six months below grade level, however).

The Carolina Abecedarian Project

The Abecedarian Project was an intensive infant, preschool, and elementary school intervention. It is especially of interest because the design contrasted four treatment groups over the years from birth through 6 years old. The design entailed two treatments: infant/preschool and elementary based. The CC, the true control group, received no preschool or special school-age program. The EC group received only the experimental infant/preschool program. The CE group received only the school-age program, and finally the EE group received the experimental preschool and school-age program.

The comparison between the CC and the EE groups indicates the effect of participation in the full program continuously from birth through the end of first grade. In terms of differences in IQ scores, the experimental group had an average IQ of 101 at age 4, whereas the control group had an IQ of 88, or an effect size of .93. By the first grade, these scores were 98 and 92, respectively. On the PPVT, the EE group scored at the 50th percentile at both kindergarten and first grade, whereas the CC group scored at the 38th percentile at kindergarten and the 36th percentile at first grade. The EC group, which stopped participation in the program upon entry into kindergarten, declined from the 50th percentile to the 48th percentile. The children who did not receive early intervention but did receive the school-age intervention improved from the 38th to the 40th percentile. Children who received no intervention went from the 38 to the 36th percentile.

The school-age intervention (kindergarten and first grade) by itself was not very effective in changing the relative position of the participants. The preschool intervention itself helped start the children higher. Without continued intervention they showed a minor decline in percentile score, from the 50th to the 48th percentile.

The results of this study indicated that the addition of a school-age program added little to the effectiveness of the preschool and infant program. Furthermore, for the children without early intervention, the school-age intervention was not sufficient to bring the children up to the level of normal achieving peers or to the level of the children who had received the intervention in infancy and during preschool. We cannot tell if the infant or the preschool treatment was more important, as these treatments are not separated in the Abecedarian study.

EFFECTS OF PRESCHOOL OR EFFECTS OF DIFFERENT AGES FOR STARTING SCHOOL?

For the Deutsch, Gray, Weikart, and Beller studies the most robust effects for preschool have been found on IQ scores after the end of one year of participation—that is, on short-term measures of cognitive performance. Note that the comparison being made is between one population that is in school with another population that has not yet started school. Ceci (1991) has recently argued for an interpretation of the relationship of IQ and schooling that is important here. Traditionally, the argument has been made that a large portion of the IQ-schooling connection is due to the effect of IQ on schooling, through such avenues as higher number of years of schooling and persistence related to IQ. Ceci argues that although IQ has been traditionally viewed as affecting schooling, it is equally true that schooling exerts a substantial influence on IQ formation and maintenance. He uses the relationship between the amount of school and IQ changes to bolster his argument. The data in Ceci's article are primarily drawn from naturally occurring variations in the amount of school.

He reviews eight types of evidence to show the influence of IQ on schooling: (1) the correlation between IQ and years in school, (2) the influence of summer vacation, (3) the effect of intermittent school attendance, (4) the effect of delayed onset of school, (5) the effect of early termination of schooling, (6) the similarity of aptitude and achievement test scores, (7) cohort effects associated with schooling and IQ, and (8) historical changes in the schooling-IQ link. The portion of his argument that is of most interest here is that pertaining to studies of the effects of delayed onset of school on IQ.

The first study reviewed by Ceci concerned children whose schooling was delayed because of various external events, such as school closings due to war or segregation efforts. DeGroot (1951) examined the effect of the closing of many of Holland's elementary schools during World War II.

TABLE 3.4   Change in IQ Score for Treatment and Control for Year of School Entry

Program	Experimental IQ Change	Year or Age	Control IQ Change	Year or Age
Early Training Project (Gray)	7 (89 to 96)	Enter summer program	3 (87 to 90)	Enter first
Perry Preschool Project (Weikart)	15 (79 to 94)	Enter preschool	8 (79 to 86)	Enter kindergarten
Institute for Developmental Studies (Deutsch)	7 (92 to 99)	Enter preschool	1 (92 to 93)	Enter kindergarten
Philadelphia Study (Beller)	7 (92 to 99)	Enter preschool	3 (91 to 94) −1 (90 to 89)	Enter kindergarten, enter fist grade
Abecedarian Project	−1 (102 to 101)	Enter kindergarten (change from day care to school)	5 (89 to 94)	Enter kindergarten

He found that during this period of school closing there was a drop in IQ for school children of around seven points. The same type of effect was documented by Ramphal (1962) who found that children in a South African village who had been denied schooling for up to four years because of the unavailability of teachers dropped five IQ points for each year out of school. Ceci reviewed several other studies of missed or delayed schooling, including schooling in East Indian settlements (Schmidt, 1967) and the closing of the Prince Edward County, Virginia, schools to avoid integration during the early 1960s (Green, Hoffman, Morse, & Morgan, 1964). In these cases, as in the DeGroot study, there was a corresponding drop in IQ for missed schooling, with the greater missed schooling resulting in lower IQ scores. The magnitude of the effect on IQ varied across the studies, but Ceci argues that it is consistently large and should amount to about five points per missed year of school.

Ceci's thesis has some implications for understanding the effects for preschool attendance. First, if one has equivalent control groups with equated IQ scores, one should find that the IQ of the preschool group will go up about five points with respect to their initial score and in comparison to the control group. Second, one should find that the no preschool group, when looked at longitudinally, should have a similar increase in IQ in the year they enter school.

If attending school is assumed to cause a one-time increase in IQ of five points, then effects of particular preschool models might be evaluated against this standard. The increase in IQ score for the relevant year of entry in school for the studies just presented is provided in Table 3.4. Increases in IQ are seen for both the experimental and control groups, as Ceci's thesis predicts. However, the increase for the experimental group is generally larger than the control group. The differences in IQ between the experimental and control group at the end of the first school year therefore include effects due to different school entrance ages, program effects, and test and testing procedure effects.

COGNITIVE EFFECTS OF DIFFERENT ARRANGEMENTS OF SERVICES FOR FOUR-YEAR-OLDS

Table 3.2 summarizes the cognitive effects for the six programs just discussed. The IQ differences for the experimental and control programs are given at the end of prekindergarten as well as at the end of third grade, where available. The proportion of students in the two treatments assigned to special education or retained in grade are supplied as well. Lastly, cognitive effects of the programs are summarized in the far right-hand column.

In Table 3.5, we collapse these individual studies into three broad categories. The first category includes preschool-only programs. These are the programs that had an intervention targeted primarily at the children before formal schooling began. Here, we include the Perry Preschool study, the Gray study, and the Beller study. The Gray study actually was a summer school program in which the children might have been enrolled after the start of formal schooling; however, it most resembles a preschool-only category. The second category consists of studies that had preschool and elementary school interventions.

Lastly, we group together studies that include infant programs, preschool, and elementary school efforts. The two programs in this category are the Milwaukee and the Abecedarian studies. These are the most intensive programs, both in terms of the length of time they intervened with the children and the intensity of the intervention itself.

The preschool-only studies find large immediate effects for preschool. These effect sizes are in the range of .8 to 1 standard deviation, or roughly 12 to 15 points on an IQ test. By grade 3, these effects have been reduced appreciably. There is minimal evidence for the effect of preschool only on long-term academic achievement as measured by achievement tests. The Gray study does not show effects, the Weikart study shows nonsignificant effects, and in both cases the treatment group is still performing well below the average for the age or grade. Except for the Beller study, the differences between the control and experimental groups have disappeared by the end of the third or fourth grade. The Beller study finds its most consistent results in grades for girls but not for boys.

The Deutsch study provides information on another type of service, that of providing preschool and then follow-up into elementary school. There are modest achievement effects that persist until the third grade for this model. However, the magnitude of the effects is relatively small by the

TABLE 3.5 Summary of Cognitive Effects by Arrangement of Services

Program	IQ End PK	IQ End 3rd	Special Education	Grade Retention	High School Completion	Academic Achievement
Preschool	(.81) (1.01)	(.51) (.11)	+ +, NS	NS, NS		NS, NS
Preschool and Elementary	(.57)	(.27)	No data	No data	No data	Effect sizes in range .5
Infant, preschool, and elementary	(2.0) (.86)	(1.2)	+ +	+ +, + +	No data	+ +

third grade, even with continued intervention (.26). In this study, we do not know if the lack of effects was due to the failure to implement the program or if the program was not effective for these children.

The most intensive interventions are the ones that started at birth, provided educational day care, and then followed up with an elementary school program. The two programs fitting this description showed positive, consistent, and large effects across the different outcome measures. The Milwaukee and the Abecedarian programs both had an infant and a preschool program, so it is not possible to learn what the relative impact of each of these factors were. However, the review of birth to age 3 programs indicates that early intervention programs with continued follow-up have long-term effects for children, whereas those without long-term interventions are not generally successful in helping children maintain their success in school.

CONCLUSION

This look at the effects of various combination of services suggests that indeed preschool is not enough. Preschool and elementary school interventions may not be enough to create the magnitude of effect that is needed. The largest effects come about from the infant and preschool and elementary programs. This appears to support a view of the need for continuing intervention as opposed to a one-time shot in the arm.

Continuing intervention may be needed because the challenges that youngsters face in different environments and at different ages may in reality be very different. Programs at one stage or age may or may not prepare students for later experiences. For example, preschool may present a very different environment than elementary school. Ideally, the learning situation in preschool will foster independence and child-initiated activities. Competence in this environment may not mean that the child will be successful in first-grade classrooms, especially in reading. Raising IQ scores does not necessarily prepare children for reading and there is still an uncertain connection between the early preschool experiences and the first-grade expectations. The requirements and tasks change across the years; students may have special difficulty with making the transitions to different environments and may lack support in the family or community to help develop coping skills necessary to navigate in these environments.

With intensive efforts such as in the Milwaukee and Abecedarian Projects, there are continuing effects for intervention. However, the experimental groups in these studies were still performing below grade level, although they were continuing to perform better than the untreated control group. This should be sobering information for those who see one year of preschool as a primary means to reduce the education gap. It should temper the optimistic view that a brief stint in an ordinary prekindergarten class in inner-city public schools run in the normal way by normal teachers is likely to produce the life changing sort of effects that have often been suggested and trumpeted in the literature, the popular press, and in the political arena.

REFERENCES

Beller, E. K. (1983). The Philadelphia Study: The impact of preschool on intellectual and socioemotional development. In the Consortium for Longitudinal Studies (Ed.), *As the twig is bent . . . Lasting effects of preschool programs* (pp. 333–376). Hillsdale, NJ: Erlbaum.

Ceci, S. J. (1991). How much does schooling influence general intelligence and its cognitive components? A reassessment of the evidence. *Developmental Psychology, 27,* 703–722.

DeGroot, A. D. (1951). War and the intelligence of youth. *Journal of Abnormal and Social Psychology, 46,* 596–597.

Deutsch, M., Deutsch, C. P., Jordan, T. J., & Gullo, R. (1983). The IDS Program: An experiment in early and sustained enrichment. In the Consortium for Longitudinal Studies (Ed.), *As the twig is bent . . . Lasting effects of preschool programs* (pp. 377–410). Hillsdale, NJ: Erlbaum.

Fuerst, J. S. (1992, April). Why Head Start is not enough. *Newsweek.*

Fuerst, J. S., & Fuerst, D. (1991). *Chicago experience with early childhood program: The special case of the Child Parent Center Programs.* Unpublished manuscript. Loyola University, Chicago.

Garber, H. L. (1989). *The Milwaukee Project: Preventing mental retardation in children at risk.* Washington, DC: American Association on Mental Retardation.

Gray, S. W., Ramsey, B. K., & Klaus, R. A. (1983). The Early Training Project 1962–1980. In the Consortium for Longitudinal Studies (Ed.), *As the twig is bent . . . Lasting effects of preschool programs* (pp. 36–69). Hillsdale, NJ: Erlbaum.

Green, R. L., Hoffman, L. T., Morse, R., & Morgan, R. F. (1964). *The educational status of children in a district without public schools* (Co-operative Research Project No. 2321). Washington, DC: Office of Education, U.S. Department of Health, Education, and Welfare.

Haskins, R. (1989, February). Beyond metaphor: The efficacy of early childhood education. *American Psychologist,* 274–282.

Lazar, I., & Darlington, R. (1982). Lasting effects of early education. *Monographs of the Society fro Research in Child Development, 47,* (2–3, Serial #195).

Lubeck, S., & Garrett, P. (1989). *Pre-kindergarten programs in North Carolina: Preferences of superintendents and principals.* Chapel Hill, NC: University of North Carolina at Chapel Hill, Frank Porter Graham Child Development Center.

Ramey, C. T., & Campbell, F. A. (1987). The Carolina Abecedarian Project: An educational experiment concerning human malleability. In J. J. Gallagher & C.

T. Ramey (Eds.), *The malleability of children* (pp. 127–139). Baltimore: Paul H. Brookes.

Ramphal, C. (1962). *A study of three current problems in education.* Unpublished doctoral dissertation, University of Natal, India.

Schmidt, W. H. O. (1967). Socio-economic status, schooling, intelligence, and scholastic progress in a community in which education is not yet compulsory. *Paedogogica Europa, 2,* 275–286.

Schweinhart, L. J., & Weikart, D. P. (1983). The effects of the Perry Preschool Program on youths through age 15—A summary. In the Consortium for Longitudinal Studies (Ed.), *As the twig is bent . . . Lasting effects of preschool programs* (pp. 71–101). Hillsdale, NJ: Erlbaum.

▶ 4

Issues in Kindergarten Organization and Curriculum

NANCY L. KARWEIT

Kindergarten attendance is nearly universal in the United States today,*
but the kindergarten experience itself is far from uniform. Kindergarten is
most often a half-day program, although the frequency of full-day attendance is on the rise.† In some districts, kindergartners follow a full-day,
every other day schedule. Some students attend two years of kindergarten
prior to first grade, either due to placement in extra-year kindergarten
programs or as a result of kindergarten retention. The typical age for
kindergarten entrance also varies by state, ranging from being age 5 by July
1 to being age 5 by December 31. Finally, there are clear differences in
curricular approach and emphasis in the kindergarten, especially with
respect to reading and math instruction.

Which of these differences in kindergarten organization and curriculum matter for the children who experience them, either in the short run

---

*Among first- and second-graders in the spring of 1990, approximately 98 percent attended
kindergarten (Office of Educational Research and Improvement, National Household Education Survey, 1991).

†Approximately 58 percent of students who were in first and second grades in 1990 attended
half-day kindergarten (Office of Educational Research and Improvement, National Household
Education Survey, 1991).

or later on? This chapter summarizes available research findings of the effectiveness of these different practices and policies. We first discuss research related to organizational characteristics of kindergarten, such as length of the kindergarten day and entrance age, followed by a discussion of internal features of kindergartens, such as curriculum and instruction.

ORGANIZATIONAL FEATURES OF KINDERGARTEN

Mandatory Kindergarten

Currently, kindergarten attendance is mandatory in eleven states as well as the District of Columbia, and in one other state it must be attended if a student does not pass a specific test.* Despite the lack of widespread compulsory attendance legislation, the majority of students attend kindergarten nonetheless. A shift to mandatory kindergarten, although affecting a small total number of students, might have large impacts in specific areas due to the distribution of attendance. For example, in Maryland (which has mandatory kindergarten), it is estimated that between 10 to 20 percent of the students in Baltimore do not presently attend kindergarten.

As states move to mandatory kindergarten, however, it is not clear what the long-term effects will be. Those who favor mandatory kindergarten argue that universal attendance will help even out the current disparities in readiness for first grade.

Despite these intentions, mandatory kindergarten may increase, not decrease, the diversity of students as they enter first grade. When attendance is optional, not all students are expected to be ready for first grade and there is probably a fairly fluid, loose set of expectations about appropriate accomplishments and attributes of first-graders. When kindergarten attendance is mandatory, the expectations for performance for entering first-graders are likely to rise as well as the expectations that all children will be able to meet these new standards. One unintended effect of mandatory kindergarten may thus be an acceleration of the kindergarten curriculum. We are unaware of any study that has documented the effects, intended or unintended, of mandatory kindergarten on the curriculum and standards.

---

*Kindergarten attendance is required in Arkansas, Delaware, Florida, Louisiana, Maryland, Ohio, Oklahoma, Oregon, South Carolina, South Dakota, Tennessee, and the District of Columbia; it must be attended or readiness demonstrated in West Virginia (Education Commission of the States, 1992).

Full-Day Versus Half-Day Kindergarten

Initially, kindergarten teachers taught the children in the morning and visited the children's homes in the afternoon. The day was shortened to a half-day during World War II due to a shortage of teachers and building space and a growing birth rate (Oelerich, 1979). By the early 1960s, about 90 percent of all kindergartens were half-day programs. Increasing interest in compensatory programs and the need for child care increased the percentage of full-day programs. Today, the majority of children (58 percent) still attend half-day programs.

A modest number of quality research studies exist to address the issue of the effects of full-day versus half-day programs. Studies that used random assignment or equivalent matched group design (Johnson, 1974; Holmes & McConnell, 1990; Winter & Klein, 1970; Oliver, 1980) find modest, though not always consistently positive, effects for full-day programs (see Table 4.1). In 13 other studies, which employed a pre- to postcomparison with a control group, modest effects in favor of full-day attendance are seen, after controlling for initial differences. These effects were most consistent in studies that focused on disadvantaged students (see Table 4.2).

There is little evidence of *long-term* effects of full-day kindergarten attendance, even as of the end of first grade. The pattern of short-term effects is consistent with other research on early intervention efforts (McKey et al, 1985; Lazar & Darlington, 1982). The lack of robust effects for additional time is also consistent with research on the effects of allocated time on achievement (Karweit, 1983; Karweit, 1988; Berliner, 1990). The length of the school day merely defines the opportunities for learning, not what actually takes place in classrooms. Meyer (1985), for example, found that some half-day kindergartens had more high-quality instructional time than did full-day kindergartens. In addition, Puleo (1988) reports that time on task is lower in full-day classes (64 percent) than in half-day classes (80 percent).

The observation that even short-term academic benefits of full-day kindergarten are most clearly demonstrated in at-risk populations is important to bear in mind as districts think about implementing full-day programs. There is little evidence to suggest that full-day kindergarten has any positive effect with middle-class children. Other putative advantages of full-day kindergarten—such as consistent schedules in the school, helping working parents with a longer school day, and the possibility of more individualized attention for young children—need to be examined carefully. Full-day kindergarten will have to compete among many other alternative early intervention strategies such as establishing prekindergartens, reducing class size in early grades, or providing tutors in early grades.

(Text continues on page 86.)

TABLE 4.1 Summary of Effects of Full-Day and Half-Day Kindergarten Programs: Random Assignment/Matched Control Group Studies

Study	Sample	Treatment	Effects	Size	Notes
Johnson (1974)	Princess Anne, MD:	EXP = full day (5'15")	Fall/Spring Walker Readiness K		
Pre-post	20 students matched on	CTL = half day (2'30")	Cohort 1 posttest	.66	p < .05
Random assignment	age, race, SES, sex, and	Same curriculum enrichment given full	2	.58	ns
Replicated	ability assigned to TRT (full	day	3	.08	ns
Longitudinal effects	day) or CTL (half day)		Spring Stanford Achievement		
	3 experiments: 1970, 1971,	Measures:	Cohort 1 posttest only	.13	ns
	& 1972	Walker Readiness	2	.28	ns
		Stanford Achievement	3	.59	ns
		Reading group grade 1	Readiness Group Placement 1st		
			Cohort 1	.00	ns
			2	.06	ns
			3	.57	ns
Winter & Klein (1970)	Two studies:	CTL = attendance am/pm	Metropolitan at end of K	+3.01	p < .005
Screened; then ran-	1) Disadvantaged treat-	TRT = regular + 90 minutes academic	Stanford at end of K	.62	ns
dom assignment to	ment and control selected	pgm	Stanford at end of 1st	.62	ns
treatment/control	from lowest 10% of K class	No pretest difference			
	TRT: n=6				
	CTL: n=7				

Continued

TABLE 4.1 *Continued*

Study	Sample	Treatment	Effects	Size	Notes
	2) Advantaged selected treatment and control from those most able to benefit TRT: $n=26$ CTL: $n=29$	CTL = attendance regular TRT = regular + 90 minutes academic pgm Significant pre-test Differences favoring TRT	Pretest Peabody Picture Metropolitan at end of K (adj post) Stanford at end of K (adj post) Stanford at end of 1st (adj post)	1.28 $p<.05$ – ns – ns 1.03 $p<.05$	
Oliver (1980) Pre-post ANCOVA No pretest differences Comparable program	Cambridge, MA: 61 students in 4 classes, half day 98 students in 6 classes full day	EXP = full day with structured curric. 117 minutes/day CTL = half day with same structured curriculum 83.8 minutes per day	Clymer-Barrett Prereading Inventory Murphy-Durrell Prereading	2.84 $p<.05$ 1.16 $p<.05$	Effect size inflated by use of class means
Holmes & McConnell (1990)	10 schools full day 10 schools half day Randomly assigned to treatment	Half day vs. full day pretest Brigance ns diff	CAT at end of K Visual Recognition Sound Vocabulary Comprehension Language Experience Math Concepts	ns ns ns ns ns +.26	

TABLE 4.2 Summary of Effects of Full-Day and Half-Day Kindergarten Programs: Nonmatched Groups/Pre-Post Studies

Study	Sample	Treatment	Effects	Size	Notes
Carapella & Loveridge (1978) ANCOVA Both groups eligible, control group of non-participants who were eligible	St Louis public schools: 507 students who scored below 50th percentile on CPI who were eligible for attendance at extended day—273 enrolled, 234 control	Supplementary instruction for kindergarten pupils using small group and individual instruction in extended day	Comprehensive Test of Basic Skills Mathematics Reading	.43 $p < .001$ .32 $p < .001$	
Nieman & Gastright (1981) Existing sample Longitudinal Post only with evidence initial equivalence	551 K students in 16 Cincinnati schools receiving Title I Full-day students had preschool experience, half-day did not.	EXP = full day K (n = 410) CTL = half day K (n = 141) EXP also had preschool	Pretest (Sept. Kinder "Goal card") Boehm (Dec. Kinder) Metropolitan (April Kinder) Metropolitan (4th grade—70% sample) Metropolitan (8th grade—50% sample) Grade retention Special education	NS .35 $p < .001$ .35 $p < .001$ .25 $p < .01$ .25 $p < .01$ .13 $p < .01$ .25 $p < .001$	
Hatcher (1980) ANCOVA ad hoc sample	4 school districts in Texas, 2 having half-day K and 2 having full-day K—60 students selected at random	Half-day vs full-day No information on curriculum or on differences in treatments	Metropolitan Readiness California Test of Personality Valett Developmental Survey Basic	ns ns ns	
Adcock (1980) ANOVA ad hoc sample	189 urban and rural K children in 5 Maryland local education agencies Comparison of existing full-day and half-day Ks	EXP = full day (n = 131) CTL = half day (n = 58) Measures: Metropolitan (pre and post)	Results ANCOVA Post = pre + K type	.56 $p < .001$	Estimated setting $t = 3.09$, minimum value for $p < .001$

Continued

TABLE 4.2 Continued

Study	Sample	Treatment	Effects	Size	Notes
Jarvis & Molnar (1986) ANOVA Half-day sample schools in process of going full day	New York City: 1807 full-day K 223 half-day K Citywide conversion to full-day K, half-day were ones unable to convert	Contrasts: Half day/language Full day/language Measures: Brigance Pre/Pst LAB Pre/Post	Result ANCOVA Brigance English speakers Non-English speakers LAB	.09 ns .45 p<.05 .38 p<.05	
Evans & Marken (1984) Pre-post ANCOVA Students are at different points beyond K	Metropolitan school district in Wash. state, mostly white, middle class: 174 1st, 2nd, 3rd in 2 diff elem schools who had different K pgms	Contrasts: Full day (n=87) Half day (n=87) Measures: Ability test (kinder CAT (1, 2 or 3) Early Chd School Sentiment Teacher ratings Reading attitude	Results ANCOVA CAT Reading attitudes Referral special education	– ns + –.26 p<.05	
Derosia (1980) Pre-post ANCOVA Students are at different points beyond K	Jefferson City, Colorado: 384 students in K, 1st and 2nd grades having full or half-day K	Full day (n=67) Half day (n=93)	Boehm (adjusted for pretest, SES, age) CTBS (Grade 1) CTBS (Grade 2)	.36 p<.05 ns ns	
Warjanka (1982)	30 students who scored < 65 on Metropolitan Readiness Test and 40 students who were in same K classes with scores > 65	Six-month treatment, regular K + extended day curriculum based on participant's ability	At pre-test, FDK group 1 standard deviation lower than other group (37.8 vs 20.5) on Metropolitan Readiness Test. After six-months of treatment, EKD group and regular group were same (54.3).	(+)	

Study	Sample	Treatment/Design	Results	Effect	Notes
Slaughter (1983)	96 students who were identified as at risk and 191 other K students	Additional instruction (119 to 242 hours) Smaller classes (15:1) Curricular change—whole language approach	Pre-post design At pre-test FDK group significantly lower than regular group on CAT listening skills subtest (In NCEs, (24 vs 45). At post-test FDK made significant gains, while regular group declined. (36 NCE to 42 NCE)	(+)	
Lysiak & Evans (1976) Convenience sample Replicated two years	Fort Worth, TX: 916 students in 111 K classes	Comparison of 6 curricular models, for students of differing SES, ethnicity, and full day and half day	Full day > half day for low SES and for high SES	(+)	
Alper & Wright (1979)	Phoenix, Ariz: 98 K students in extended day and regular	Full day had longer day (5 vs. 2½) and smaller classes (12–25) Teacher visits to homes Three-month study	Metropolitan Readiness Test Extended day > regular No report of significance level	(+)	No significance levels computed
May (1989)	5 school FD, 5 schools HD, match SES and ach. level school	Half day vs. full day	ITBS at end of K Work Analysis Math Total	(+.) (+.) (+.)	
Azumi (1987)	Nonequivalent groups, FD are more advanced having had PK experience ANCOVA adjusts for age, readiness	Half day vs. full day	CTBS at end of K Visual Recognition Sound Vocabulary Oral Math Concepts	+.86 +.35 +.77 +.50 +.50	Not equivalent groups

Unfortunately, there is little research directly comparing the relative effectiveness of these differing approaches.

Two-Year Kindergarten Programs

Young children differ markedly in their experiences and development as they enter kindergarten. One response to this student diversity is to give the less ready children an extra year before entering first grade. There are three commonly used types of two-year kindergarten programs:

1. *Developmental kindergartens* screen children prior to the kindergarten year and place them in a two-year route to first grade. The first year of kindergarten and second year of kindergarten are differentiated in approach and curriculum.
2. *Kindergarten retention* recycles a child through kindergarten after experiencing failure the first time through.
3. *Transitional first or junior kindergartens* place children in a differentiated program after they have had difficulty in kindergarten, but prior to first-grade entry.

The research on extra-year programs suffers from the same difficulties as research on retention: selection bias (lack of random assignment or equivalent control group) and failure to adequately identify the basis of comparison (comparison of comparable children after equal time or at equal age). Selection bias is often an issue as matched control groups for students in extra-year programs are typically constructed from students who are recommended for retention or two-year placement, but whose parents refused retention or placement. The mere fact of parental refusal suggests preexisting (and uncontrolled for) differences between the groups on such factors as social economic status (SES) and parent involvement and beliefs.

Chapter 5 reviews studies related to extra-year kindergarten programs. The major conclusion of that chapter is that across the methodologically adequate studies, there was little evidence that extra-year kindergarten programs were beneficial to children. However, simply promoting children was also not very helpful. Children do not outgrow academic problems; ignoring their problems and promoting them anyway is also not an effective strategy.

Entrance Age

Typically, children in the United States begin kindergarten when they are 5 years old. States routinely have debates about raising and lowering the entrance age to help make children "ready" for school. Studies of the effect of age do not support this as an effective strategy. Although the youngest children in the classroom do show a lower score on first-grade reading tests (Shepard & Smith, 1986), these differences disappear by third grade. Moreover, moving the starting age up or down does not solve the problem of being the youngest in the classroom, it simply defines another group of children as the young students. The kindergarten population today is older than it was 30 years ago due to changes in regulations governing starting ages (Shepard & Smith, 1986). Moving the age up has not decreased the number of nonready children. In fact, the retention rate in kindergarten has risen over the same period, probably because of the escalation of difficulty of the kindergarten curriculum (Shepard & Smith, 1986).

More Time, Higher Quality?

The lion's share of kindergarten reform efforts have in some way or another focused on the amount and scheduling of time. Adding time to the kindergarten, making attendance mandatory, changing the starting age— all focus on changes in school time. On the whole, these temporal innovations do not seem to be particularly effective in accomplishing the major challenge to kindergarten education, namely that of providing an individually and developmentally appropriate curriculum for all children.

For example, in the case of extending the kindergarten day, although there have been short-term positive effects, we suspect that the extension of the kindergarten day was also accompanied by a shift in the curriculum to a more academic focus. Thus, it is unclear to what extent the change involved time alone or time and curriculum.

By and large, changes in the current *organization* of kindergarten will have some, but probably only modest, effects. More long-lasting and far-reaching change will have to involve what goes on *inside* kindergartens.

INSIDE KINDERGARTENS

Many changes are currently being advocated for the kindergarten curriculum. There are two movements that appear to be going on at the same time, sometimes in harmony and sometimes in conflict with one another. The first movement rejects the pushing down of the methods and content of the elementary curriculum into the kindergarten. In particular, this part of the kindergarten reform movement wants to ensure that classroom practice is age and developmentally appropriate. The second movement, aimed at early intervention to prevent school failure, wants to ensure that students in kindergarten receive the skills they need to succeed in first and later grades. The two goals are not necessarily incompatible—one can have developmentally appropriate kindergartens in which students acquire the necessary skills to be on the way to success—however, they often do result in conflict over content and methods in the curriculum.

The instructional methods part of this debate, as it is seen in kindergarten, primarily involves the balance of teacher-directed versus child-initiated activity. The content part of this debate involves the relative merits of focusing children's attention on the communicative function of written language or on the form of the written language (Stahl & Miller, 1989; Chall, 1989; Carbo, 1989; Turner, 1989). In the current version, this debate is seen as a square-off between advocates of phonics and whole language. Stahl and Miller (1989) carried out a meta-analysis of the effects of whole language/language experience approaches in comparison to more traditional curricula. In kindergarten they incorporated studies that compared whole language/language experience to use of a basal series. They found that in 17 studies the whole language/language experience approach was favored; in 14 studies there was no difference; and 2 studies favored the basals. Thus, this meta-analysis endorses the use of whole language/language experience approaches in kindergarten in comparison to basals.*

Debates about approaches to reading instruction are long standing and frequently take on an ideological fervor. The continuing debate between advocates of whole language and more phonetic approaches to beginning reading provides a current example of the heated debate over approaches to beginning reading. Adams (1990) suggests the importance of striking a balance. The issue, for her, is not whether whole language or phonics is more effective but when and how much of each is effective.

The sticky part in this debate does seem to be the approach by which young readers come to understand the phonetic principles of the language. The ability to analyze words into their constituent sounds is a necessary skill for beginning readers to acquire. Many beginning readers experience difficulty in accessing the phonemic units of a word. The basic task facing the beginning reader is to develop an understanding of the link between the "sounds of speech and the signs of print" (Ball & Blachman, 1988). Some students have a great deal of difficulty with this task. Intervention studies in kindergarten suggest that specific strategy training in phonemic segmentation is beneficial in this process. Ball and Blachman (1988) carried out an interesting study in which kindergarten children received specific intervention training in phonemic awareness. Students were assigned to one of three groups: phoneme training, no control, and language development control. The phoneme group received specific training in developing decoding skills. At the end of the intervention, the phoneme training

---

*We note that they did not make the same conclusion about first grade, although several authors disputed the analyses and conclusions (McGee & Lomax, 1990; Schickedanz, 1990).

group scored significantly higher than the other groups on tests of reading performance. Several other studies document the singular importance of phonemic segmentation, suggesting agreement among reading researchers on the centrality of this task for beginning readers (Adams, 1990).

The debate, then, may be less about the importance of the particular skill and more about the method of presentation. Decontextualized phonics instruction is especially objectionable to proponents of whole language. Unfortunately, the debate about the method of presentation should not obscure the important fact that beginning reading is facilitated by phonemic awareness and that many children have difficulty with this task. Disadvantaged children in particular seem to have difficulty with grasping this concept (Wallach et al., 1977). Moreover, it is not clear that teachers who claim to be presenting "phonics in context" actually present the material in a systematic and thorough enough way to be comprehensible to the children. Studies contrasting these approaches to building phonemic awareness are needed.

Beginning reading approaches used in kindergarten, therefore, need to be carefully attentive to building needed skills, but in a manner appropriate for the kindergarten child. Certainly kindergarten children need to understand that print conveys meaning before they start on the task of decoding. Otherwise, the activity is disconnected from any meaningful purpose for the children.

Many publishers, districts, and teachers are producing new curricular materials in the kindergarten that aim to be more appropriate to the kindergarten-age child and to incorporate the type of balance between whole language and phonics, which Marilyn Adams and others suggest. However, we do not know the actual extent to which actual classroom practice has been altered, as opposed to teachers simply philosophically embracing new ideas. Studies of teachers' beliefs and actual practices suggest that the two may not necessarily be the same. For example, in a study of preschool, Robinson (1990) found in a survey of preschool teachers that 62 percent of them stated that they used the emergent literacy perspective in their classroom. Yet a significant portion of these same teachers thought that exposing children to written language was developmentally inappropriate. Robinson concludes that these inconsistencies suggest that there is still considerable controversy among practitioners about how to prepare children for reading. It is unclear whether these inconsistencies arise from an incomplete understanding of the method or an incomplete adoption due to other pressures or district directives. Other studies that document this same disparity between teacher belief and practice suggest that the disparities arise because of differences in beliefs, not failure to implement (Hatch & Freeman, 1988).

EXAMPLES OF EFFECTIVE PROGRAMS

An earlier chapter (Karweit, 1989a) reviews effective programs and practices for kindergarten students. In that work, we looked at the programs that had been certified as effective by the Joint Dissemination Review Panel (JDRP). These are the programs that have been reviewed by a panel of educational experts and judged, on the basis of submitted evidence, to be effective. The volume *Educational Programs that Work* describes the currently validated programs (JDRP is now called PEP). In the current *Educational Programs that Work*, we found that there are surprisingly few new additions since the 1970s. An earlier examination of JDRP-validated programs (Karweit, 1989a) found some 21 programs that had been validated for kindergarten. In the current *Educational Programs that Work*, we found that 7 of those original programs were still active (KITE, TALK, CLIMB, STAMM, Early Prevention of School Failure, KINDERMATH, and Kenosha Model). Of the 7, only 2 had substantial modifications made to the program since the initial certification (KITE, which integrates Astra's Magic Math and Alphaphonics, and Early Prevention of School Failure, which added a first-grade component). A summary of salient features of these programs is provided in Table 4.3.

In the next section, we describe the operation and effectiveness of four kindergarten programs: Kindergarten Integrated Thematic Experiences (KITE), Early Prevention of School Failure (EPSF), Writing to Read (WTR), and Story Telling and Retelling (STaR). These programs were selected because they represent a range of intensity of services and costs; they all have evidence of effectiveness, and they involve contrasting methods.

Kindergarten Integrated Thematic Experiences (KITE)

KITE incorporates Astra's Magic Math and Alphaphonics, two widely used and well-evaluated programs. (See Karweit, 1989a, for a more complete discussion of these programs and their evaluations.) KITE integrates the entire kindergarten day through thematic units emphasizing language, cognitive physical development, and socioemotional development. KITE provides a thematic program pack with lesson materials for each day. Teachers utilize a KITE integration matrix for literature, beginning reading, and science. Through the use of a webbing process, the teacher learns to plan and integrate the day around the theme. This open-ended planning fosters creativity and gives teachers supportive materials and a framework for planning.

The original evaluation of the math and reading components contained random assignment to treatment and control groups, as well as follow-up

(Text continues on page 96.)

TABLE 4.3 Effective Kindergarten Programs

Name	Developer	Content	Instructional Strategy	Evaluation Design	Measures	Effects	Cost/Training	Adoptions/Activity
KITE								
(incorporates Alphaphonics & Astra's Magic Math) 2/90 90–11	South San Francisco Unified School	Rdg. Math	Integrated, thematic approach, multisensory, child centered, hands-on experiment	Comparison control group using pre-post	CTBS Math KITE CTL Reading KITE	+22 NCEs +6 NCEs +27 NCEs	$390/classroom	
CLIMB								
9/85 (recertification) 1–44	Middlesex, NJ	Rdg. Math	Diagnostic/prescription approach	Spring to spring achievement compared to nat'l norms & compensatory growth	CTBS	+		781 (1982–6) from sponsor
TALK								
7/79 1/85 78–189	Rockford, Illinois, school system	Lang.	Specialist works in classroom 4 wks ½ hour for 6 months	Pre-post ANCOVA trt, matched controls	PPVT 75 76 WISC 75 75 PPVT 75 76 (K) 75 76	.25 .42 .38 .46 .26 .74 .38 .55	$50 manual ½ day	572 districts

Continued

TABLE 4.3 *Continued*

Name	Developer	Content	Instructional Strategy	Evaluation Design	Measures	Effects	Cost/Training	Adoptions/Activity
STAMM								
12/84 (recertification) 76-87	Lakewood, Co	Math	Continuous progress math with mgt system	Pre-post implementation scores for district & adoption site as consumables, pre-post design, fall-to-spring	CAT	+	# stdts × 7, avg startup. # stdts × cf if wkbks used	41 states, 1,500 adoptions
Kenosha Model								
78-184	Kenosha, WI	Lang.	Extended day K 2-3 hrs in afternoon, additional time for remedial instruction	Pre-post gains compared to expected	PPVT TOBE	+ NCE gain Avg = 8	$10/student	34 states
EPSF								
4/77 74-46R	Peotone District, IL	Rdg. Math	Early identification of developmental needs & learning styles of 4-, 5-, & 6-year-olds	Improvement per month on different scales – no comparison data either w/ a control group or preimplementation	PLS (Pre-school language scale) PPVT (Peabody) VMI (Visual)	+	2-day trng $500/bldg $5/student	From sponsor, 50,000 classrooms

Continued

On the Way to Success in Reading	6/90			Supplementary 1st-grade program focusing on reading literature, writing, & appropriate practice			1-day trng $125/class $5/student
Interdependent Learning Model	8/77 77–121	Fordham University	Rdg. Math	Instructional games and pupil self-management methods to teach traditional academic skills, positive socio-cultural attitudes & behaviors Components: (Reading) Linguistic Pattern Series —Getting Ready —Beginner Sequence —Introductory Sequence Literature Series Workbook Series Small group (4–6) Emphasis modeling Emphasis games Frequent feedback Imp. monitoring	Comparison with control, district (Atlanta). After two years in program, 90% of first-graders at 50th percentile. At beginning, 45% were. In comparison to Atlanta schools in general, the increase in number of students scoring above but ILM made significantly higher gains!	Comparison proportion at 50 percentile on CTBS 90% first-graders in ILM at 50 percentile; two years before, 45% were. Better than control.	Trainer, $250/day (1½ days minimum) Materials, reading, $25/student Reading Linguistic Series Classroom Management Manual Training Manual Games Conversation games manual

TABLE 4.3 *Continued*

Name	Developer	Content	Instructional Strategy	Evaluation Design	Measures	Effects	Cost/Training	Adoptions/Activity
First Level Math								
84-1 (Kindermath)	PRIMAK Educational Fndt.	Math	Sequential curriculum & mgt system wchich is diagnostic/prescriptive. Instructional grps formed on basis of pre-tests. Instruction in 3–4 grps for about 20–30 minutes.	Pre-post design, fall to spring	CIRCUS	+ Not possible to compute	$35/kit	
Right to Read								
74-93	Glassboro, NJ	Rdg.	Diagnostic, prescriptive, indiv. progress model, ungraded	No control 325 children pre-post	CRI (Classrm Reading Inv)	Avg gain = 1.52 yrs	20 hrs inservice + 1 hr/wk	No data
Perception +								
6/74 74-78	ERIC Sewell, NJ	Making experiences meaningful	15 minutes 3 times/week	No data provided			$115/kits; kits for 2 levels	

STAY						
4/73 73–43	Moore, OK	Alternative to K reten. Verbal Math Human rel Fine arts Small class (20), 2 tchrs, aide	Spend morning regular first, afternoon in STAY	Pre-post NCE growth no control	Stanford Ach NCE growth = 34 NCEs	$2,000 each student
Precision Teaching						
5/75 5/79 (recertification) 75–25	Great Falls, MT	Suitable for all curricular areas	Measurement procedures daily assessment, charting strategies	Comparison district avg over 4-year period	ITBS Reading Y4 20 pts Math Y4 40 pts	Not provided

of children through third grade. The effects were uniformly significant and large (effect sizes = .89 to 1.11)

The evaluation of KITE looked at NCE (normal curve equivalent) gain scores in comparison to an equated control. The average growth for the KITE group was around 25 NCEs; for the control group, it was 6. This corresponds roughly to an effect size of .90.

Three features of KITE are noteworthy. First, it relies on a systematic approach to the introduction of letters and letter-sound correspondence. Second, it encourages teacher input, modification, and creativity so that teacher "ownership" is possible. Finally, it has a reasonable enough evaluation and a long enough continued history of operation that is likely that teachers utilizing this method will replicate the results in their classrooms.

Early Prevention of School Failure/On the Way to Success in Reading and Writing

The Early Prevention of School Failure/On the Way to Success in Reading and Writing (EPSF-Success) program is designed for at-risk kindergarten and first-grade students. EPSF is a kindergarten program that focuses on early identification of developmental needs and learning styles. Its companion first-grade program is called On the Way to Success in Reading and Writing. We comment on this program even though it is a first-grade program because it is closely connected to the kindergarten program.

> The Success resource kit provides the program teacher with effective teaching strategies and student-centered activities for an integrated literature-based classroom program. The strategies used in Success include a literature-based reading and writing program, use of themes and units, higher process thinking activities, and the researched steps of teacher-directed instruction for children with similar needs. The program is based on child growth and development and the principles of learning which focus on children's different rates of learning and different learning styles. (Werner, 1991, p. 1)

Writing to Read (WTR)

IBM's Writing to Read program is widely used in kindergarten and first grade, in particular in urban areas. The primary goal of Writing to Read is to increase the reading and writing skills of kindergarten students. Each school that adopts WTR has a lab with computer terminals, printers, and other work stations. Students work in the lab for an hour each day. There are five work stations in the lab. In one station, the students learn phonics by means of computer drill games. In the second station, students use a word processor on the computer to enter stories they are writing. In a third station, students listen to tape-recorded stories while they follow the text in a book. In a fourth station, they can write their stories with pencil and paper, and in the fifth station, additional practice with phonics is provided.

Slavin (1991) reviewed the evaluations of Writing to Read. He separated the studies into those looking at kindergarten and those involving first-graders. For kindergarten students, Slavin notes that the median effect size was +.23. He states that this effect size is likely to be inflated due to the fact that the comparison groups were unlikely to be focusing on the same academic objectives as the WTR group. A fairer comparison would be with kindergartens that were emphasizing the same goals and skills, using different methods. Also evaluation in first grades and follow-up evaluations of kindergarten and first-grade implementations have shown few effects. Slavin noted that Writing to Read, in comparison with other kindergarten programs such as Alphaphonics, is vastly more expensive and not as effective.

Story Telling and Retelling (STaR)

STaR is an interactive story-reading program for prekindergarten through first-grade students that was developed as a part of the Success for All program (see Chapter 7). The goals of the program are to introduce children to books and the conventions of print, to motivate prereaders to want to become readers by involving them in high-interest books, to provide experience with language used in books, and to help develop and improve comprehension skills and strategies.

STaR was developed to help provide an enjoyable introduction to literature, especially for children who were likely to have little experience with print and books. The program consists of specific strategies to involve children in story reading before, during, and after the story. It also contains hands-on materials and sequence cards that are particularly useful aides to help children talk about and retell the story.

Matched pre- and posttest studies of children in classrooms using STaR compared with regular kindergarten classrooms indicate positive effects on individually administered tests of language development and comprehension. The effect sizes for the Test of Language Development (TOLD) Picture Vocabulary was +.24; for Sentence Imitation, +.59; for Grammatic Completion, +.69; and for the Merrill Language, +.43. A full description of the program and evaluation are found in Karweit (1989b).

CONCLUSION

This chapter has examined a wide range of dimensions along which kindergartens differ. It has suggested that although the greatest policy emphasis has been on changing the external conditions of kindergartens, more substantial reform will result from attending to the activities and daily routines that take place within kindergartens. Building quality kindergartens will not automatically occur through creating uniform attendance and full-day kindergartens or altering the entrance age. Building quality kindergartens requires attention to what goes on each and every day in the kindergarten classrooms.

There are several impediments to creating quality kindergartens. First, there is the continuing and even heightened emphasis on creating better kindergartens and schools through external avenues, such as increasing the kindergarten day, lowering or increasing entrance age, and requiring kindergarten attendance. This is understandable as these features of kindergartens can be manipulated by changing laws, not by the more difficult task of changing what people believe, how they behave, or the activities in which they engage. Although it is certainly useful to guarantee that all children have the same opportunities for the same amounts of kindergarten education, the real issue is the quality of the experience. Assuring comparable quantity is important, but it does not solve the quality problem.

Second, there may be limited appreciation on the part of curriculum reformers of the importance of the contribution of the last wave of reforms. In the enthusiasm to put new ideas in place, educators still need to incorporate, not discard, previous models. Is good practice in the schools of the future revolutionary or evolutionary? Whether one tosses out all the old or attempts to incorporate what was learned in the last several decades of educational research and evaluation, one thing seems clear. Change focusing on only one facet will fail because the necessary enabling conditions are neglected. Effective practice involves simultaneous attention to multiple facets of learning, teaching, school context, and environment. Advocates of curricular reform may have the right message, but may never be heard unless the enabling school conditions are there as well.

A third impediment to creating quality kindergartens remains the lack of staff development and opportunities for staff interaction and collaboration. Despite understanding the importance of effective staff development, it appears that "two days in August" remains the major way in which most staff development is done. This seems especially troubling for kindergarten teachers where there is significant change occurring in the organization and structure of the school day. What do I do now that I have a full day kindergarten? is a typical question asked. While it is not clear how teachers adapt to new time allocations, it is possible that they simply extend existing time allocations and do not take full advantage of the opportunities more time could bring.

A fourth impediment is the lack of research in the kindergarten area. Increasing attention is being focused on preparation for school and the role of kindergarten in this preparation. However, there simply is not an adequate, replicated research base on which to base decisions about kindergarten education. Curricular reform in particular seems likely to be underevaluated, perhaps because of the ideological fervor behind such reforms. Advocates of specific approaches may be blinded by the vision they hope educators will see. But, in order for reform to be sustained and expanded, the vision must be backed by data.

REFERENCES

Adams, M. (1990). *Beginning to read: Thinking and learning about print.* Cambridge, MA: MIT Press.

Azumi, J. (1987). *All-day kindergarten evaluation report.* Newark, NJ: Division of Research, Evaluation, and Testing, Newark Board of Education.

Ball, E. W., & Blachman, B. A. (1988). *Kindergarten training in phoneme segmentation effect on reading readiness.* Presented at the annual meeting of American Educational Research Association, New Orleans, LA.

Banerji, M. (1990). *Longitudinal effects of a two-year developmental kindergarten program on academic achievement.* Paper presented at the Annual Meeting of the American Educational Research Association, Boston, April 16–21.

Berliner, D. C. (1990). What's all the fuss about instructional time? In M. Ben-Peretz, & R. Bromme (Eds.), *The nature of time in schools.* New York: Teachers College Press.

Carbo, M. (1989, October). An evaluation of Jean Chall's response to "Debunking the great phonics myth." *Phi Delta Kappan,* 152–157.

Chall, J. (1989, October). The uses of educational research: Comments on Carbo. *Phi Delta Kappan,* 158–160.

Education Commission of the States. (1992). State characteristics: Kindergarten. *Clearinghouse Notes.*

Hatch, J. A., & Freeman, E. B. (1988, October). Who's pushing whom? Stress and kindergarten. *Kappan,* 70, 145–147.

Holmes, C. T., & McConnell, B. M. (1990). *Full-day versus half day kindergarten: An experimental study.* Paper presented at the Annual Meeting of the American Educational Research Association, Boston, April 16–21.

Johnson, E. (1974). *An experimental study of the comparison of pupil achievement in the all-day kindergarten and one half-day control group.* Walden University. (ERIC Document Reproduction No. ED 115 361)

Karweit, N. (1983). *Time-on-task: A research review* (Technical Report No. 322).

Baltimore: Center for Social Organization of Schools, The Johns Hopkins University.

Karweit, N. (1988). *Full or half day kindergarten: Does it matter?* (Technical Report No. 11). Baltimore: Center for Research on Elementary and Middle Schools, The Johns Hopkins University.

Karweit, N. (1989a). Effective kindergarten programs and practices for students at risk. In R. E. Slavin, N. L. Karweit, & N. A. Madden (Eds.), *Effective programs for students at risk.* Boston: Allyn and Bacon.

Karweit, N. (1989b, October). The effects of a story-reading program on the vocabulary and story comprehension skills of disadvantaged prekindergarten and kindergarten students. *Early Education and Development,* 1, 2.

Karweit, N. (in press) Retention in grade. In Marvin C. Alkin (Ed.), *Encyclopedia of Educational Research,* 3944–3959. Naples, FL.

Lazar, I., & Darlington, R. (1982). Lasting effects on early education. *Monographs of the Society for Research in Child Development,* 47 (2–3, Serial No. 195).

Mantzicopoulos, P., & Morrison, D. (1991). *Longitudinal effects of kindergarten retention: Academic and behavioral outcomes.* Paper presented at the Annual Meeting of the American Educational Research Association, Chicago, April 17–22.

May, C. (1989). *All-day kindergarten.* Wichita Public Schools.

McGee, L., & Lomax, R. (1990). On combining apples and oranges: A response to Stahl and Miller. *Review of Educational Research,* 60 (1), 133–140.

McKey, R., Condelli, L., Ganson, H., Barrett, B., McConkey, C., & Plantz, M. (1985). *The impact of Head Start on children, families, and communities.* DHHS Publication No. (OHDS) 85–31193.

Meyer, L. (1985). *A look at instruction in kindergarten: Observations of interactions in three school districts.* (ERIC Document Reproduction No. ED 268 489)

Oelerich, M. (1979). *Kindergarten: All day every day?* Paper presented at the National of the Association for Childhood Education International, St. Louis.

Office of Educational Research and Improvement, U.S. Department of Education. (1991). Experiences in child care and early childhood programs of first and second graders prior to entering first grade: Findings from the 1991 National Household Education Survey. *Statistics in Brief*

Oliver, L. S. (1980). *The effects of extended instructional time on the readiness for reading of kindergarten children.* Unpublished doctoral dissertation, Boston University School of Education.

Puelo, V. T. (1988). A review and critique of research on full-day kindergarten. *The Elementary School Journal,* 8 (4), 427–439.

Robinson, S. (1990). *A survey of literacy programs among preschools.* Paper presented at the Annual Meeting of the American Educational Research Association, Boston.

Schickedanz, J. A. (1990). The jury is still out on the effects of whole language and language experience approaches for beginning reading: A critique of Stahl and Miller's study. *Review of Educational Research,* 60 (1), 127–131.

Shepard, L. (1989). A review of research on kindergarten retention in L. A.

Shepard & M. C. Smith (Eds.), *Flunking grades: Research and policies on grade retention*. New York: Falmer Press.

Shepard, L., & Smith, M. (1986). Synthesis of research on school readiness and kindergarten retention. *Educational Leadership, 44*, 78–86.

Slavin, R. (1986). Best evidence synthesis: An alternative to meta-analytic and traditional reviews. *Educational Researcher, 15*, 9.

Slavin, R. (1991). Reading effects of IBM's Writing to Read program: A review of evaluations. *Educational Evaluation and Policy Analysis, 13* (1), 1–11.

Stahl, S., & Miller, P. (1989). Whole language and language experience approaches for beginning reading: A quantitative research synthesis. *Review of Educational Research, 59* (1), 87–116.

Turner, R. L. (1989, December). The "great" debate: Can both Carbo and Chall be right? *Phi Delta Kappan*, 276–283.

Wallach, L., Wallach, M. A., Dozier, M. G., & Kaplan, N. E. (1977). Poor children learning to read do not have trouble with auditory discrimination but do have trouble with phoneme recognition. *Journal of Educational Psychology, 72* (1), 1–15.

Werner, L. (1991). *Early prevention of school failure. Awareness packet*. 114 North Second St., Peotone, IL.

West, J. (1991). *National household education survey*. National Center for Educational Statistics, Washington, D.C.

Winter, M., & Klein, A. (1970). *Extending the kindergarten day: Does it make a difference in the achievement of educationally advantaged and disadvantaged pupils?* Bureau of Elementary and Secondary Education, Washington, D.C. (ERIC Document Reproduction No. ED 087 534)

► 5

Extra-Year Kindergarten Programs and Transitional First Grades

NANCY L. KARWEIT   BARBARA A. WASIK

How to best provide an appropriate learning environment for kindergarten-age children who are thought not to be ready to begin school is a perennial issue faced by schools and parents. Despite the universality of the problem, there are few agreed upon solutions. Much debate over the definitions and conceptualizations of *readiness* continues. This chapter reviews the research on one approach for the nonready child—providing an extra year of kindergarten.

The meaning of being "not ready" varies from school to school, but incorporates dimensions of social and academic immaturity, such as impulsiveness, inattentiveness, fidgetiness, poor social and emotional adjustment, and the inability to recognize and name colors, letters, and numerals. Various tests and procedures are used by individual districts to determine which children are not ready. Being not ready in Baltimore probably is defined differently than it is in Boston or in Denver. Readiness is therefore situationally, not universally, defined.

In fact, there is substantial disagreement concerning the readiness construct. Critics argue that readiness is poorly measured by most tests designed to measure it (Cunningham, 1989). In addition, even if test validity and reliability were not an issue, focusing on children's readiness for school helps foster the view that schools need only worry about educating children when they are ready. In fact, it is *the schools who must be ready for children;* they are charged with educating all children, not just those who meet certain standards.

In addition, the practices aimed at accommodating student diversity vary greatly from place to place. In some districts, all students are placed in the same kindergarten curriculum, regardless of readiness status, whereas in others, special tiers or kindergarten tracks are created to accommodate student diversity. The prevailing view of child development and the belief in the possibility of intervention probably exert an appreciable influence on these practices. In particular, districts following a maturational view of child development, such as that proposed by the Gesell Institute, will consistently be in favor of approaches that define readiness in terms of developmental, not chronological age, and will favor programs that allow children "more time" as a strategy for getting ready. Following this philosophy, there is little point in intervening to remediate nonreadiness because each child's development has its own timetable that cannot be hurried up or altered. Approaches that are consistent with this point of view do not try to remediate deficiencies but allow the child more time to develop. Typically, these approaches involve providing the nonready child with the gift of time in the form of an extra year in kindergarten or prior to first grade. Such programs as transitional first grades, developmental kindergartens, or kindergarten retention follow this maturational point of view.

The number of children who take an extra year in kindergarten is considerable. Meisels (in press) reports that in North Carolina in 1989, 8.6 percent of the students were retained and that kindergarten retention rates in California ranged from 0 to 50 percent.

Critics of the "gift of time" approach argue that the only thing that will happen while one is waiting for children to mature is that they will fall more and more behind their agemates. In addition, the criticism is voiced that these extra-year programs do not in fact bring children up to the same level as their peers, whether one is looking at children who are held back due to academic delays or behavioral immaturity (Shepard & Smith, 1986). Despite these criticisms of extra-year programs, many districts remain convinced that immature or academically not ready children will benefit from an extra year in kindergarten.

The precise nature of the extra-year program varies, depending on when the decision for additional time is made and the nature of the program. Students may be selected for programs prior to the entrance to kindergarten (developmental kindergarten) or after kindergarten has been completed (retention and transitional first-grade programs). Programs may either be differentiated (developmental kindergarten and transitional first grade) or may present the same material and use similar methods (kindergarten retention). Because of these differences in the timing and the focus of the program, it is appropriate to consider the effects of these programs separately. Table 5.1 presents this typology of extra-year programs, by timing of the program and the nature of the program.

Are any of these programs effective for students who seem to be at risk of future school failure? What evidence is there to support the use of extra-year programs? What evidence is there to show that these programs are ineffective or harmful? In comparison to the extensive literature on retention in elementary school, there are relatively few reviews of kindergarten extra-year programs. Perhaps the most influential review is that of Shepard (1989). (See also Shepard and Smith [1986], which concludes that none of the extra-year programs is effective.)

Despite the definitiveness of these conclusions, several issues remain unsettled by the Shepard review. First, the type of program was not considered as a factor. Separate analyses were not conducted for the three program types: kindergarten retention, transitional first grade, and developmental kindergarten. Second, in arriving at this conclusion of ineffectiveness, studies were combined that used different bases of comparison. Some studies compared students after equal time in school but at different ages, while other studies used students of the same age but different grade comparisons. This is always a dilemma in studies of retention; should a retained student be compared to his or her original (promoted) classmates or to his or her new, younger classmates? Because these bases of comparisons are looking at very different outcomes, it is not appropriate to combine these different studies. Finally, attention must focus on possible differences in effects for students of different backgrounds and competencies. In this chapter, we therefore look at extra-year programs with a careful eye toward possible differential effects due to program type, student characteristics, and basis of comparison.

We group studies into those looking at effects of retention, at developmental kindergarten, and at transitional first grade. Within these categories, we explore whether different effects are noted for specific groups of students. In particular, we examine whether there is any evidence that extra-year programs are more effective for immature students than they are for academically delayed students. The basis of comparison—that is, which

TABLE 5.1   Typology of Extra-Year Programs

	Special Program	Recycling
Decision Made Before Kindergarten	Developmental kindergarten	
Decision Made After Kindergarten	Transitional first grade	Kindergarten retention

students are being compared, on what measure, and at what time interval—is also identified. We note that districts may have specific objectives that influence the choice of the basis of comparison used in the evaluation. For example, if a district is interested in giving students an extra year to catch up with their regular classmates, the success of that program may be judged by comparing the attainments of the extra-year students to regular progressing classmates in the same grade who make normal progress. A more usual method to create a matched comparison group is to create a comparable "potential failure group" of students eligible for an extra year but who did not participate. The progress of those experiencing the extra-year program and those who were promoted are then compared. The same-grade comparisons compare children after the same grade (unequal age); the same-age comparisons compare children after equal age (unequal grade). Table 5.2 depicts same-age and same-grade comparisons.

There are several issues in the creation of a matched control group in studies of extra-year programs. First, the potential failure group, created from a pool of students who were eligible but whose parents refused the placement, cannot be argued to be an equivalent group to those who experienced the extra-year placement. The fact of parental refusal probably indicates a preexisting difference in parent involvement and childrearing practices that may affect children's success in school (Powell, 1991). If this is so, one can expect that the promoted students will probably do as well or better than the extra-year students in part because the groups were really not equivalent at the outset.

Another issue is when students should be compared. The same-age comparison and the same-grade comparisons address different issues. Often, results are collapsed across both of these issues. The same-grade comparison, because it is looking at students of different ages, addresses the question of comparability of performance at the same grade level, irrespective of age. This will likely favor the older, retained student who is often taking the same test for a second time. Typically, grade, not age, norms are used, so that the older students can be seen to have an advantage in this comparison.

TABLE 5.2 Basis of Comparison in Extra-Year Studies

Group	Year 1	Year 2	Year 3	Year 4
Retained	Kindergarten	Kindergarten	Grade 1	Grade 2
Promoted	Kindergarten	Grade 1	Grade 2	Grade 3

Diagonal lines indicate same-grade comparisons; straight lines indicate same-year comparisons.

Studies that utilize the same-age comparison may also be problematic. Often it is not clear whether the same or a different test is being given to the students who are the same age but are in different grades. If the students take the *same* test, then the promoted students will probably perform better because of their exposure to more advanced material. If the students take *different* tests, then there may be problems of comparability across the two tests so that interpretation is an issue.

In this review, we look primarily at studies that identified a control group and provided information to indicate who was being compared, when the comparison was being made, and what test was used. We emphasize again that the adequacy of the control group is a central problem in limiting the usefulness of most studies of extra-year programs and transitional first programs.

KINDERGARTEN RETENTION

Three adequately controlled studies were located that contrasted students who had been retained in kindergarten with those who had been recommended for retention, but whose parents refused retention. In all three studies, students were compared at the end of the first grade. They used same-grade comparisons—that is, the nonretained students were younger than the retained ones.

Shepard and Smith (1985, 1987) compared the academic and other outcomes of a matched sample of 40 students in a Colorado district. They matched schools within the district on social economic status (SES) level, the percent for whom English was a second language, and historical differences in the retention rates. Ten such schools were paired, five high-retaining schools with five low-retaining schools. Within each school, they matched retained and nonretained students on Santa Clara score, gender, birthday, kindergarten readiness, eligibility for free lunch, and use of language other than English.

The Shepard and Smith study looked for global effects of extra-year programs. They combined students who were in developmental kindergartens, transitional first grades, and retained in kindergarten. Separate analyses by type of program were not presented. Matching was done of children in the same school, but children across schools (and therefore programs) were combined into this sample. If there were different effects by program, the Shepard and Smith analysis was not designed to find them. The overall population in this study was achieving at about the national average.

The study compared the academic progress of these 40 matched pairs on several dimensions at the end of first grade. Specifically, they examined differences in the Comprehensive Test of Basic Skills (CTBS) reading and math as well as teacher ratings of reading and math performance, social maturity, learner self-concept, and attention. They found that on all but one outcome measure, there were no differences.

The significant difference was detected between the two groups on the CTBS reading test. The effect size was +.41, indicating that the retained students scored 41 percent of a standard deviation higher than their younger, nonretained counterparts. Although the magnitude of this effect might suggest an educationally significant difference, the difference between the two groups amounted to a difference between the 63rd percentile and the 56th percentile, or a grade equivalent of 1.9 versus 1.8. On the basis of the size of the difference, Shepard and Smith conclude that an extra year in kindergarten was not effective. It is important to keep in mind that Shepard and Smith did find a statistically significant difference in reading that went against the proposed hypothesis and that the study combined together several types of extra-year programs, not just kindergarten retention (recycling).

Mantzicopoulos and Morrison (1991) examined the effects of kindergarten retention using 53 pairs of students who were retained and promoted and who were matched on school, gender, birthday, SES, reading, and at-risk status (as measured by a screening device for learning disabilities called SEARCH). They followed this sample of children through the first and second grades and carried out analyses after equal time in school as well as equal grade. The equal-grade comparisons and the same-age comparisons favored the retained students in the first year of the comparison and showed no differences in the second and third years.

At the end of the kindergarten year, after the retained children had been in kindergarten the second time, the retained children scored significantly higher than their nonretained peers (ES = +1.95 for reading). But the advantage of the retained group did not continue into the first and second grades (ES = +.11 and +.08, respectively). A similar pattern appeared for math. These comparisons do not support the effectiveness of kindergarten retention for long-term improvement of academic difficulties.

Same-age comparisons were also carried out by Mantzicopoulos and Morrison (1991). These comparisons contrasted students at the same age who were in different grades due to kindergarten retention. Because different tests were being compared, the metric used was expressed as the number of standard deviation units above or below the mean on the reading and math tests. The same-age comparisons indicated a positive and significant effect for retention (in reading and in math). This compares the relative performance of students at the end of the retained kindergarten year with those who went ahead to first grade. The comparison of first- and second-graders was not significant, indicating that whatever advantage there may have been to retention, it did not continue into the next year.

Mantzicopoulos and Morrison also compared retained and promoted students on teacher ratings on the Revised Behavior Problem Checklist (Quay & Peterson, 1967). The retained group was rated as demonstrating significantly more immature and behavior problems than their same-age peers during the first year in kindergarten. This initial difference faded during the second kindergarten year. In the later comparisons, they report that the two groups were not rated differently by their teachers.

The matched comparison groups were not matched on behavior rating. In fact, it was impossible to construct a matched sample given this added matching variable because children could not be matched simultaneously on all the variables. This suggests that the behavior problem may have been a factor in the retention decision. Further, it may be the case that retention may have helped the behavior problems. But, because there was not a sample of students matched on inattention and immaturity in both treatments, it is not known if the same decline in behavioral problem ratings would occur if the retained children had been socially promoted.

An earlier study by Turley (1979) compared retained students with a recommended but refused placement matched control group. In this study, the children were recommended for retention on the basis of their score on a developmental test that included subtests from the Stanford-Binet, Wechsler Intelligence Scale for Children, Detroit Tests of Learning Ability, Monroe Readiness, Wide Range Achievement Test, and Gesell inventory. Turley compared the students' progress at the end of first grade to that of their younger classmates (equal grade, unequal age). The retained group scored significantly higher than the promoted group on the Stanford Achievement Test (SAT) reading (ES = +.84) and math (ES = +.98) scales. Turley's overall population was primarily upper SES, high-performing children. The grade equivalent scores for reading for the retained and nonretained groups were 2.8 and 1.8, respectively, and for math were 2.9 and 2.0, respectively. Turley did not perform a follow-up study with the children in later grades, so it is not possible to know if these effects vanished with time, as did the effects detected by Mantzicopoulos and Morrison.

Table 5.3 summarizes the results for studies of kindergarten retention. The studies reviewed here include those studies that had an identifiable control group, provided a clear indication of what groups were being compared, and indicated whether same-grade and/or same-age comparisons were being used. Across the three controlled studies, the results indicate that there is a favorable result for kindergarten retention on academic achievement in the year of retention. However, these effects do not

TABLE 5.3 Studies Comparing Kindergarten Retention to Equivalent Controls

Study Author(s) and Date	Sample	Matching Factors	When Compared	Measures Compared	Effect Sizes: Retained vs. Promoted	Notes
Shepard & Smith (1987)	40 matched pairs who had either been retained or promoted in K.	Schools matched SES and on percent English as a second language and paired to contrast school with different retention rates. 10 schools thus paired, 5 high-retaining with 5 low-retaining students within school pairs were matched on Santa Clara score, sex, birthday, K readiness, free lunch, language other than English, and contrasted on retention	*First Grade* *Same Grade* Unequal time	Teacher Ratings Reading Math Social Maturity Self-Concept Attention CTBS Rdg CTBS Mth	+.11 NS +.09 NS +.14 NS +.29 NS +.07 NS +.41 $p<.05$ -.17 NS	On all but one outcome measure, there were no differences CTBS reading is statistically different
Turley (1979)	Comparison of those retained in K with those recommended for retention but refused. High SES district.	PEPP (contains draw a person, visual-motor, VMI & WISC)	*First grade* *Same grade,* Unequal time	SAT reading SAT math	End first grade +.84 ($p<.0$) +.98 ($p<.00$)	Conclusion: Favors retention
Mantzicopoulos & Morrison (1991)	Comparison of those retained in K with matched nonretained group.	School, sex, age, SEARCH, SES, reading, & match ach.	*First Grade & Second Grade* *Same Grade* Unequal time	SAT reading SAT math CTBS reading CTBS math Z scores	K 1.95 ($p<.0001$) G1.11 (NS) G2.08 (NS)	Conclusion: Favors retention fades out by grade 1 & 2. Extra year K gave children chance to improve behavior and mature socially.

persist. This suggests that the main longitudinal effect of retention is that the retained children are one year older than their classmates.

DEVELOPMENTAL KINDERGARTEN

Developmental kindergarten refers to the practice of screening students who are entering kindergarten in specific developmental areas (e.g., visual, motor, language, behavior, social, emotional) and placing students in differentiated kindergartens on the basis of this assessment. The actual practices vary from place to place, but typically involve placement of developmentally immature children into a two-year route to first grade. The first year in kindergarten, often termed *young kindergarten* or *junior kindergarten,* may be similar in organization and emphases to nursery schools or other prekindergarten programs. In the second year, before first grade, these "young kindergartners" (now actually "old kindergartners") may join a regular kindergarten class of younger students or, in some versions of this practice, may attend a second year of alternative kindergarten.

Developmental kindergarten is based on the belief that children should be placed in school on the basis of developmental, not chronological, age. Because rates of development are so varied, children of the same chronological age may vary widely in their developmental age. In addition, a child may have uneven rates of development across developmental areas, being advanced in some areas and delayed in others.

The Gesell Institute is the most widely known proponent of developmental screening and placement. Many districts use the Gesell Preschool Readiness Test as the basis for placement decisions. This test has been criticized on several grounds, including its lack of appropriate psychometric properties and its overlap with IQ tests (Kaufman, 1985).

Developmental screening and placement are based on a belief in a nativist, maturational view of child development. In this view, growth and development are determined by the child's inner timetable. As a result, there is little point in rushing or interfering with the timetable by early intervention. Thus, in this nativist view, the best environment and best practice schools can follow for these immature children is the gift of time. Interference with the process of development, in this view, is not only wasted effort but it may be injurious to children. The idea is that developmental placement allows children time to let development unfold at its own pace.

There are no current data on the prevalence and characteristics of developmental kindergartens in the United States. The impression is that states and districts vary greatly in the use of this practice. However, the practice is receiving a growing body of criticism. Part of the criticism is derived from the current ongoing general negative reaction to retention and with the equating of developmental kindergarten with retention (Shepard & Smith, 1986). Shepard (1989) lumps developmental kindergarten into the general practice of retention and concludes, "It is still retention—and still ineffective."

There are only two studies of developmental kindergartens that have used a clearly identifiable control group (May & Welch, 1984; Banerji, 1990). Both studies matched students placed in developmental kindergarten with those recommended for placement but whose parents refused placement. The children were followed longitudinally.

May and Welch (1984) compared the achievement of students who were screened using the Gesell instrument and placed in developmental kindergarten with those who were recommended for placement but refused and went to regular kindergarten. Some 223 students, grades 2 through 6, formed the sample for this study. Students were classified into three groups: TR, the regular attending kindergartners, not recommended for placement; BAY, the developmentally placed students (for buy a year); and the OP children, recommended for placement but refusing it (for "overplaced" children). The basis for developmental placement was the Gesell screening test. The OP children had a significantly higher developmental score than the BAY children, indicating that the groups were not equivalent at the outset. The BAY students in the developmental kindergarten were a year older than the comparison students on all posttest comparisons. At the end of the kindergarten year and at the end of the first grade, these initial differences remained. By the end of the third grade, the BAY children still were the lowest group of the three, even though they were a year older. That is, the additional year did not seem to be beneficial in reducing the performance gap between the TR and BAY children or in overcoming the initial differences the BAY children had with respect to the OP children.*

Banerji (1990) reports on a four-year longitudinal study of the effects of placement in developmental kindergarten. She matched 34 pairs of students on ethnicity, SES, gender, age, and school achievement at school entry. She compared the achievement of these students at the end of grades 1, 2, and 3 both to younger students of the same grade and to students of the same age. The developmentally placed students spent an extra year in kindergarten, so the comparisons here are of students of different ages but at the same grade. She found positive effects for attending the program at the end of the first grade, but found that these effects

---

*Standard deviations were not presented in this article so that computation of effect sizes is not possible.

TABLE 5.4 Studies Comparing Developmental Kindergarten to Equivalent Controls

Study Author(s) and Date	Sample	Matching Factors	When Compared	Measures Compared	Effect Sizes: Retained vs. Transit		Notes	
					Developmental	Traditional	ES	
Banerji (1990)	34 matched pairs (n = 68) with 4-year follow-up data	Schools matched on geographic location, by proportion of free lunch and by presence/absence DK. Students from DK and non-DK individually matched on ethnicity, SES, gender, age, and SESAT at entry to school.	*Same grade* Grade 1 Grade 2 Grade 3	SAT (NCEs) SAT (NCEs) SAT (NCEs)	50.46 50.76 44.69	33.23 (P <.05) Ns 45.51 Ns 43.40 NS	+.79	Two-year program benefits children at beginning of first grade but effects are short-lived.
	Study of two-year K program with developmental placement (DK)		*Same age* Year 2 Year 3 Year 4	SAT (NCEs) SAT (NCEs) SAT (NCEs)	76.68 50.46 50.76	33.23 (P <.05) NS 45.51 NS 43.40 NS	+2.06	Large boost in NCEs due to taking test again and being a year older.
May & Welch (1984)	233 students in grades 2–6 in suburban homogeneous mid-class	Gesell Screen used to identify eligible students, OP (refused), and BAY (Buy a year)	Beg K (same age) End K (same grd) End 1 (same grd) End 3 (same grd) End 3 (same grd)	Gesell Gesell Gesell Gesell Stanford	55.50 69.91 70.05 59.29 143	57.93 65.36 74.50 64.96 151		Non-equivalent groups OP>BAY. Differences maintained throughout third grade.

+ = effect retention

– = effect promotion

were not sustained in grades 2 and 3. The same-grade comparisons yielded an effect size of +1.92, favoring the DK attenders in the first year. The same-age comparisons also favored the DK group, with an effect size of +.82. On neither of these comparisons were effects sustained into the second and third grade; the differences were no longer significant after the first grade.

These studies of developmental kindergarten suggest that the two-year route to first grade provides, at best, a short-term temporary boost in academic achievement, followed by a fade-out. If developmental kindergartens only placed a small number of students, perhaps one might argue that a temporary boost may be beneficial, or at least not harmful to the few students who go into this two-year route. However, districts may developmentally place a third or more of their students (Remmey & McIlhenny, 1987). Certainly, the current and usual dire financial straights of many school districts, coupled with the demonstrated lack of effects for developmental kindergartens, lead one to question the wisdom of two years of kindergarten for as many as one-third of the students. It is interesting that although a belief in the positive effects of developmental kindergarten on children's self-regard is often used as a motivation for the practice, we are unaware of any controlled study that has actually examined the effect of these programs on this factor.

Table 5.4 summarizes the results for these two controlled studies. It indicates that developmental kindergarten, although involving screening prior to kindergarten attendance, has a similar pattern of effects as does kindergarten retention: positive effects in the year of retention followed by a fade-out over time.

TRANSITIONAL FIRST GRADE

Many districts offer a transitional program between kindergarten and first grade. Children attend regular kindergarten but then are placed in a transitional first grade or other "half-step" program prior to first grade. Children are often placed in transitional first grades because they are developmentally young or immature or because they are felt not to be academically ready for first grade. Transitional first-grade classrooms are often smaller in size (15 or so students) and may utilize alternative curricula. Transitional first grades differ in actual practice and intent, in some cases being more a remedial program and in other cases being more an intervention or alternative program.

In our examination of the effects of transitional first grade, we excluded studies that did not utilize a control group. The matched control group was usually comprised of children for whom transition had been recommended, but whose parents had refused placement. In some cases a control group was made up of children who were deemed eligible for placement but for whom there was no available program.

Raygor (1972) compared the achievement of third- and fourth-graders in a suburban district who had used different routes to the first grade, including a transitional first grade, kindergarten retention, and regular progression. This study used both same-grade and same-age comparisons. Raygor first compared children who had attended transitional first with those who had been retained in kindergarten. There were no differences on any dimensions between these groups on measures taken at the end of first and third grades. Raygor concludes that retention and transition, at least as practiced in this district, had equivalent effects.

In subsequent analyses, these two extra-year groups were grouped together. At the end of grade 1, the transition/retained group was significantly higher than a "potential failure group," a group identified as possible candidates for retention or transition. The potential failure group had an average of 1.5 (expressed in grade equivalents), whereas the transitional and retained groups were 2.6 and 2.8, respectively. Of course, the transitional and retained groups were taking the same test a year later, so the higher test scores are not too surprising. Computing the average effect sizes across these six subtest provides an estimate of +.77 for the effect of an extra year. At the end of Raygor's study, when the transitional and the retained students were in grade 3 and the potential failure group was in grade 4, the teacher rating of the children's ability and competencies were similar, except that the teachers rated the reading ability of the retained/ transitioned group as higher than the potential failure group.

Interestingly, the potential failure group's actual achievement at the end of the fourth grade was almost identical to that of the regular fourth-graders. The same could not be said for the retained and transitional groups at the end of the third grade, as they were not on an even par with the regular third-graders (who were a year younger).

Raygor's study suggests three conclusions: (1) retention and transition have similar effects, (2) there is a boost and then a fade-out effect for an extra-year program when children are compared at the same grade, and (3) the potential failure children do catch up to their regular classmates. See Table 5.5 for a summary of Raygor's results.

Caggiano (1984) compared the achievement and behavior of children in a suburban New Jersey district who had been in a transitional program. Using the Iowa Test of Basic Skills, he found that the performance of the transitional and matched potential failure group were similar at grades 2, 4, and 6, and that both lagged behind the regularly promoted students. For the second grade, the students performed at the 81st, 78th, and 87th percentiles, respectively; at grade 4, these numbers were 74, 74, and 85,

TABLE 5.5 Studies Comparing Transition Eligible but Refused to Transition Eligible and Complied

Study Author(s) and Date	Sample	Matching Factors	When Compared	Measures Compared	Effect Sizes: Retained vs. Transit	Notes
Raygor (1972)	"Potential failures," students recommended for retention in K whose parents refused, and eligibles who were either retained in K or attended transitional first grade	Candidates for retention ($N = 30$) vs. those retained in K ($N = 30$)	End grade 1 (unequal time same grade).	Stanford Ach (different ages), same grade	Retained/transition vs. promoted $+.77$ Average across six subtests on the Stanford Ach test show positive effects for extra year	At end of first-grade year, transition/retained students spend an additional year in school. They do score higher on the Stanford Achievement Test at the end of the first grade than their younger counterparts who were not retained.
Carlson (1988)	59K students who were identified as good candidates for K–1 transition class were followed up 4 years later, 43 were found. 21 not retained (NR) 22 retained (R) K or 1 NR sample grade 3 R sample grade 2	Eligible, identified for participation K–1 class	Compared after equal time but not same grade (grade 3 for nonretained, grade 2 for retained).	Walker McConnell Ratings Teacher pref soc beh Peer pre soc beh Sch adj beh Total	Retained/transition vs. promoted $+.57$ ns $-.08$ ns $+1.06$ $p < .01$ $+.72$ $p < .01$	Positive effects for retention on letter sound and teacher perception.

Continued

TABLE 5.5 *Continued*

Study Author(s) and Date	Sample	Matching Factors	When Compared	Measures Compared	Effect Sizes: Retained vs. Transit	Notes

Bell (1972)	Students identified as in need of readiness room but who attended a school where one was not available	Students in readiness program in six schools (64), regular instructional program in one school (12 students)	Same age and time but in different grades. Comparison of readiness room attendees and regular class attendees.	SESAT II
				environment
				mathematics
				letter/sounds
				aural comp.
				word reading
				para reading
				Total
				vocab
				word study
				self-concept
					+ 1 yr *+ 2 yr*
					−.16 ns
					−.06 ns
					−.38 sn
					−.09 ns
					−.99 (p<.05)
					−.44 ns −.43 ns
					−.64 ns −.49 ns
					          −.30 ns
					          −.32 ns
					0 (ns) −.52 (p<.05)
						SESAT ns diff except on word reading which favored the students who were promoted.
						
						Significant decline in self-concept for children retained, while scores slightly increased for promoted students.

Mossburg (1987)	Post hoc formation of comparison groups at fifth grade of those attending transitional class and those not attending	Sex, SES, ability and age		SAT composite at G1 G2 G3 G4	*Same grade, diff. age* 0 −.37 −.48 −.59	Readiness is not effective in long term, start out equivalent (i.e., no difference in grade 1, but then spread apart).
Matthews (1977)	Post hoc formation control groups G1 = eligible G3 = retained first E = transition		*Same age* E vs. G3 *Same grade* E vs. G1	Gates-Mac CAT-Total	*Same age* *Same grade* +.66 +.66 +.74 +.88	Maximum class size 15, diagnostic testing, individualized instruction.
Leinhardt (1980)	Targeted transition 44 transit 9 1st NRS 23 1st basal	Screening reading difficulties	Equal time, unequal grade.	SAT Total Reading	Basal NRS −.41 −1.07	Positive effects promotion; positive effects NRS, small number of cases.

and at grade 6, they were 73, 74, and 85. He also compared these different groups on teacher ratings using the Revised Behavior Problem Checklist. No clear pattern was discernible for transitional first grade on the dimensions of this checklist (motor excess, attention problems, conduct disorder, or anxiety withdrawal).

Caggiano's results suggest that there is a small, nonsignificant advantage to transitional first grade that rapidly fades, despite the fact that the transitional students are a year older than the potential failure comparison group. His study also suggests that neither the transitional nor the potential failures catch up with the regular students. However, we note that these children were performing at a relatively high level initially.

Carlson (1988) compared the ratings on the Walker McConnell scale of students who were eligible for transition classes and did not attend with those who were eligible and did attend. The students compared were of the same age and had spent an equal time in school. He found positive effects for the transition students on teachers perception of positive student behavior (ES = +.76).

Bell (1972) examined the role of transition room placement and attendance on student self-esteem and achievement. Students were identified as being in need of a transition room, but attended a school where none was available. She compared students having the transition room experience with those who did not, using a same-age comparison. The students in the transitional room scored lower than their counterparts in the first-grade classroom; similarly, at the end of the second year, the students in the first grade scored lower than those in the second grade. The only significant difference, however, was in a test of word reading. This study looked only at same-age comparisons; we therefore do not know how these students compared when they were in the same grade. Bell also looked at the effect on self-concept and found that the children who were in the transitional room experienced a significant decline in self-concept that was not experienced by the promoted children. Bell's study is one of the few studies to examine effects on children's self-concept of extra-year placement. Contrary to the usual prediction of positive effects on children's self-esteem, Bell found a negative one for placement in transitional first-grade programs.

Mossburg (1987) carried out a same-grade comparison for a group of children who were in transitional first grades and a matched potential failure group. All children who attended a specific district in a mid-size midwestern town were included. The students covered a range of SES levels. The matching characteristics were gender, SES, and ability. At the end of grade 1, the transition group was slightly higher than the potential failure group on the composite Stanford Achievement Test, although these differences were not statistically significant. Starting at grade 2 and continuing through to grade 4, the differences between the two groups were significant and favored the potential failure group, with effect sizes of − .37, − .48, and − .58. That is, the same-grade comparisons in this case favor the promoted students despite the fact that they were a year younger than the transition students. Furthermore, at the end of fifth grade, teachers judged the potential failure students significantly higher than the readiness students on behavioral characteristics that reflect social, emotional, and academic readiness for middle school.

Matthews (1977) provided an important study because of the number of different control groups he utilized. He focused on children who were then in the second and third grade and identified five distinct groups. The experimental children were those who had gone through a transitional first grade. This program had a maximum class size of 15, individualized instruction, and placement on the basis of diagnostic testing. Four comparisons groups were identified. Group 1 consisted of children who had been identified for transition but who were not placed either because space was unavailable or because of parental refusal. Group 2 was a group of normally progressing and achieving students. Group 3 consisted of students who were retained in the first grade. Group 4 consisted of students who entered kindergarten a year later than the experimental and other control groups.

The tests used were the Gates-MacGinitie (second grade) and the California Achievement Test (third grade). Gredler (1984), in looking at Matthews's results, contends that retention is not effective, primarily because he compared the achievement of the experimental children to the regular children and noted that they were unable to catch up. However, if the more traditional criteria of comparing the children to children with a like starting point is used, a different story might be told. Using same-grade comparisons, we found a positive effect of retention on both tests (ES = + .66 and + .74 for second grade and third grade, respectively). Comparisons of those retained in first grade also show positive effects for transition (ES = + .66 and + .88, respectively). While it is true that the students who were in transitional classes did not make up or catch up with the classmates who were not deemed in need of transitional classes, they did perform better, using the same grade as a comparison, than their classmates who were recommended for transitional and were not so placed, and better than those who were retained in first grade. It is interesting in contrast with most such studies that these results persist into the second and third grades. However, Matthews does not provide evidence of initial comparability among the different groups; therefore, we do not know the extent to which the continuing differences reflect these initial differences.

Leinhardt (1980) made an interesting comparison of three groups of transition-eligible students. One group attended the transition class, a self-contained, alternative program ($n = 44$). A group of transition-eligible students who refused placement went into first grade ($n = 32$). Some of these students received the regular, basal instructional program ($n = 23$), while others received an individualized reading approach ($n = 9$). At the start of the year, all students took a screening test; the three groups did not differ from each other on the screening test but did differ significantly from the students attending regular first grade. At the end of the year, these same students were given the Stanford Achievement Test (SAT) total reading battery. The scores on this test indicated that the regular first-graders scored the highest (mean = 99.7), followed by the students in the individualized reading program (mean = 71.3), the students in the regular first grade (mean = 56.3), and finally by the transition-room attendees (mean = 49.9). These statistics support two conclusions: (1) the transition room attendees did not fare as well as the children who went on to regular first grade using a same-age, different-grade comparison; and (2) the students receiving the individualized reading program in the first grade did the best of the three approaches, but these children still scored about one standard deviation below the mean for the first grade. Thus, although the promoted group did better than the transitional group, neither group caught up with the rest of the class.

These studies of transitional rooms support the following conclusion. In the majority of studies that utilize same-grade comparisons (Matthews, Caggiano, & Raygor, but not Mossburg), the students in transitional programs had higher achievement than their younger classmates in the first grade, but these effects faded after the first grade. In studies that utilized same-age comparisons (Bell, Raygor, & Leinhardt), the effects were either zero or favored the promoted children. Thus these studies do not support the long-term effectiveness of transitional rooms as an educational intervention.

CONCLUSION

Looking across the separate extra-year programs, there is no evidence that kindergarten retention, developmental kindergarten, or transitional first-grade programs are more effective than simply promoting the children. It should be emphasized that this conclusion does not therefore suggest that these children should simply be promoted in hopes that their problems will go away. The longitudinal evidence does not support this conclusion. Students who were retained, either by kindergarten retention, developmental kindergarten, or transitional first grade, *as well as children who were not retained even though they were recommended for retention,* continue to show academic difficulties into the elementary grades. They do not, in short, outgrow their academic problems by buying a year. They also do not circumvent their academic problems by being promoted anyway. These children continue to lag behind their peers. Long-term, continued intervention and supportive help when it is needed may provide a better model for appropriate instruction for these children than an additional extra year waiting to mature or a frustrating year at the bottom of the heap.

REFERENCES

Banerji, M. (1990). *Longitudinal effects of a two-year developmental kindergarten program on academic achievement.* Paper presented at the Annual Meeting of the American Educational Research Association, Boston, April 16–21.

Bell, M. (1972). *A study of readiness room program in a small school district in suburban Detroit, Michigan.* Unpublished doctoral dissertation.

Caggiano, J.A. (1984). *A study of the effectiveness of transitional first grade in a suburban school district.* Unpublished doctoral dissertation, Temple University.

Carlson, R. (1988). *At risk in kindergarten: A study of selection, retention, transition and promotion.* Paper presented at the Annual Meeting of the American Educational Research Association, New Orleans.

Cunningham, A. E. (1989). Eeny, meeny, miny, moe: Testing policy and practice in early childhood. In B. R. Gilford (Ed.), *Imperfect measures and absolute decisions.* Boston: Klywer Academic Publishers.

Gredler, G. (1984). Transition classes: A viable alternative to the at-risk child? *Psychology in the Schools, 21,* 463–470.

Kaufman, N. L. (1985). Review of Gesell preschool test. In J. V. Mitchell, Jr. (Ed.), *The ninth mental measurements yearbook: Volume I* (pp. 607–608). Lincoln: University of Nebraska Press.

Leinhardt, G. (1980). Transition rooms: Promoting maturation or reducing education? *Journal of Educational Psychology 72,* (1), 55–61.

Mantzicopoulos, P., & Morrison, D. (1991). *Longitudinal effects of kindergarten retention: Academic and behavioral outcomes.* Paper presented at the Annual Meeting of the American Educational Research Association, Chicago, April 17–22.

Matthews, H. W. (1977). *The effect of transition education, a year of readiness, and beginning reading instruction between kindergarten and first grade.* Unpublished doctoral dissertation, St. Louis University.

May, D., & Welch, E. (1984). The effects of developmental placement and early retention on children's later scores on standardized tests. *Psychology in the Schools 21,* 381–385.

Meisels, S. J. (in press). *Doing more harm than good: Iatrogenic effects of early childhood enrollment and promotion policies.* The University of Michigan.

Mossburg, J. W. (1987). *The effects of transition room placement on selected achievement variables and readiness for middle school.* Doctoral dissertation, Ball State University.

Powell, D., (1991). *Strengthening parental contributions to school readiness and early school learning.* Paper presented for Office of Educational Research and Improvement. Washington, DC: U.S. Department of Education.

Quay, H. C., & Peterson, D. R. (1967). *Behavior problem checklist.* Champaign, IL: Children's Research Center, University of Illinois.

Raygor, B. (1972). *A five year follow-up study comparing the school achievement variables and school adjustment of children retained in kindergarten and children placed in transition class.* Unpublished doctoral dissertation, University of Minnesota.

Remmey & McIlhenny (1987). *Two-year developmental kindergarten program.* Paper presented at annual conference of the Association for Supervision and Curriculum Development, New Orleans, LA. March 21–24.

Shepard, L. A. (1989). A review of research on kindergarten retention in L. A. Shepard & M. L. Smith (Eds.), *Flunking grades: Research and policies on grade retention.* New York: Falmer Press.

Shepard, L. A., & Smith, M. L. (1985). *Boulder Valley kindergarten study: Retention practices and retention effects.* Boulder, CO: Laboratory of Educational Research, University of Colorado, Boulder.

Shepard, L. A., & Smith, M. L. (1987, October). Effects of kindergarten retention at the end of first grade. *Psychology in the Schools,* 346–357.

Shepard, L. A., & Smith, M. L. (1986). Synthesis of research on school readiness and kindergarten retention. *Educational Leadership, 44,* 78–86.

Turley, C. C. (1979). *A study of kindergarten children for whom kindergarten retention was recommended.* Unpublished doctoral dissertation, University of San Francisco.

► 6

School and Classroom Organization in Beginning Reading

Class Size, Aides, and Instructional Grouping

ROBERT E. SLAVIN

Several of the most hotly debated issues surrounding the education of children in the early elementary grades have to do with the organization and staffing of schools and classrooms. Such questions as class size, use of instructional aides, and ability grouping between and within classes have been argued for decades. From a policy perspective, changes in school and classroom organization are always attractive options, as they are policies that can be set at the statehouse or district office without the requirement for long, messy, and uncertain staff development involved in other types of reforms. In particular, reducing class size is a policy that, although expensive, has widespread political support because it makes sense to educators and taxpayers alike.

This chapter reviews research on class size, use of instructional aides, and ability grouping as these policies are applied in kindergarten and first grade to examine the degree to which they may influence student success in reading.

CLASS SIZE*

The achievement effects of class size have been studied since the 1920s and have certainly been debated much longer. However, class size has come to the fore in recent years for several reasons. One is the publication in 1978 of a meta-analysis on the subject by Glass and Smith challenging the then-conventional wisdom (among researchers, at least) that class size made little or no difference in achievement. More recently, statewide experiments involving substantial reductions in class sizes in the early grades have taken place in Tennessee, Indiana, and Nevada. Changes in Chapter 1 regulations have allowed high-poverty schools to use their Chapter 1 dollars to serve all students, and most schools that have taken advantage of this "schoolwide project" provision have used the opportunity to reduce class size (Committee on Education and Labor, 1990). Further, the class size discussion is central to school finance cases, which have begun in several states to successfully challenge unequal funding among districts in the same state. Clearly, the achievement effects of class size reduction are not merely an academic question. Conclusions in this issue have very real policy and legal consequences.

Why Class Size Should Matter and Why It Shouldn't

If class size were known to have substantial effect on student achievement, this finding would probably be considered one more case of educational research confirming the obvious. Since the earliest research on the question, advocates have noted the likely benefits of smaller classes: more opportunities for teachers to focus on individual needs, more opportunities for students to actively participate, fewer problems of classroom management, and higher morale among teachers and students. More recently, many reviewers have added to this list the possibility that smaller classes may allow teachers to use innovative practices that they would be less likely to use with large classes. As one example of this, some (e.g, Anderson & Barr, 1989) have linked teachers' willingness to teach completely heterogeneous (untracked) classes to a reduction in class size.

On the other hand, the main reason one might not anticipate substantial effects of class size reduction is that teachers do not generally teach very differently in class sizes of, say, 15 than in larger classes. Observational studies of teacher behaviors in large and small classes (e.g., Cahen,

---

*This section is adapted from Slavin (1990). Copyright © 1990 by Robert Slavin and *Contemporary Education*.

Filby, McCutcheon, & Kyle, 1983; Evertson, Folger, Breda, & Randolph, 1990) find only subtle and inconsistent differences in the actual teaching strategies or behaviors of these teachers. Still, the evidence of improved morale among teachers and students (e.g., Glass, Cahen, Smith, & Filby, 1982; Johnston, 1990), in addition to common sense concerning the teacher's ability to help individual children, would provide a basis for predicting improved achievement in small classes.

It might be argued that class size would make a particularly large difference in the early grades, where students' lack of independent work skills and diverse ways of learning may make smaller classes especially important. In fact, a review of research on class size conducted by the Educational Research Service (Robinson & Wittebols, 1986; Robinson, 1990) concluded that while small classes made little difference in grades 4 and up, they did increase achievement in grades K through 3.

Effects of Class Size on First-Grade Reading Achievement

The reviews of research on the achievement effects of class size have combined many grade levels and subjects. What is the evidence specifically relating to the potential of major reductions in class size to enhance the reading achievement of students in the primary grades? To answer this question, we attempted to locate all studies that compared first grades of different sizes, focusing on studies in which the difference between large and small classes was at least 20 percent (e.g., a reduction from 29 to 23 or from 24 to 19). The studies also had to present evidence that the students in the larger and smaller classes were initially equivalent, either by using random assignment to large or small classes or by matching on achievement or socioeconomic status.

All studies that met these criteria are summarized in Table 6.1. A total of four randomized and seven matched studies were located. The randomized studies are listed in descending order of sample size, and then the matched studies are listed similarly. If the study involved maintaining smaller class sizes in other grades (beyond first), effects for these grades are also presented.

The largest of the randomized experiments is a Tennessee statewide study called STAR, for Student-Teacher Achievement Ratio (Word et al., 1990; Finn, 1990). In this study, 6,500 kindergartners were randomly assigned to large classes (22 to 25), large classes with aides, or small classes (13 to 17). The students remained in their designated class sizes for four years, through grade 3. Reading effects favored the smaller classes in all grades, reaching a maximum effect size of $+0.34$ at the end of the first grade and diminishing to $+.24$ at the end of third grade. A follow-up study

TABLE 6.1 Studies of Class Size and Reading Achievement in the Early Grades

Article	Grades	Location	Sample Test	Class Sizes	Design	Effect Sizes	
Studies Using Random Assignment							
Word et al., 1990; Finn, 1990	K–3	Tennessee (Statewide)	6,500 students	L = 23 S = 15	Students and teachers in same schools randomly assigned to large or small classes. Same students followed for 3 years.	Kdg. Grade 1 Grade 2 Grade 3	+ .21 + .34 + .26 + .24
Johnson & Roan-Quintana, 1978	1	South Carolina (Statewide)	50 cl.	L = 29 S = 21	Students and teachers in same schools randomly assigned to large or small classes.	(0)	
South Carolina State Dept. of Education, 1977	1	South Carolina (Statewide)	46 cl.	L = 29 S = 21	Students and teachers in same schools randomly assigned to large or small classes.	(+)	
Carrington et al., 1981	1	Virginia Beach, VA	16 cl.	L = 29 S = 21	Students and teachers in same schools randomly assigned to large or small classes.	(+)	
Studies Using Matching							
Farr et al., 1987	K–3	Indiana (Statewide)	1128 sch.	L = 23.5 S = 18	Project PRIME TIME. Small classes matched with earlier cohorts.	Kdg. Grade 1 Grade 2 Grade 3	+ .09 (+) (+) + .06
Jarvis et al., 1987	1	New York City, Low SES	99 sch., exp. 22 sch., ctrl.	L = 26 S = 16	Compared students in small classes to matched regular classes.	+ .09	

Continued

TABLE 6.1 *Continued*

Article	Grades	Location	Sample Test	Class Sizes	Design	Effect Sizes
Studies Using Matching (cont.)						
Mazareas, 1981	1	City near Boston, MA	146 cl.	L>30 S<20	Compared students in large and small classes, controlling for IQ.	−.12*
McDermott, 1977	1–2	Irving, TX	35 cl.	L=29 S=23	Compared classes reduced to less than 25 to same teachers' larger classes in previous year.	.00*
Whittington, Bain, & Achilles, 1985; Bain et al., 1988	1–3	Nashville, TN	14 cl.	L=25 S=15	Compared students in small classes to matched regular classes. Same students followed for three years.	Grade 1 +.57 Grade 2 (0) Grade 3 (0)
Christner, 1987	K–1	Austin, TX Chapter 1 students	2 sch., exp.	L=22 S=15	Compared students in Chapter 1 schoolwide projects to all other Chapter 1 students. Classes compared for six years.	Kdg. (0) Grade 1 (0)
Tillitski et al., 1988	1–3	Princeton, IN	193 students	L=21–24 S=17–20	Part of Project PRIME TIME. Students in smaller classes matched with earlier cohort; same students followed for 3 years.	Grade 1 +.19 Grade 2 +.17 Grade 3 −.07

Source: Adapted from Slavin (1990). Copyright ©1990 by Robert Slavin and *Contemporary Education.*
Key: (+) Results favored small classes   (−) Results favored large classes
      (0) No differences   * Effect sizes approximate, estimated from ANCOVA's

found that by the end of fourth grade, students who had been in smaller classes in grades K through 3 were only slightly ahead of students who had been in larger classes (mean ES = +.13) (Finn, Fulton, Zaharias, & Nye, 1989).

Observational studies of teacher behaviors in large and small second- and third-grade classes were conducted by Evertson, Folger, Breda, and Randolph (1990). They found few differences between large and small classes in terms of time spent on reading, lesson format, or teacher-student interactions.

Two randomized statewide studies of class size in first grade were conducted in South Carolina. Johnson and Garcia-Quintana (1978) randomly assigned first-grade students in two classes in each of 25 school districts to large (n = 29) or small (n = 21) classes. Teachers were also randomly assigned to large or small classes. The experiment was repeated twice. In the 1975–1976 school year, small positive effects (about a quarter of a standard deviation) were found in reading for the smaller classes, but in the 1976–1977 cohort, there were no significant differences. (Effect size was approximately +.08.)

In a randomized study patterned on the South Carolina experiments, Carrington, Meekins, and Lovelace (1981) compared first-graders randomly assigned to classes of 29 or 21 in the Virginia Beach, Virginia, school district. As in South Carolina, teachers as well as students were randomly assigned to large or small classes. The results favored the small classes by about two points (out of 48) on the California Achievement Test Total Reading Scale. In contrast to the findings of the Tennessee study, differences favoring small classes were larger for white students (2.14 points) than for nonwhite (0.74 point), although the small number of nonwhite students involved (32) means that this result should be considered tentative at best.

Project PRIME TIME in Indiana was, like the Tennessee class size experiments, an attempt by the state to assess the impact of class size reductions in the early grades. The study compared students in small classes (average size = 18) from grades 1 through 3 with students in a previous cohort who were in larger classes (average size = 23.5).

Statewide assessments of Project PRIME TIME found small positive effects of reduced class size in first and second grades (Farr, Quilling, Bessel, & Johnson, 1987). A study of third-graders who had been in small classes for three years (Farr et al., 1987) found that the reading achievement of these students was virtually identical to that of students in earlier cohorts who had been in larger classes (ES = +.06). This study also found few effects of reduced class size on kindergarten prereading skills (ES = +.09). An independent study of PRIME TIME conducted by a rural school district found patterns similar to those of the larger assessment. This study

(Tillitski, Gilman, Mohr, & Stone, 1988) followed the same children for three years and compared them to students in an earlier cohort, before PRIME TIME. Small positive reading effects were found in first grade (ES = +.19) and in second grade (ES = +.17), but by third grade the differences were gone (ES = −.07).

Another very large study of significant class size reductions was an experiment done in New York City (Jarvis, Whitehurst, Gampert, & Schulman, 1987). First-grade classes in 99 schools (633 classes) serving students low in socioeconomic status were reduced in size to an average of 15 students or, if space considerations did not allow this, they were given a half-time aide or teacher to team with the regular classroom teacher during reading and math periods. The achievement of students in these classes was compared with that of students in 22 schools (100 classes) where first-grade class sizes averaged 26. The overall difference on the Metropolitan Achievement Test was very small (ES = +.09). Unfortunately, this study did not separate outcomes for classes with aides (17.3 percent of the experimental classes) from those that reduced class sizes. However, since the great majority of classes did have reduced class sizes, it is reasonable to assume that most of the experimental-control difference is due to reduced class size. As in the Tennessee study, this study included observations of teachers in large and small classes, and it found few differences in their teaching behaviors.

Mazareas (1981) compared the achievement of first-graders in classes with 30 or more students to that in classes of 20 or less, controlling for IQ and other variables, in a "semi-industrialized city north of Boston." He found that on standardized reading measures, students in the smaller classes performed slightly *worse* than students in larger classes.

In a study in suburban Irving, Texas, McDermott (1977) compared first- and second-graders in classes reduced to less than 25 students to the same teachers' classes the previous year, when class sizes were 27 or more. A test of general ability was used as a covariate. Reading outcomes on the *SRA* were essentially identical in the larger and smaller classes. This was true for both grades and for students of all ability levels.

In a small pilot study for the Tennessee STAR experiment, students in matched large (*n* = 25) and small (*n* = 15) classes in Nashville were compared over a three-year period. As of the end of first grade, the results looked promising (Whittington, Bain, & Achilles, 1985), but in second and third grades, the differences disappeared, even though the experimental students remained in their small classes (Bain, Achilles, Dennis, Parks, & Hooper, 1988).

Beginning in 1980–1981, the Austin, Texas, school district designated its two highest poverty schools as Chapter 1 schoolwide projects, which means that they could use their Chapter 1 dollars (supplemented by district matching funds) to serve all children. The schools used the money to reduce average class size to 15. First-year test results strongly favored the smaller classes in grades 2 through 6 (Doss & Holley, 1982), but continuing evaluations over a six-year period found few differences in achievement between students in the small classes and similar students in other schools, including students in kindergarten and first grade (Christner, 1987).

Conclusions: Effects of Class Size on Reading Achievement in the Early Grades

The conclusion from the 11 studies summarized in Table 6.1 must be that the effects of significantly reducing class size in first grade has a positive effect on student reading achievement, but the effect is small and short lived. Of the 11 studies, 7 found positive effects on reading in first grade, 3 found no differences, and 1 found a small effect favoring larger classes. Across the 5 studies from which effect sizes could be computed, the median effect size is +.14. However, of the 4 studies that kept students in small classes throughout the primary grades (grades 1 through 3), only 1, the large Tennessee experiment, found an effect different from zero by the end of three or four years of smaller classes. Correlational studies of the effects of class size on early reading achievement resulted in similar conclusions to those of the experimental studies. The correlations were either very small (e.g., Farr et al., 1987) or zero (e.g., Madison Public Schools, 1976).

It is possible that the standardized tests used in all of the class size studies are too insensitive to register any true effect of class size reduction in the early grades. However, standardized tests should become more, not less, sensitive to student achievement in the later grades, and effects of class size are consistently greater in first grade than in any other grade (see Slavin, 1990; Robinson & Wittebols, 1986). It is also interesting to note that the effects of class size on mathematics achievement are very similar to effects on reading achievement (Slavin, 1990).

A trend noted in the Tennessee study (Finn, 1990) was for effects to be larger for minority students, mostly African-American students, than for whites. However, just the opposite trend was seen in the Virginia Beach study (Carrington et al., 1981), and other studies with mostly minority samples found no differences (Jarvis et al., 1987; Christner, 1987).

The relatively large (but still quite modest) effects seen in the statewide Tennessee study provide the greatest cause for optimism about the potential of class size reductions to increase reading achievement. What was unique about this study that could account for these findings? One factor may be that the amount of reduction was particularly great in the Tennessee project. Among the large randomized studies, this is the only one to study class sizes reduced by nearly half (40 percent), and with small classes of only 15. The Virginia Beach and South Carolina randomized studies involved class sizes reduced from 29 to 21 (28 percent) and the Indiana statewide studies involved a reduction from 23.5 to 18 (23 percent). However, other studies (Jarvis et al., 1987; Christner, 1987; Bain et al., 1988) evaluated class size reductions as great as those in the large Tennessee study, and these studies ended with students in small and large classes achieving at about the same level.

Reducing class size in first grade may well be an important part of an overall strategy to prevent early reading failure, but it must not be seen as a sufficient solution to the problems of beginning reading instruction. If class size is to be reduced, first grade appears to be the grade on which to focus, but class size reductions must be accompanied by other changes in curriculum, instruction, and supportive services if it is to have a major and lasting impact on students at risk for school failure.

AIDES

One of the most common investments of Chapter 1 dollars is in instructional aides, or paraprofessionals. The roles of aides can vary widely. They can help with clerical activities or other noninstructional tasks to help free teachers to teach; they can help students with seatwork or otherwise provide "as-needed" assistance to students; and they can tutor individual students or small groups. Some aides have little more than a high school diploma; others may be fully certified teachers who are not teaching because their certification is from another state, because they cannot find a job, or for any number of other reasons. Because of the diversity in the qualifications and roles of aides, it is hard to generalize about their effectiveness. However, research on the most common uses of aides to assist in first-grade reading classes revealed few effects on student reading performance.

The largest and best-designed study of the use of aides was a part of the Tennessee class size study (Word et al., 1990; Folger & Breda, 1990). In this experiment, kindergartners in schools throughout Tennessee were randomly assigned to small classes ($n = 15$), large classes without an aide ($n = 25$), or large classes with an aide ($n = 25$). The outcomes comparing small and large classes were reported earlier.

After kindergarten, students in the large classes with or without aides were again randomly assigned to the two groups, and then remained in the same type of class for three years. The aides averaged three years of experience, and their education ranged from high school (55 percent) to some college (37 percent) to college degree (8 percent). They reported spending an average of 4.8 hours per week in custodial activities (e.g., supervising lunch), 10.6 hours in clerical activities (e.g., grading papers), and 7.4 hours in instructional activities (e.g., tutoring individual children or working with small reading or math groups).

The differences in overall reading achievement between classes with and without aides were essentially zero in kindergarten (ES = +.05). Only at the first-grade level did aides make a statistically significant difference, but the effect was small (ES = +.15). By the end of third grade, students who had been in classes with aides for three years were virtually identical in achievement to students who had been in classes of the same size without aides (ES = +.05).

Other studies of the effects of instructional aides on first-grade reading achievement have similarly revealed effects ranging from zero to very small. Mazareas (1981) found that students in classes with aides performed slightly worse than those in classes without aides. Hicks (1976) also found no differences in first-grade reading between classes with and without aides. Miller (1970) found that first-graders in classes without aides achieved somewhat better than students in classes with aides (ES = −.21). A review of the literature involving all grade levels by Schuetz (1980) found few consistent effects of the use of aides.

Although research does not generally support the use of aides as they are most often used, there is evidence that aides implementing structured one-to-one tutoring programs can substantially increase the achievement of at-risk first-graders. This evidence, summarized in Chapter 7, would suggest that aides *can* be a part of a program to ensure the reading success of young children, but not if they are used in the ways aides are usually employed. The structured one-to-one tutoring programs implemented over periods of several months have little in common with the "strolling trouble-shooter" instructional role played by most classroom aides, and have even less in common with the clerical and custodial activities that occupy the bulk of aides' time.

ABILITY GROUPING

Ability grouping is one of the most important and controversial elements of school and classroom organization. In the early elementary grades, ability grouping can refer to several quite distinct practices intended to reduce the range of student performance in an instructional group (see Slavin, 1987). One is *ability-grouped class assignment,* where students are assigned on the basis of ability or achievement to one self-contained class. For example, this might mean that a school has high, average, and low first-grade classes. Alternatively, students might be assigned to heterogeneous classes most of the day but are *regrouped for reading* according to reading performance. A particular form of regrouping is the *Joplin Plan,* in which students are regrouped for reading across grade lines, so that a second grade, first semester reading class might include first-, second-, and third-graders. Each homogeneous class is taught as one reading group, without within-class grouping. The nongraded primary, which has features in common with the Joplin Plan, is discussed in a later section.

The most common form of ability grouping in elementary schools is *within-class ability grouping* in reading (and sometimes in math or other subjects). Until recently, the use of reading groups in primary classes was virtually universal, and as of this writing it is still nearly so, although increasing numbers of teachers are experimenting with whole-class instruction for at least part of the reading period. A statewide survey of Pennsylvania schools by McPartland, Coldiron, and Braddock (1987) found that approximately 95 percent of first grades used reading groups. In contrast, 47 percent of classes used some form of homogeneous class grouping in reading, including 23 percent which used regrouping.

Research on grouping in first-grade reading finds that the effects depend entirely on the type of grouping used. The following sections discuss the research on each major form of grouping.

Ability-Grouped Class Assignment

In an earlier review of the literature on ability grouping in the elementary grades, Slavin (1987) found the effects of ability-grouped class assignment to cluster closely around zero for all students. High, average, and low achievers all performed the same in ability-grouped or heterogeneous classes. Looking at the first-grade studies, the conclusion is little changed. Bremer (1958) compared the reading achievement of ability-grouped first-graders in Amarillo, Texas, to that of first-graders the previous year (before ability-grouped class assignment was introduced). The results slightly favored the heterogeneous classes (ES = −.10). Flair (1964) compared ability-grouped first-graders in suburban Skokie, Illinois, to matched students in a school that used heterogeneous grouping, and found essentially no differences in reading achievement (ES = +.03).

Regrouping for Reading

Slavin (1987) found the limited evidence on regrouping for reading to be inconclusive. None of the studies of regrouping included first-graders.

Reading Groups

Unfortunately, there are no methodologically adequate studies comparing the use of reading groups to whole-class instruction in reading. This is probably due in large part to the fact that until recently, few teachers would consent to teach a heterogeneous reading class as a single group. Recently, whole-class instruction in reading has sometimes been a recommended practice in whole-language methods. Evaluations of such ungrouped programs are still few in number and tend to find no differences in reading performance (e.g., Stice & Bertrand, 1987). However, whole-language studies completely confound curriculum and instruction with grouping strategies, so they cannot directly address the question of the effects of within-class ability grouping in reading.

Joplin Plan

The Joplin Plan (Floyd, 1954), in its simplest form, is an extension of regrouping for reading to allow for grouping by reading level across grade-level lines. This practice typically creates reading classes in which all students are working at the same or, at most, two reading levels, so that within-class ability grouping may be reduced or eliminated. The trade-off between within-class (reading groups) and between-class (Joplin) ability grouping is a pivotal issue in studies of the Joplin Plan, which may be conceptualized not as ability grouping versus heterogeneous grouping but as between- versus within-class grouping (see, for example, Newport, 1967). In contrast, studies of regrouping for reading within grades maintain reading groups within the class, although there may be some reduction in the number of reading groups used.

Overall, studies of the Joplin Plan support the use of this strategy. Slavin (1987) found a median effect size of +.45 in favor of the Joplin Plan (in comparison to heterogeneous classes using multiple reading groups within the class). Studies involving first-graders also support this strategy. These are discussed below.

Hillson, Jones, Moore, and Van Devender (1964) randomly assigned first- and second-grade students and teachers to Joplin or traditional classes. Students in the nongraded classes were assigned to heterogeneous classes but regrouped across grade levels for reading. They proceeded through nine reading levels and were continually regrouped on the basis of their reading performance. Within each reading class, teachers had multiple reading groups and used traditional basal readers and instructional methods.

The results of this study supported the efficacy of the Joplin Plan program. After three semesters, reading scores for experimental students on three standardized scales were considerably higher than for control students (ES = +.72, or about .41 grade equivalents). After three years in the program, experimental-control differences had diminished, but were still moderately positive (ES = +.33) (Jones, Moore, & Van Devender, 1967).

Ingram (1960) evaluated a Joplin program very similar to that studied by Hillson and colleagues (1964). Students in grades 1 through 3 were assigned to one of nine reading levels without regard to age. As students moved from grade to grade, they began where they had finished in the previous year. Teachers generally had more than one reading group within their reading classes. As in the Hillson and colleagues' (1964) study, the results strongly supported the nongraded approach. By the end of three years, students in the nongraded program were achieving approximately .7 grade equivalents ahead of similar students in earlier years before nongrading (ES = +.61) on standardized reading tests.

In a study by Halliwell (1963), students in grades 1 through 3 were regrouped for reading only, and they remained in heterogeneous classes the rest of the day. Spelling was also included in the regrouped classes for second- and third-graders. The article is unclear as to whether within-class grouping was used in regrouped reading classes, but there is some indication that reading groups were not used. Results indicated considerably higher reading achievement in Joplin classes than in the same school the year before nongrading was introduced (ES = +.59). Scores were higher for Joplin students at every grade level, but by far the largest differences were for first-graders who exceeded earlier first-grade classes by .94 grade equivalents (ES = +1.22).

In the three studies including first-graders, the effects of the Joplin Plan on reading achievement are remarkably positive. Only the Halliwell (1963) study presented data that indicated effects on first-graders separately from second- and third-graders, and in this study the effects were extremely positive (ES = +1.22). For the other two studies, effects across grades 1 through 3 were also very positive. For grades 1 through 3, the median effect size across the three studies was +.61.

Conclusions: Effects of Ability Grouping on Reading Achievement in the Early Grades

The evidence presented here points to an interesting conclusion. Traditional forms of ability grouping, such as assigning students to homogeneous classes for all or part of the day, have little if any impact on student reading achievement. However, there are strong positive effects of the Joplin Plan. Why might this be so?

In understanding the effects of the Joplin Plan, it is important to recall that the evaluations of this strategy do not compare ability grouping to no grouping but rather compare one form of grouping to another: within-class ability grouping (i.e., use of reading groups). As traditionally applied, reading groups create a serious problem. While the teacher is working with one group, the others have typically been given workbooks or other seatwork. The value of this seatwork is questionable (see Anderson, Brubaker, Alleman-Brooks, & Duffy, 1985). This may be particularly true in first grade, where students' lack of independent reading and work skills may make seatwork especially ineffective. By grouping students across classes and grade lines, the Joplin Plan allows teachers to use whole-class instruction in a group all at one reading level. The potential negative social effects of ability grouping may be alleviated by the flexibility of groupings typical of Joplin Plan implementations, by the fact that teachers rarely teach homogeneous high or low classes (since they have advanced young students, students at grade level, and older students performing below grade level in the same class), and by the fact that the regrouping is only for the portion of the school day devoted to reading, so that students identify with a heterogeneous class.

However, the consistently positive effects of the Joplin Plan open another intriguing possibility. If the Joplin Plan works because it allows for whole-class instruction in reading, then perhaps whole-class instruction is effective even without the cross-grade grouping. In light of the substantial variation in readiness levels in most first-grade classes this seems impractical, but in combination with tutoring or other interventions to accelerate the reading progress of low achievers, such a strategy may be effective. It is certainly worth evaluating.

THE NONGRADED PRIMARY

An innovation of the late 1950s and 1960s, the nongraded or ungraded primary is an idea that is experiencing a resurgence in the 1990s (see Willis, 1991; Pavan, 1992). The term *nongraded* or *ungraded* refers to a variety of related grouping plans. In its original conception (Goodlad & Anderson, 1963), nongraded programs are ones in which grade-level designations are entirely removed, and students are placed in flexible groups according to their performance level, not their age. Full-scale nongraded plans might use team teaching, individualized instruction, learning centers, and other means of accommodating student differences in all academic subjects. Students in nongraded programs might complete the primary cycle (grades 1 through 3) in two years, or may take four years to do so. The curriculum in each subject may be divided into levels (e.g., 9 or 12 levels for the primary grades) through which students progress at their own rates, picking up each year where they left off the previous year. This "continuous progress" aspect of nongrading gives students a feeling that they are always moving forward; for example, rather than being assigned to the low reading group each year, a low-achieving student simply progresses from level to level at a slower rate.

Some of the nongraded programs evaluated in the 1960s and early 1970s did use the flexible, complex grouping arrangements envisioned by

Goodlad and Anderson (1963), while others did not. For example, several programs described by their authors as "nongraded" were in fact indistinguishable from the Joplin Plan. That is, students were assigned to heterogeneous classes most of the day but regrouped across grade lines for reading. All three of the studies of the Joplin Plan reviewed above actually identified their interventions as nongraded primaries.

Throughout its history, the concept of nongradedness has been presented as an ideal to which schools may aspire rather than as a specific program which they may implement. Many of the studies of nongraded plans, especially of the Joplin-like variations, apologize for their failure to fully live up to the nongraded ideal. As noted earlier, implementations of programs described as nongraded have ranged from simple regrouping plans for reading to very complex interventions. For example, Carbone (1961) poses the following six questions to be considered in discussing the concept of nongrading:

1. Do we have clear statements of our instructional objectives organized in a realistic sequence and covering the entire span of our program?
2. Do we have a sufficient variety of instructional materials on different levels of sophistication so that each teacher can adjust instruction to the range of abilities found in each classroom?
3. Are we able to move toward greater individualization of instruction so that pupils can actually progress at individual rates?
4. Are we willing to use grouping practices that are flexible enough to allow easy movement from group to group within a class and from class to class within a school?
5. Do we have evaluation devices, based on our instructional objectives, that will provide clear evidence of pupil attainments and thus facilitate our decisions on grouping and progress?
6. Are we sufficiently committed to that educational shibboleth— recognizing individual differences—to do something about the difference that we have so long only "recognized"? (p. 88)

Examples of recommended practices grouped under these six questions include use of self-teaching and self-testing materials; independent study on projects appropriate to students' interests, abilities, and needs; use of independent study or instruction to very small groups (2 to 6 students) at least two-thirds of the day; and variable amounts of time in which students graduate. In this ideal form, the nongraded elementary school is closer in conception to individualized instruction or to the open school than it is to the Joplin Plan, which does not use individualized instruction and reduces or eliminates within-class ability grouping.

Research on nongraded elementary school programs was recently reviewed by Gutiérrez and Slavin (1992). This review of 56 studies that compared nongraded and graded programs divided programs into four major categories. Positive effect sizes were found for the simplest forms of nongrading, the Joplin-like plans affecting only one subject (almost always reading; median ES = +.46). Programs using cross-grade grouping for multiple subjects were also associated with significant achievement gains (median ES = +.34). However, more complex programs emphasizing individualized instruction (median ES = +.02)—including studies of Individually Guided Education (median ES = +.11)—were markedly less successful than the simpler grouping plans.

Overall, the data from studies of comprehensive nongraded primary programs support their use, although the effects are neither as consistent nor as large as those for the simpler Joplin Plan. Since the nongraded primary in its fullest realization contains many distinct elements, it is hard to know which contribute to the effectiveness of the model and which do not. Some of the elements often seen in nongraded primary schools, such as individualized instruction, have been separately researched and found to be ineffective (e.g., Horak, 1981). In fact, the most comprehensive implementations of the nongraded primary closely resemble the open classroom (see Goodlad & Anderson, 1987), which did not generally produce achievement gains for students (Giaconia & Hedges, 1982). On the other hand, the cross-grade grouping for reading and the use of a continuous-progress sequence of skills that the nongraded primary shares with the Joplin Plan are well supported by research, and they may account for much of the effectiveness of the nongraded programs. This conclusion is supported by the finding of the Gutiérrez and Slavin (1992) review, which noted a tendency for the largest positive effects of the nongraded primary to occur in relatively simple forms of the model.

For example, the largest positive effect for a study including first-graders was obtained in a study by Machiele (1965), which used only the cross-grade grouping and continuous-progress elements of the nongraded plan. Studies by Lawson (1973), Hickey (1963), and Brody (1970) used similar procedures and also obtained positive effects. In contrast, Bowman (1971) and Wilt (1971) evaluated nongraded primary programs incorporating individualized instruction, team teaching, learning centers, and other features in addition to cross-grade grouping and continuous progress, and neither found achievement effects for primary students.

A serious problem in research on the nongraded school is the fact that while, in concept, students in nongraded schools should be able to take more or less time to complete their studies, few experiments have reported how many students actually took more or less time than usual. One survey of eight New York districts using nongraded or graded primaries found that acceleration was rare in both types of school, whereas deceleration (due to retention) was more common in the graded schools (McLoughlin, 1970). Similarly, a study by Enevoldsen (1961) found that there was a higher proportion of students retained in the traditional graded program than were in the fourth year of the normatively three-year nongraded primary. Thus, it is not at all clear that the nongraded program has served in practice to give students more time to master the primary curriculum (also see Chapter 5).

CONCLUSION

The research reviewed in this chapter covers a broad range of issues of school and classroom organization. The major conclusions drawn are as follows:

Class size. The effects of substantial reductions in class size on reading in the early grades are clearly positive but small, and they tend to fade beyond the first grade even if students remain in small classes.

Aides. Provision of instructional aides to assist classroom teachers has rarely been found to have any effect on achievement, although it may improve the quality of life for teachers. On the other hand, aides using structured one-to-one tutoring programs can make a substantial difference in student reading achievement (see Chapter 7).

Ability grouping. Assignment of students to classes on the basis of ability or achievement level has few effects on student achievement. Regrouping for reading and use of within-class ability grouping (reading groups) have not been adequately studied at the early grade levels to permit any conclusions to be drawn. However, there is evidence of strong positive effects of the Joplin Plan (in comparison to use of multiple reading groups within the classroom). The Joplin Plan involves grouping students across grade lines according to reading levels, so that whole-class instruction (or at least a smaller number of reading groups) can be used.

Nongraded primary. The term *nongraded primary* or *elementary school* refers to a range of practices intended to allow students to move through the grades at their own pace, progressing through a series of levels in major content areas rather than following a lockstep grade-to-grade progression. Some nongraded programs have used individualized instruction, learning stations, team teaching, multi-age grouping, and other strategies, whereas others have simply used nongraded grouping as a means of flexibly grouping students across grade lines for instruction. Research is inconsistent but generally supports the simpler forms of nongraded programs that most resemble the Joplin Plan.

Clearly, changing school and classroom organization practices is not in itself an adequate strategy for preventing early reading failure. However, in combination with other interventions, such practices as reducing class size in first grade and using grouping methods that allow for whole-class instruction in reading while providing instruction appropriate to students' needs can contribute to the chances that students will be successful in reading the first time they are taught, and as such they can be important elements of a comprehensive prevention strategy.

REFERENCES

Anderson, C. S., & Barr, R. (1989, March). *Teacher response to proposed changes in grouping: Impact on policy and practice.* Paper presented at the annual meeting of the American Educational Research Association, San Francisco.

Anderson, L. M., Brubaker, N. L., Alleman-Brooks, J., & Duffy, G. G. (1985). A qualitative study of seatwork in first-grade classrooms. *Elementary School Journal, 86,* 123–140.

Anderson, R. H. (1973). *Opting for openness.* Arlington, VA: National Association of Elementary School Principals.

Bain, H., Achilles, C. M., Dennis, B., Parks, M., & Hooper, R. (1988). Class size reduction in Metro Nashville: A three-year cohort study. *ERS Spectrum, 6* (4), 30–36.

Bowman, B. L. (1971). A comparison of pupil achievement and attitude in a graded school with pupil achievement and attitude in a nongraded school, 1968–69, 1969–70 school years. *Dissertation Abstracts, 32,* 86-A. (University Microfilms No. 71-20, 958)

Bremer, N. (1958). First grade achievement under different plans of grouping. *Elementary English, 35,* 324–326.

Brody, E. B. (1970, April). Achievement of first- and second-year pupils in graded and nongraded classrooms. *Elementary School Journal, 70,* 391–394.

Cahen, L. S., Filby, N., McCutcheon, G., & Kyle, D. (1983). *Class size and instruction.* New York: Longman.

Carbone, R. F. (1961). A comparison of graded and non-graded elementary schools. *Elementary School Journal, 62,* 82–88.

Carrington, A. T., Meekins, P. E., & Lovelace, D. W. (1981). *Class size project, 1980–1981.* Virginia Beach, VA: Virginia Beach Public Schools. (ERIC No. ED 237 251)

Christner, C. A. (1987, April). *Schoolwide projects: The almost revolution (?) six years later.* Paper presented at the annual convention of the American Educational Research Association, Washington, DC.

Committee on Education and Labor (1990). *Chapter 1 survey of the Hawkins-Stafford school improvement amendments.* Washington, DC: U.S. House of Representatives.

Doss, D., & Holley, F. (1982). *A cause for national pause: Title I schoolwide projects.* Austin, TX: Office of Research and Evaluation, Austin Independent School District. (ERIC No. ED 214 996)

Enevoldsen, C. L. (1961). *An evaluation of the ungraded primary program in the Lincoln, Nebraska public school system.* Unpublished doctoral dissertation, University of Nebraska.

Evertson, C. M., Folger, J. K., Breda, C., & Randolph, C. (1990, April). *How does inservice training affect teachers' instruction in small, regular, and regular/aide classes?* Paper presented at the annual convention of the American Educational Research Association, Boston.

Farr, B., Quilling, M., Bessel, R., & Johnson, W. (1987). *Evaluation of PRIME TIME: 1986-1987.* Final report. Indianapolis: Advanced Technology, Inc.

Finn, J. D. (1990, April). *Who is helped the most by small classes?* Paper presented at the annual convention of the American Educational Research Association, Boston.

Finn, J. D., Fulton, D., Zaharias, J., & Nye, B. A. (1989). Carry-over effects of small classes. *Peabody Journal of Education, 67* (1), 75–84.

Flair, M. D. (1964). The effect of grouping on achievement and attitudes toward learning of first grade pupils. *Dissertation Abstracts, 25,* 6430. (University Microfilms No. 65-03, 259)

Floyd, C. (1954). Meeting children's reading needs in the middle grades: A preliminary report. *Elementary School Journal, 55,* 99–103.

Folger, J., & Breda, C. (1990, April). *Do teacher-aides improve student performance? Lessons from Project STAR.* Paper presented at the annual convention of the American Educational Research Association, Boston.

Giaconia, R. M., & Hedges, L. V. (1982). Identifying features of open education. *Review of Educational Research, 52,* 579–602.

Glass, G., Cahen, L., Smith, M. L., & Filby, N. (1982). *School class size.* Beverly Hills, CA: Sage.

Glass, G. V., & Smith, M. L. (1978). *Meta-analysis of research on the relationship of class size and achievement.* San Francisco: Far West Laboratory for Educational Research and Development.

Goodlad, J. I., & Anderson, R. H. (1963). *The nongraded elementary school* (rev. ed.). New York: Harcourt, Brace, & World.

Goodlad, J. I., & Anderson, R. H. (1987). New introduction to the revised edition. In J. I. Goodlad & R. H. Anderson (Eds.), *The non-graded elementary school* (3rd ed.). New York: Teachers College Press.

Gutiérrez, R., & Slavin, R. E. (1992). Achievement effects of the nongraded elementary school: A best-evidence synthesis. *Review of Educational Research, 62,* 333–376.

Halliwell, J. W. (1963). A comparison of pupil achievement in graded and nongraded primary classrooms. *Journal of Experimental Education, 32,* 50–64.

Hickey, M. P. (1963). An evaluation of pupil progress of the ungraded primary program in the diocese of Pittsburgh. *Dissertation Abstracts, 23,* 2817-A. (University Microfilms No. 63-208)

Hicks, J. S. (1976). *Early identification program.* Brooklyn: New York City Public Schools. (ERIC No. ED 141 479)

Hillson, M., Jones, J. C., Moore, J. W., & Van Devender, F. (1964). A controlled experiment evaluating the effects of a nongraded organization on pupil achievement. *Journal of Educational Research, 57,* 548–550.

Hopkins, K. D., Oldridge, O. A., & Williamson, M. L. (1965). An empirical comparison of pupil achievement and other variables in graded and nongraded classes. *American Educational Research Journal, 2,* 207–215.

Horak, V. M. (1981). A meta-analysis of research findings on individualized instruction in mathematics. *Journal of Educational Research, 74,* 249–253.

Ingram, V. (1960). Flint evaluates its primary cycle. *Elementary School Journal, 61,* 76–80.

Jarvis, C. H., Whitehurst, B., Gampert, R. D., & Schulman, R. (1987, April). *The relation between class size and reading achievement in first-grade classrooms.* Paper presented at the annual convention of the American Educational Research Association, Washington, DC.

Johnson, L. M., & Garcia-Quintana, R. A. (1978). *South Carolina first grade pilot project 1976–77:* The effects of class size on reading and mathematics achievement. Columbia, SC: South Carolina Department of Education.

Johnson, L. M., Mandeville, G. K., & Quinn, J. L. (1977). *South Carolina first grade pilot project 1975–76:* The effects of class size on reading and mathematics achievement. Columbia, SC: South Carolina Department of Education.

Johnston, J. M. (1990, April). *What are teachers' perceptions of teaching in different classroom contexts?* Paper presented at the annual convention of the American Educational Research Association, Boston.

Jones, C. J., Moore, J. W., & Van Devender, F. (1967). Comparison of pupil achievement after one and a half and three years in a nongraded program. *Journal of Educational Research, 61,* 75–77.

Lawson, R. E. (1973). *A comparison of self-concept and achievement in reading of students in the first, third, and fifty year of attendance in graded and nongraded elementary schools.* Unpublished doctoral dissertation, Ball State University.

Machiele, R. B. (1965). A preliminary evaluation of the non-graded primary at Leal School, Urbana. *Illinois School Research, 1,* 20–24.

Madison Public Schools. (1976). *Effects of class size on reading achievement in grades 1–3 in the Madison Metropolitan School District (1974–1976).* Madison, WI: Author. (ERIC No. ED 140 256)

Mazareas, J. (1981). *Effects of class size on the achievement of first grade pupils.* Unpublished doctoral dissertation, Boston University.

McDermott, H. T. (1977). *The effect of a reduction in class size among first and second-grade students.* Unpublished doctoral dissertation, Texas Women's University.

McLoughlin, W. P. (1970). Continuous pupil progress in the non-graded school: Hope or hoax? *Elementary School Journal, 71,* 90–96.

McPartland, J. M., Coldiron, J. R., & Braddock, J. H. (1987). *School structures and classroom practices in elementary, middle and secondary schools* (Tech. Rep. No. 14). Baltimore, MD: Johns Hopkins University, Center for Research on Elementary and Middle Schools.

Miller, J. L. (1970). *A comparison of how first grade classroom teachers with and without full time teacher aides utilize instructional time and the effect of aide utilization upon academic performance of children.* (ERIC No. ED 043 595)

Morris, V. B. (1969). An evaluation of pupil achievement in a nongraded primary plan after three, and also five years of instruction. *Dissertation Abstracts, 29,* 3809-A. (University Microfilms No. 69-7352)

Newport, J. F. (1967). The Joplin Plan: The score. *Reading Teacher, 21,* 158–162.

Pavan, B. N. (1992). The benefits of nongraded schools. *Educational Leadership, 50* (2), 22–25.

Remacle, L. F. (1971). A comparative study of the differences in attitudes self-concept, and achievement of children in graded and nongraded elementary schools. *Dissertation Abstracts, 31,* 5948-A. (University Microfilms No. 71-12, 649)

Robinson, G. E. (1990). Synthesis of research on class size. *Educational Leadership, 47* (7), 80–90.

Robinson, G. E., & Wittebols, J. H. (1986). *Class size research: A related cluster analysis for decision making.* Arlington, VA: Educational Research Service.

Ross, G. A. (1967). A comparative study of pupil progress in ungraded and graded primary programs. *Dissertation Abstracts, 28,* 2146-A. (University Microfilms No. 67-16, 428)

Schuetz, P. (1980). *The instructional effectiveness of classroom aides.* Pittsburgh, PA: University of Pittsburgh, Learning Research and Development Center.

Skapski, M. K. (1960). Ungraded primary reading program: An objective evaluation. *Elementary School Journal, 61,* 41–45.

Slavin, R. E. (1987). Ability grouping and student achievement in elementary schools: A best-evidence synthesis. *Review of Educational Research, 57,* 293–336.

Slavin, R. E. (1990). Class size and student achievement: Is smaller better? *Contemporary Education, 42,* 6–12.

Stice, C. F., & Bertrand, N. P. (1987, December). *The effects of a whole language program on the literacy development of at-risk children.* Paper presented at the annual meeting of the National Reading Conference, St. Petersburg, FL.

Tillitski, C., Gilman, D., Mohr, A., & Stone, W. (1988). Class size reduction in North Gibson School Corporation: A three-year cohort study. *ERS Spectrum, 6* (4), 37–40.

Vogel, F. X., & Bowers, N. D. (1972). Pupil behavior in a multi-age nongraded school. *Journal of Experimental Education, 41,* 78–86.

Whittington, E. H., Bain, H. P., & Achilles, C. M. (1985). Effects of class size on first-grade students. *ERS Spectrum, 3,* 33–39.

Willis, S. (1991). Breaking down grade barriers: Interest in nongraded classrooms on the rise. *ASCD Update, 33* (3), 1, 4.

Wilt, H. J. (1971). A comparison of student attitudes toward school academic achievement, internal structures and procedures: The nongraded school vs. the graded school. *Dissertation Abstracts, 31,* 5105-A. (University Microfilms No. 71-8406)

Word, E., Johnson, J., Bain, H. P., Fulton, B. D., Zaharias, J. B., Lintz, M. N., Achilles, C. M., Folger, J., & Breda, C. (1990). *Student/Teacher Achievement Ratio (STAR): Tennessee's K–3 class size study, final report.* Nashville: Tennessee State Department of Education.

Preventing Early Reading Failure with One-to-One Tutoring

A Review of Five Programs

BARBARA A. WASIK   **ROBERT E. SLAVIN**

Tutoring is the oldest form of instruction. Parents have always provided one-to-one instruction to their children, and learning settings that range from driving instruction to on-the-job training typically employ one teacher for each learner for at least part of the learner's instruction. In elementary and secondary instruction, one-to-one tutoring exists around the margins of group instruction. For example, teachers often work with individual children during seatwork periods, recess, study hall, or after school. Parents sometimes hire tutors to work with their children. Tutoring is often used in special education, and sometimes in other remedial programs such as compensatory education.

The topic of tutoring has come to the fore in recent years because of a renewed focus on students who are at risk of school failure, coupled with a renewed commitment to see that all students learn basic skills in the early grades. In particular, modest effects of traditional Chapter 1/Title I pull-out programs (Carter, 1984) and loosening of restrictions on uses of Chapter 1

An earlier version of this chapter was presented at the annual convention of the American Educational Research Association, Boston, April 1990.

funds have contributed to a broader range of services being provided under Chapter 1 funding. One-to-one tutoring is one option often considered or implemented.

One particularly important application of tutoring that has increased in recent years is the use of tutors with first-graders to prevent early reading failure. First grade is a critical year for the learning of reading, and reading success in the early grades is an essential basis for success in the later grades. Disadvantaged third-graders who are significantly behind in reading or have been retained have little chance of ultimately graduating from high school (Lloyd, 1978). Observing how much progress is made in reading between the first and last days of first grade by the average reader, it seems obvious that students who fail to learn to read during first grade are far behind their peers and are unlikely to ever catch up. Research on Chapter 1 programs suggests that remediation of learning deficits after the primary grades is largely ineffective (see Kennedy, Birman, & Demaline, 1986). It makes much more sense to prevent learning deficits in the first place than to attempt to remediate them in the later grades.

The major drawback to tutoring is its cost. Providing tutoring to large numbers of students across the grade span would, of course, be prohibitive. But if there is a "critical period" for learning to read and tutors can be used to substantially increase the proportion of students who successfully navigate it, the use of this expensive intervention may be cost effective.

The importance of understanding the effects of first-grade tutoring goes far beyond the pedagogical and technical issues involved. Ron Edmonds's (1981) statement that every child can learn and Benjamin Bloom's (1981) assertion to the same effect contributed to a variety of discussions among policy makers about learning as an entitlement for all children, on the basis that if every child can learn, the schools have an ethical and perhaps legal responsibility to see that every child does learn. One manifestation of this point of view is a document produced by the Council of Chief State School Officers (1987) that describes model state statutes to entitle every child not only to an appropriate education but to success in achieving an acceptable level of performance (also see Council of Chief State School Officers, 1989). If success is seen as an entitlement, educators must have methods that produce success for all nonretarded children regardless of home background, no matter how expensive these methods may be. In any discussion along these lines, one-to-one tutoring for at-risk students is sure to be one element of the strategy to ensure success for all.

Few would doubt that one-to-one tutoring from trained adults would have a positive effect on student achievement. What is more important to know is how large the effect of tutoring is (in comparison to plausible alternatives), to what degree effects of tutoring maintain over time, and which specific tutoring programs and practices produce the largest gains in student reading achievement. The purpose of this chapter is to review the research on the effectiveness of one-to-one tutoring programs to identify what is currently known about the answers to these and other questions.

WHY SHOULD TUTORING BE EFFECTIVE?

Vygotsky's theory of cognitive development provides a framework for explaining why the tutoring model may be effective. According to Vygotsky's theory, children can often complete tasks when working with another person that they could not complete if they were working alone (Vygotsky, 1978). He suggested that abilities children demonstrate when given assistance are in the process of being internalized. These abilities are not yet crystallized, but are in the process of forming. The distance between what the child can do when working alone and what he or she can do with the assistance of another person is labeled as the *zone of proximal development*.

An effective teacher teaches within a child's zone of proximal development (Day, Cordon, & Kerwin, 1989; Vygotsky, 1978). In other words, the teacher neither teaches children at their actual level, because they would not be challenged, nor does the teacher teach beyond what the children are currently capable of doing. Instead, the effective teacher instructs the students in their zone of proximal development with material that is well within their grasp but that also challenges their potential.

With a group of 25 to 30 students who all have varying cognitive abilities, it is difficult to teach within *each* student's zone of proximal development. However, the one-to-one tutoring dyad creates the perfect situation for working within a student's zone of proximal development. The tutor can determine what the child knows about reading, what reading strategies he or she uses, and how he or she processes information. The tutor can tailor the instruction for each student's needs.

Working in the child's zone of proximal development, the tutor uses scaffolding as an essential strategy. *Scaffolding* is the process of helping the student practice already mastered strategies as well as providing the opportunity to work on nascent skills (Greenfield, 1984; Vygotsky, 1978). Scaffolding is most effective in one-to-one tutoring. The tutor can listen to the child read, help with words he or she cannot read, ask specific comprehension questions, and determine if the child is understanding what is read. The tutor can also help the student identify strategies such as self-correction or rereading that will help the student become a successful reader. This on-line interaction of working with the student one-to-one can help the child achieve a goal that would be beyond his unassisted efforts.

Wood, Bruner, and Ross (1976) directly apply the scaffolding concept to tutoring. They identify six functions of the tutor in this scaffolding role: recruit the child to work on the task; reduce the task demands for the learner; motivate and engage the child; point out relevant features of the task as well as the discrepancies between the child's production and the correct solution; control the frustration level of the learner; and model the correct solution to the task. Regardless of the specific differences among the tutoring programs, these functions generally describe what takes place in a tutoring session. Although the most effective teachers attempt to do this in their classrooms, the demands of teaching many learners at the same time make it difficult to effectively reach individual children. In one-to-one tutoring, the tutor has the opportunity to work at the individual child's level and, therefore, in Vygotskian terms, the tutoring session becomes the means for the social transmission of knowledge.

Review Methods

This chapter's review uses a set of procedures called *best-evidence synthesis,* which combines elements of meta-analysis with those of traditional narrative reviews (Slavin, 1986). Briefly, a best-evidence synthesis requires locating all research on a given topic and discussing the substantive and methodological issues in the research as in a narrative review. A priori criteria for germaneness to the topic at hand and for methodological adequacy are typically applied. Whenever possible, study outcomes are characterized in terms of effect size (ES), the difference between experimental and control means divided by the control group standard deviation (see Chapter 1 for more on this).

Inclusion Criteria.   Studies were included in the present review if they evaluated one-to-one instruction delivered by adults (certified teachers, paraprofessionals, or volunteers) to students in the first grade who were learning to read for the first time. In some cases, tutoring or other services may continue beyond the first grade, but such studies were included as long as the tutoring began in first grade. Studies had to compare tutoring to traditional instruction in elementary schools over periods of at least four weeks on measures of objectives pursued equally in experimental and control conditions. The duration requirement did not exclude any studies of first-grade tutoring, and the first-grade requirement excluded only three studies (Bausell, Moody, & Walzl, 1972; Fresko & Eisenberg, 1983; Shaver & Nuhn, 1971), which looked at remedial tutoring in the third grade and higher. Studies of cross-age and same-age peer tutoring (e.g., Cloward, 1967; Maheady, Sacca, & Harper, 1987; Harrison & Gottfredson, 1986) and special education studies (see Polloway, Cronin, & Patton, 1986; Scruggs & Richter, 1985) were also not included. Therefore, this best-evidence synthesis included all studies of one-to-one tutoring ever conducted that focused on instruction delivered by adults to first-graders. In a complete review of published as well as unpublished studies, a total of 16 studies met the inclusion criteria. Note that the methodological inclusion criteria applied in the present review are essentially identical to those applied in earlier best-evidence syntheses on mastery learning (Slavin, 1987b) and ability grouping (Slavin, 1987c, 1990).

RESEARCH ON PREVENTIVE TUTORING PROGRAMS

All of the studies that met the inclusion criteria specified above evaluated specific tutoring programs, which incorporated instructional materials as well as provision of one-to-one tutors. Five such programs have been researched. Some of the major characteristics of these programs are summarized in Table 7.1. As is apparent from the table, the five programs vary widely in curriculum, integration with classroom instruction, use of certified versus paraprofessional tutors, and other factors not intrinsically related to the one-to-one setting. As a result, we make no attempt to combine findings across studies in any way, but instead review the research on each model of tutoring separately.

Reading Recovery

The preventive tutoring program that has received the most attention and use in recent years is Reading Recovery. This program was originally developed by Marie Clay (1985) in New Zealand, and it is widely used in that country. In 1984–85, Marie Clay and a colleague, Barbara Watson, spent a year at Ohio State University. They trained a group of teachers to use the program, and trained several Ohio State faculty members to train others. Since that time, research on Reading Recovery has been conducted at Ohio State, and the program has rapidly expanded in use.

As applied in the longitudinal studies, Reading Recovery provides one-to-one tutoring to first-graders who score in the lowest 20 percent of their classes on a program-developed diagnostic survey. The tutors are certified teachers who receive training for 2½ hours per week for an entire academic year. Students are tutored for 30 minutes each day until one of two things happens. If students reach the level of performance of their classmates in the middle reading group, they are "discontinued." If they

TABLE 7.1   Characteristics of Preventive Tutoring Programs

Program	Location of Evaluations	Tutors	Tutees	Duration	Tutoring Methods and Curriculum
Reading Recovery	Ohio; Chicago	Certified Reading Teachers	Lowest 1st-graders	30 minutes/day ranging from 12 to 20 weeks	Learning to read by reading. Reading short stories and connecting writing activities to reading. Tutors guide children to learn metacognitive strategies. No connection to classroom instruction.
Success for All	Inner-city Baltimore	Certified Teachers	Lowest 1st- & 2nd-graders	20 minutes/day evaluated on 8-week cycle	Learning to read by reading. Closely integrated with structured classroom curriculum. Emphasis on metacognitive strategies.
Prevention of Learning Disabilities	New York; Ohio; California	Certified Teachers	Lowest 1st- & 2nd-graders	30 minutes/3 to 5 times/week	Use directed activities to teach specific perceptual and spatial skills involved in reading. Emphasis on skill acquisition. No emphasis on reading connected text. No connection with a classroom curriculum.
Wallach Tutorial Program	Inner city Chicago; rural North Carolina	Paraprofessionals	Lowest 1st-graders	30 minutes/day, 1 year	Phonics-based tutoring program. Emphasis on systematic mastery of phonetic skills. Does not focus on reading-connected text. Not integrated with classroom instruction.
Programmed Tutorial Reading	Inner-city Indianapolis; Lenoir City, North Carolina	Paraprofessionals	All 1st-graders	15 minutes & 30 minutes/day	Highly detailed and prescribed lessons with corresponding materials; includes sight-reading program, comprehension, and word analysis. Emphasis on skills. Partially integrated with classroom instruction.

receive 60 lessons without achieving this level of performance, the students are released from the program but considered "not discontinued." Such students may be retained or assigned to special education.

The tutoring model emphasizes "learning to read by reading" (Pinnell, 1989; Pinnell, DeFord, & Lyons, 1988). For the first few tutoring sessions, the teacher and student "roam around the known," reading and writing together in an unstructured, supportive fashion, to build a positive relationship and to give the teacher a broader knowledge of the child. After this, teachers begin to use a structured sequence of activities, as follows:

The child rereads familiar books. The child reads again several favorite books that he or she has previously read. The materials are story books with natural language rather than controlled vocabulary. Books within a lesson may range from quite easy to more challenging, but the child is generally reading above 90 percent accuracy. During this time, the child has a chance to gain experience in fluent reading and in using strategies "on the run" while focusing on the meaning of the text. The teacher interacts with the child during and after the reading, not correcting but talking with the child about the story and supporting the effective actions the child has taken.

The teachers analyzes reading using the running record. Each day the teacher takes a running record of a book that was new for the child the previous day. The running record is a procedure similar to miscue analysis (Goodman, Watson, & Burke, 1987). Using a kind of shorthand of checks and other symbols, the teacher records the child's reading behavior during oral reading of the day's selected book. The teacher examines running records closely, analyzing errors and paying particular attention to behavior such as self-correction. In this way, the teacher determines the strategies the child is using to gain meaning from text. This assessment provides an ongoing picture of the progress the child makes. While the child is reading, the teacher acts as a neutral observer; the child works independently. The accuracy check tells the teacher whether the text has been well selected and introduced the day before.

The child writes messages and stories and then reads them. Every day the child is invited to compose a message and to write it with the support of the teacher. Writing is considered an integral part of gaining control over messages in print. The process gives the child a chance to closely examine the details of written language in a message that he or she has composed, supported by his or her own language and sense of meaning. Through writing, the child also develops strategies for hearing sounds in words and using visual information to monitor and check his or her reading.

After the construction of the message, the teacher writes it on a sentence strip and cuts it up for the child to reassemble and read. This activity provides a chance to search, check, and notice visual information. Using plastic letters on a magnetic board, the teacher may take the opportunity to work briefly with the letters to increase the child's familiarity with the names of letters and their use in known words such as the child's name. This work will vary according to the knowledge the child already has.

The child reads new books. Every day the child is introduced to a new book that he or she will be expected to read without help the next day. Before reading, the teacher talks with the child about the book as they look at the pictures. The teacher helps the child build a frame of meaning prior to reading the text. The purpose of the introduction is not necessarily to introduce new words but to create understanding in advance of reading so that it will be easier to keep a focus on meaning (Pinnell, DeFord, & Lyons, 1988, pp. 10–11).

Every child's program differs. Children do a great deal of reading but not from a graded sequence. No child reads the same series of books. The small books are carefully selected by the teacher for that child at that time. In writing, children work on their own messages, so they are writing and reading works that are important to them individually. The major difference within and across lessons lies in the teacher's ability to follow each child and to respond in ways that support acceleration and the development of strategies. Strategies may include directional movement, one-to-one matching, self-monitoring, cross-checking, using multiple cue sources, and self-correction. The Reading Recovery teacher uses instructional techniques designed to help the child develop and use such strategies.

The tutoring model in Reading Recovery is separate from the instruction provided in the regular classroom. Most often, Reading Recovery teachers tutor students half time and either teach small groups of Chapter 1 students or teach a regular class the other half. The tutees may thus have the same teacher as their reading teacher and as their tutor, but in general this does not occur.

Tutor training in Reading Recovery is extensive. During the first year, in addition to teaching a reading class and tutoring four students, the tutors attend weekly seminars during which they receive training in observational, diagnostic, and assessment techniques and are schooled in the reading philosophy of Marie Clay. The tutors also participate in weekly "behind the glass" demonstration lessons where they observe actual tutoring sessions behind a one-way mirror and have the opportunity to critique and discuss the lesson. Considerable time is spent learning about the reading process and learning how to implement appropriate strategies to meet the needs of individual children. Follow-up in-service training continues after the first year. Additional training is required of Teacher Leaders who are certified to train Reading Recovery tutors in their areas. Teacher Leaders participate in a one-year internship at the Ohio State University training center (other states such as New York are establishing regional centers) where they participate in reading and writing seminars and learn to train tutors using the "behind the glass" technique.

Research evaluating Reading Recovery in New Zealand (Clay, 1985) focused entirely on the "discontinued" students (those who were successful in the program) and therefore greatly overstates the effectiveness of the intervention. However, the U.S. research has included "discontinued" and "not discontinued" students—all of the students who either graduated from the program or received at least 60 lessons.

The Ohio State group has conducted two longitudinal studies comparing Reading Recovery to traditional Chapter 1 pull-out or in-class methods. The first (pilot) study (Huck & Pinnell, 1986; Pinnell, 1988) of Reading Recovery involved 21 teachers trained by Marie Clay who worked in six inner-city Columbus, Ohio, schools. Each school provided one Reading Recovery class and a matched comparison class. The lowest 20 percent of students in each class served as the experimental and control group, respectively. Students were pretested in September and December, 1984, but the tutoring did not begin until the spring semester of 1985.

The second longitudinal study (Pinnell, Short, Lyons, & Young, 1986; DeFord, Pinnell, Lyons, & Young, 1988) involved 32 teachers in 12 schools in Columbus; 12 of these teachers had been tutors in the pilot cohort. In this study, students in the lowest 20 percent of their classes were randomly assigned to Reading Recovery or control conditions. The research design originally made a distinction between students in the experimental and control groups who had Reading Recovery-trained versus non-Reading Recovery-trained teachers in their regular reading program. However, there were no differences on this factor. Thus, the analyses focused on tutored versus untutored children, regardless of who their regular reading teacher was.

The results at the end of the first implementation year for the two Ohio State studies are summarized in Table 7.2. The measures used were all individually administered scales designed either by Marie Clay and her associates or by the Ohio State researchers. Reading Recovery students substantially outperformed control students on almost all measures. The exceptions were tests of letter identification and a word recognition scale

TABLE 7.2   First-Year Evaluations of Reading Recovery

Measure	Effect Sizes	
	Pilot Cohort	*Second Cohort*
Letter Identification*	+.36	−.04
Word Test*	−.13	+.40
Concepts about Print	+.60	+.65
Writing Vocabulary	+.62	+.69
Dictation	+.57	+1.03
Text Reading	+.72	+.91

Note: Pilot cohort data are from Huck and Pinnell, 1986. Second cohort data are from Pinnell, Short, Lyons, and Young, 1986.

*There are apparent ceiling effects on these measures.

that had apparent ceiling effects in both conditions (i.e., average scores were near the maximum possible score for each scale).

Each spring for two years following the implementation year, all children were assessed on Text Reading Level, an individually administered test in which students are asked to read from books with progressively more difficult content. This measure yields a reading level (e.g., second grade, first semester). The results on this measure, summarized in Table 7.3, show an interesting statistical paradox. By the criterion of effect size, the effects of Reading Recovery are clearly diminishing each year. By the end of the third grade, the effect size for the pilot cohort has diminished from +.72 to +.14, and in the second cohort the effect size diminished from +.78 to +.25. On the other hand, the difference in raw units between Reading Recovery and control students remained about the same across all three years, hovering around two points in the pilot cohort and three in the second cohort. Is the effect maintaining or not?

The difference between these two measures is that the standard deviation of the Text Reading Level measure increases each year, making the same raw difference a smaller proportion of the standard deviation. In more substantive terms, the size of the difference may not be diminishing (assuming the measure is an equal-interval scale), but the importance of the difference is diminishing. For example, a difference of three months on a standardized reading test might be a big difference at the end of the first grade but is a small one at the end of sixth grade.

Actually, there is a more complex story on the longitudinal effects of Reading Recovery. The students who succeeded in Reading Recovery, those categorized as "discontinued," were performing on average at a level like that of their classes as a whole and substantially better than the comparison group of low achievers. On the other hand, all of the "not

TABLE 7.3 **First-Year Evaluations of Reading Recovery**

	Effect Sizes (Raw Differences)	
	Pilot Cohort	*Second Cohort*
End of implementation year	+.72 (1.6)	+.78 (2.8)
One-year follow-up (Grade 2)	+.29 (2.0)	+.46 (3.0)
Two-year follow-up (Grade 3)	+.14 (1.8)	+.25 (2.8)

Note: All data are from individually administered Text Reading Level assessments developed by the program developers. Pilot cohort data are from Pinnell, 1988; second cohort data are from DeFord, Pinnell, Lyons, and Young, 1988.

discontinued" students (who had at least 60 tutoring sessions but failed to achieve at the level of the rest of their class) were still below the level of their classmates by third grade and were substantially lower than the control group. These "not discontinued" students represented 27 percent of the former Reading Recovery students tested in the third grade in the second cohort study (DeFord et al., 1988).

Effects of Reading Recovery on Promotions from Grade to Grade. Participation in Reading Recovery increased students' chances of being promoted to the second grade in comparison to the control low achievers. While 31 percent of comparison students were retained in first grade or assigned to special education, this happened to only 22 percent of Reading Recovery students (DeFord et al., 1988). However, by third grade this difference had mostly disappeared. A total of 59.6 percent of Reading Recovery children and 57.8 percent of control children were in the third grade two years after first grade. A school district evaluation in Wakeman, Ohio, found that first-grade retentions dropped from 24 to 1 in the three years after implementation of Reading Recovery.

One additional study compared Reading Recovery to control treatments in first grade. This was a study conducted in four Chicago elementary schools. As in the earlier studies, students were randomly assigned to Reading Recovery or control conditions. Because neither standard deviations nor statistical tests are presented, effect sizes cannot be computed, but program effects in comparison to control students were clearly substantial. Applying standard deviations from the Ohio studies to the same measures used in Chicago yields end-of-first-grade effect sizes of approximately +.90 on Dictation and Text Reading Level.

The most recent major study of Reading Recovery conducted by the Ohio State group (Pinnell, Lyons, DeFord, Bryk, & Seltzer, 1991) evaluated the full program in comparison to three alternative programs and a control group in 10 Ohio school districts. The treatments were as follows:

1. Reading Recovery (RR) was implemented as in earlier assessments.
2. Reading Success (RS) was the same as Reading Recovery except that teachers received a two-week training session in the summer instead of the year-long, two to three hours per week training with "behind-the-glass" demonstration teaching used in Reading Recovery. In comparison to Reading Recovery, this treatment tested the possibility that effects like those for the program as usually implemented could be obtained with far less extensive training, a major stumbling block to widespread diffusion.
3. Direct Instruction Skills Plan (DISP) was an individual tutorial program that tested the possibility that it is one-to-one tutoring, not the particulars of the Reading Recovery model, that explains the effects of the program. DISP used direct instruction in specific skills such as letter, sound, and word recognition; sequencing; filling in blanks; answering questions; and reading extended text. Teachers were encouraged to design lessons themselves to teach these and other skills.
4. Reading and Writing Group (RWG) was a small group tutorial model taught by teachers who had been trained as Reading Recovery teachers. They used Reading Recovery materials and strategies but were asked to adapt them to the small group setting in their own ways. This treatment essentially tested the effects of the one-to-one tutoring aspect of Reading Recovery holding curriculum constant.
5. Control group for each treatment was the Chapter 1 pull-out program already in existence in each school.

Four schools (one per treatment) were involved in each district. In each school that already had a Reading Recovery teacher, students were randomly assigned to RR or control (Chapter 1) treatments. In other schools, additional teachers were hired from the district's substitute lists to implement the RS or DISP tutoring models. Trained Reading Recovery teachers were added to schools to implement the Reading and Writing Group (RWG) treatment. Students were randomly assigned to treatment or control classes.

The treatments were implemented starting early in first grade. Students were then assessed in February, in May, and again the following October. The results are summarized in Table 7.4. As is clear from Table 7.4, the effects varied considerably according to measure and time of test administration. The February measures clearly favored the Reading Recovery on all measures and the Reading Success model on the two measures developed as part of the Reading Recovery program, Dictation and Text Reading Level. However, the February measures are biased in favor of the three tutoring models. By February, the tutoring was concluded, and students moved into the Chapter 1 group program. In contrast, the RWG

TABLE 7.4   Ohio Statewide Study of Reading Recovery (Adjusted Effect Sizes in Comparison to Control Groups)

	Reading Recovery	Reading Success	DISP Tutoring	Reading-Writing Group
February				
Dictation	+.65	+.45	−.05	+.14
Text Reading	+1.50	+.45	−.01	+.41
Woodcock	+.49	+.04	+.25	+.23
Gates	+.51	+.27	+.14	+.23
May				
Gates	+.19	−.14	−.05	+.34
October				
Dictation	+.35	+.00	−.25	+.29
Text Reading	+.75	+.07	+.06	+.32

Data are from Pinnell et al., 1991.

and Chapter 1 control group programs were year-long interventions, so measuring effects in February discriminates against them.

Unfortunately, the only test given in May was the standardized Gates-MacGinitie, which found few effects for any treatment.

The October follow-up provides the best indication of the effects of the four programs. The most positive effects were found for Reading Recovery on Dictation (ES = +.35) and Text Reading Level (ES = +.75). Neither of the other two tutoring methods (RS and DISP) found any positive effects. It is interesting to note that after the full program, it was the Reading and Writing Group (RWG) treatment that had the most positive effects (ES = +.29 for Dictation, +.32 for Text Reading Level). This treatment also had the largest positive effects on the May Gates-MacGinitie of all treatments (ES = +.34).

There is one important factor that may be confounded with the effects of the four programs. The teachers in the two most successful treatments, Reading Recovery and Reading and Writing Group, were experienced Reading Recovery teachers who had a year of Reading Recovery training and at least a year of experience implementing the program. In contrast, the Reading Success and DISP teachers were hired from the substitute list and may have been considerably less skilled and less experienced.

At a minimum, the Ohio statewide study provides one more convincing evaluation of Reading Recovery, showing large effects, especially on Text Reading Level, which maintain into the school year following the intervention. The findings suggest that the year-long training, the particular curriculum and instructional model used, and the one-to-one aspect of the tutoring are all critical to the success of the model, but these conclusions may be tempered by possible differences in teacher quality in the groups that received shorter training (RS) and the alternative tutoring model (DISP).

There are a few methodological issues worth raising about the Reading Recovery research. First, all measures reported were designed by the developers of the program, and therefore may be biased in favor of the kinds of skills taught in the program. This is most likely at the low levels of the Text Reading Level measure, where assessments focus on concepts of print, using pictures and patterns to guess story content, and other skills specifically taught in Reading Recovery. The finding of particularly large effects on Text Reading Level (in contrast to other measures) was especially pronounced in the Ohio statewide study (Pinnell et al., 1991).

Finally, Reading Recovery has a policy of not serving students who have already been retained in first grade and students identified for special education. One of the reports (Pinnell et al., 1986) implies that some students originally selected for tutoring failed to make adequate progress in early tutoring sessions and were excused from tutoring (and therefore excluded from the evaluation). Any of these practices might have influenced the Reading Recovery sample by excluding the very lowest achievers.

These criticisms aside, the efforts of Reading Recovery are impressive at the end of the implementation year, and they maintain for at least two years. The rapidly expanding use of Reading Recovery throughout the United States (see Lyons, Pinnell, DeFord, McCarrier, & Schnug, 1989) shows that the program is practical to use.

Success for All

Success for All (Slavin, Madden, Karweit, Livermon, & Dolan, 1990; Slavin, Madden, Karweit, Dolan, & Wasik, 1990; Madden, Slavin, Karweit, Dolan, & Wasik, in press; Slavin, Madden, Karweit, Dolan, & Wasik, 1992) is a comprehensive schoolwide restructuring program that is designed primarily for schools serving large numbers of disadvantaged students. Its main intention is to see that all children are successful in basic skills, particularly reading, the first time they are taught. One major element of Success for All is one-to-one tutoring by certified teachers for students in grades 1 through 3 who are having difficulties learning to read. The program includes many other elements, such as an innovative beginning reading program, preschool and kindergarten programs, and family support services. (These, and the broader research on Success for All, are described in Chapter 8.) However, for low-achieving first-graders, who receive most of the tutoring services, the Success for All program can be primarily seen as a preventive tutoring program.

The tutoring model used in Success for All is different in many ways from that used in Reading Recovery. One difference is that in Success for All, the tutoring model is completely integrated with the reading program. The tutor's most important responsibility is to make sure that the student is making adequate progress on the specific skills and concepts being taught in the reading class.

Another difference is that in Success for All, first-graders receive tutoring as long as they need it. Although most students receive tutoring for part of a year, some receive it all year and then continue to be tutored into the second grade. The commitment in Success for All is to see that every child succeeds, and that no child is retained or assigned to special education except under extreme circumstances.

First-graders are initially selected into tutoring in Success for All on the basis of individually administered informal reading inventories given in September. After that, however, students are assessed every eight weeks in terms of their progress through the reading curriculum. On the basis of these eight-week assessments, students who are doing well may be rotated out of tutoring as other students are rotated into tutoring. The amount of tutoring received by a given student may vary from eight weeks to the entire year or more. Students receive tutoring every day for 20 minutes. This time is usually scheduled during an hour-long social studies/science block, so that tutoring represents additional time in reading.

The tutors are certified teachers recruited in the same way as other teachers. Each tutor teaches a 90-minute reading class each day (to reduce class size for reading) and then spends the rest of the day tutoring three children per hour. Because the tutors teach a reading class, they are fully aware of what the reading program is; if a child is struggling with Lesson 37, for example, the tutor knows exactly what is required for success in Lesson 37, because he or she has taught it.

In many cases, tutors work with students who are also in their morning reading class. When scheduling does not allow this, the student's reading teacher fills out a "tutor/teacher communication form," which indicates the lesson that the student is working on in class and the teacher's assessment of the specific problems the student is having with that lesson. The tutor uses this information to plan the tutoring session. This communication ensures coordination between the classroom instruction and tutoring.

The tutors receive two days of training (along with all other beginning reading teachers) to learn to teach the Success for All beginning reading program (described below), and then they receive additional days of training on assessment and on tutoring itself. Tutors are observed and given direct feedback on the sessions, usually by their building facilitator.

Like Reading Recovery, the Success for All tutoring model emphasizes learning to read by reading (Madden & Livermon, 1990). In addition, a strong emphasis is placed on teaching comprehension strategies. The tutor's goal is to get the students to read fluently and to understand what they read. Tutors are trained to explicitly teach metacognitive strategies to help students monitor their comprehension. For example, a tutor will teach a student to stop at the end of each page and ask, Did I understand what I just read? The students learn to check their own comprehension and to go back and reread what they did not understand.

Each tutoring session is structured, but the tutor is constantly diagnosing and assessing the individual needs of each student and tailoring the sessions to fit the student's specific problem. If a student is having difficulty with fluency, the tutor will have the student do repeated reading of a story. With similar materials, a tutor may work with another child on comprehension monitoring. A typical tutoring session begins with the student reading a familiar story that he or she has read before in tutoring and in the reading class. This is followed by a *one-minute drill of letter* sounds to give the student the opportunity to practice the letter sounds taught in class. The major portion of the tutoring session is spent on reading "shared stories" that correspond to the beginning reading lessons. The shared stories are interesting, predictable stories that have phonetically controlled vocabulary in large type and other elements of the story in small type. The teacher reads the small-type sections to provide a context for the large-type portions read by the students. The tutor works with the student to sound out the phonetically regular words, asks comprehension questions about the whole story, and has the student reread passages to gain fluency. Writing activities are also incorporated into the reading activities.

As noted, the tutoring model is closely integrated with the reading program (Slavin et al., 1992) in which students are regrouped according to their reading levels. Use of tutors as reading teachers allows schools to reduce the class size to about 15 students who are all at one level, so there are no multiple reading groups in class. This allows teachers to spend the entire class period actively teaching reading, as it removes the need for the follow-up or seatwork activities typical of classes with multiple reading groups. The beginning reading program emphasizes reading to students, engaging students in discussions of story structure, and developing oral language skills. Students begin using shared stories, as described earlier. As letter sounds and sound blending strategies are taught, students can apply them in their books. Students do a great deal of partner reading and pair practice activities, and writing is taught along with reading.

The high degree of structure in the beginning reading program facilitates integration between initial instruction and tutoring. Expectations for each lesson are clear, so the teacher and tutor can know that they are working on the same objectives. As mentioned, integration is also facilitated by the use of brief tutor/teacher communication forms, on which each can tell the other about particular successes or problems a child is experiencing.

Research on Success for All.   Success for All is currently being evaluated in schools in several school districts. Evaluations most relevant to the tutoring aspect of the program relate to low achievers in two Baltimore schools that have had adequate funding to provide a high level of tutoring services for several years. Abbottston Elementary, the original pilot school, has implemented Success for All for four years. City Springs Elementary is a fully funded site whose implementation began a year after Abbottston. Each school was matched with a similar comparison school, and then students were individually matched on standardized reading measures. The student bodies at both Baltimore schools are almost entirely African American. Seventy-six percent of Abbottston's students qualify for free lunch. City Springs serves the most disadvantaged student body in the district; all its children come from housing projects, and 96 percent receive free lunch. Both are Chapter 1 schoolwide projects. Each May, students are individually assessed on scales from the Woodcock Language Proficiency Battery (Woodcock, 1984), and the Durrell Analysis of Reading Difficulty (Durrell & Catterson, 1980).

The results for the students in grades 1 through 3 who scored in the lowest 25 percent on the pretests are summarized in Table 7.5. The amount of tutoring received by these students varied depending on their needs; almost all received some tutoring, but in some cases they received eight weeks, while some second- or third-graders may have received more than a year of daily tutoring.

The results shown in Table 7.5 indicate powerful effects of the combination of tutoring, curricular changes, and family support services used in Success for All. At both schools in all years, first-grade low achievers have scored far better than their matched counterparts in control schools (mean effect size = +1.15). Second-graders who started in Success for All in the first grade or earlier also scored substantially better than control students (mean effect size = +0.82), as did third-graders in the program for three years (ES = +1.16). These second- and third-year effects should not be compared with the second- and third-year effects of Reading Recovery; the Reading Recovery data relate to the *lasting* effect of a first-grade intervention, whereas those for Success for All relate to the effects of *continuing* intervention. While effect sizes stayed at approximately the same level in

TABLE 7.5 Effects of Success for All on Low-Achieving Students

Measure	Abbottston				City Springs		
	Year 1	Year 2	Year 3	Year 4	Year 1	Year 2	Year 3
Grade 1:							
Woodcock Letter-Word	+0.42	+1.57	+1.09	+2.40	+0.08	+1.03	+0.57
Woodcock Word Attack	+1.34	+4.22	+1.00	+1.30	+0.51	+1.77	+0.71
Durrell Oral Reading	+0.99	+1.97	+0.21	+1.79	+1.14	+0.23	+0.37
Durrell Silent Reading	+1.30	+1.73	+1.06		+0.47	+0.45	
Mean	+1.01	+2.37	+0.84	+1.83	+0.55	+0.87	+0.55
Grade 2:							
Woodcock Letter-Word		+0.39	+0.37	+1.07		+0.09	+0.98
Woodcock Word Attack		+0.66	+1.78	+1.28		+0.75	+1.36
Durrell Oral Reading		+0.52	+0.71	+0.87		+0.28	+0.98
Durrell Silent Reading		+1.26	+0.64			+0.16	
Mean		+0.71	+0.88	+1.07		+0.32	+1.11
Grade 3:							
Woodcock Letter-Word			+0.57	+1.22			+0.20
Woodcock Word Attack			+1.22	+2.70			+0.50
Durrell Oral Reading			+1.11	+1.82			+0.78
Durrell Silent Reading			+1.36				
Mean			+1.07	+1.91			+0.49

Note: Data are effect sizes from Slavin, Madden, Karweit, Livermon, and Dolan, 1990; Slavin, Madden, Karweit, Dolan, and Wasik, 1990; Madden, Slavin, Karweit, Dolan, Wasik, Shaw, Leighton, and Mainzer, 1991; and Madden, Slavin, Karweit, Dolan, and Wasik, in press.

second and third grades as in first, this is an indication of a growing effect. Because standard deviations increase each year, a constant effect size means a growing difference between experimental and control groups in grade equivalents or raw scores.

In addition to effects on reading achievement, all three schools substantially reduced assignments of students to special education for learning problems and essentially eliminated retentions (Slavin, Madden, Karweit, Livermon, & Dolan, 1992).

As with Reading Recovery, there are methodological limitations to research on Success for All that may affect the results. First, because only one school was involved in each comparison, school effects could account for part of the observed differences. Lack of random assignment of schools or students also could have affected the results.

The effects of Success for All were particularly dramatic for the lowest-achieving quarter of students involved, but they were also very positive for the other students in the school (see Chapter 8). However, the effects for the higher-achieving students must be ascribed to the curriculum and other program elements, as few of them received any tutoring. Also it is important to note that schools using Success for All without extra resources for tutoring also obtained very positive results, although not as positive as those for the fully funded schools (see Slavin et al., 1992). These schools used their existing Chapter 1 funds to provide some tutoring (almost all to first-graders), but could not sustain the amount of tutoring provided to Abbottston and City Springs low achievers. A school in Philadelphia used a modified version of Success for All to work with limited English proficient (LEP) Cambodian students, and also found very positive outcomes for these students and for non-LEP students (Slavin & Yampolsky, 1991). The evaluation of Success for All shows the potential power of a tutoring program that is integrated with a structured reading program. Evaluations of additional years will be needed to determine whether the program's goal of success for every child is realistic. Follow-up studies are needed to determine the validity of the program's assumption that success through the elementary grades will have long-term consequences, but the data collected to date clearly demonstrate the program's effectiveness when used at the beginning of students' school careers.

Prevention of Learning Disabilities

Prevention of Learning Disabilities is a program developed by the Learning Disorders Unit of the New York University Medical Center that identifies first- and second-graders who are at risk for school failure and provides intensive instruction before they begin to fall behind in basic skills. Students involved in the program are screened in first grade using an instrument (SEARCH) that primarily focuses on neurological indicators of learning disabilities and on perceptual and general immaturity. Using diagnostic information from SEARCH, first-graders are given lessons either individually or in small groups that attempt to strengthen their areas of perceptual weakness. The instructional interventions, called TEACH, are designed primarily to build perceptual skills—such as recognition discrimination, copying, and recall—and are administered by certified teachers in 30-minute sessions three to five times per week.

Prevention of Learning Disabilities differs from the other tutoring models reviewed in this chapter in its focus on generalized perceptual skills rather than reading. However, improvement of reading performance is a major program goal, and reading was assessed in program evaluations. No coordination with the regular reading program is apparent in program descriptions. An evaluation of Prevention of Learning Disabilities was conducted in inner-city New York City classrooms (Hagin, Silver, & Beecher, 1978; Silver & Hagin, 1979). Students were randomly assigned to experimental or control classes, and those in the experimental group received TEACH instruction for two years. Table 7.6 summarizes the findings. On reading measures as well as on perception measures, the experimental students performed substantially better than controls. In the same study, Silver and Hagin (1979) found that students who had a full year of TEACH performed better than those who had only a half year of TEACH.

In a similar study, Silver, Hagin, and Beecher (1981) found that third-graders who received the TEACH intervention in first and second grade showed significantly greater performance in oral reading, word identification, and word attack skills when compared to a no-treatment control group.

Arnold, Barnebey, McManus, Smeltzer, Conrad, and Desgranges (1977) replicated the Prevention of Learning Disabilities program in inner-city and middle-class schools in Columbus, Ohio. Using SEARCH, 86 first-graders were identified as being at risk for reading problems and were assigned to one of three groups: (1) the TEACH intervention group, (2) a group who received academic tutoring from a teacher, and (3) a no-treatment control group. Students in the TEACH and regular tutoring group received tutoring for 30-minute sessions twice a week. Table 7.6 summarizes the findings. At the end of one year, the effects for both the TEACH intervention and the regular tutoring were minimal on the Wide Range Achievement Test (WRAT). However, at the end of the second year of the intervention, students in the TEACH group performed significantly better than the students in the regular tutoring and the no-treatment control group on the WRAT.

A more recent study by Mantzicopoulos, Morrison, Stone, and Setrakian (1990) found few effects for the TEACH intervention. In this study,

TABLE 7.6   Effects of Prevention of Learning Disabilities on At-Risk Students

Measures	Effect Sizes		
	End of Grade 1	End of Grade 2	End of Grade 3 Follow-Up
Silver and Hagin, 1979; Silver et al., 1981			
SEARCH (Perception)	+.99	–	–
WRAT (Oral Reading)	+.85	+1.06	+.95
Woodcock Work Identification	+.94	+.91	+1.38
Woodcock Word Attack	+1.39	+1.67	+1.26
SRA Comprehension	–	+.95	–
Gates-MacGinitie Comprehension	–	–	+.30
Gates-MacGinitie Vocabulary	–	–	+.15

Arnold et al., 1977	TEACH vs. Control		Reg. Tutoring vs. Control	
	End of Grade 1	End of Grade 2	End of Grade 1	End of Grade 2
WRAT	+.33	+1.09	+.16	+.11

Mantzicopoulos et al., 1990	TEACH vs. Control		Phonetic vs. Control	
Total Reading Achievement	End of Grade 1	End of Grade 2	End of Grade 1	End of Grade 2
(Combined SAT, CTBS, CAT)	+.16	+.21	+.28	+.13

first-graders who were identified as at risk for reading failure by the SEARCH screen were assigned to three groups: a TEACH group, a phonics tutoring group, and a no-contact control group. In the phonics tutoring group, students were given phonics instruction, were drilled in phonics, and read phonetically regular books. This is in contrast to the TEACH group, which worked on visual-auditory discrimination activities. In both the TEACH and phonics tutoring groups, students received one-to-one tutoring for 30-minute sessions twice a week. The findings are summarized in Table 7.6.

On reading measures and perceptual measures, students in the TEACH group did not perform any differently than the phonics tutoring group or the no-contact controls. Interestingly, the phonics tutoring group did show some significant improvement in word attack skills compared to the no-contact control. Mantzicopoulos and associates (1990) suggest that one reason for the disappointing effects of TEACH was that the high attrition rate of their students left them with a skewed sample distribution. Attrition is a factor in working with at-risk populations.

Wallach Tutorial Program

The Wallach Tutorial Program (Wallach & Wallach, 1976) is, like Reading Recovery and Success for All, based on the idea that students who fail to learn to read in first grade are seriously at risk, and that carefully structured tutoring intervention can prevent reading failure. In this model, students receive one-half hour of tutoring per day for a year. Unlike Reading Recovery and Success for All, the Wallach model uses paraprofessionals as tutors. The tutoring is directed to students who score below the 40th percentile on a standardized reading test.

The curriculum of the Wallach program emphasizes phoneme identification skills, in response to a finding in an earlier study (Wallach, Wallach, Dozier, & Kaplan, 1977) that indicated that at the end of kindergarten, most of a sample of disadvantaged students (but few middle-class students) had difficulty recognizing phonemes in words read to them, such as knowing that *man* but not *house* starts with the *mmm* sound.

The program has three parts. For about 10 weeks, children are taught to recognize starting phonemes in words read to them, to recognize letters, and to associate letters and phonemes. In the second stage, students spend 2 to 3 weeks learning to sound out and blend easy words. For the remainder of the year, the children learn to apply their skills to classroom reading materials. Thus, the Wallach model begins as a completely separate tutoring program (like Reading Recovery) but later begins to integrate tutoring with classroom instruction (like Success for All).

Two studies have evaluated the Wallach model. The results of these studies are summarized in Table 7.7. The first evaluation was a field test in two inner-city Chicago schools (Wallach & Wallach, 1976). First-graders who were identified at the beginning of the school year as low in "academic readiness" were randomly assigned to either tutoring or a no-treatment control. At the end of the school year, the children were tested individually on the Spache Diagnostic Reading Scales.

On the Spache Word Recognition Scale, the tutored students scored five months higher than the control (GE = 1.8 and 1.3, respectively) with an effect size of +.64. On the Spache Consonant Sounds Test, the tutored students also outperformed the control group, with an effect size of +.66. On the Spache Reading Passage scales, there were apparent differences favoring the tutored students, but these were obscured by a floor effect on the test (which does not measure below a grade equivalent of 1.6).

A second study (Dorval, Wallach, & Wallach, 1978) evaluated the program in rural Roanoke Rapids, North Carolina. Students who received

TABLE 7.7   Grade-Equivalent Differences and Effect Sizes for Wallach and Wallach

Measures	Grade Equivalent Differences	Effect Sizes
	Tutored vs. Matched Control	
Wallach & Wallach (1976)		
Spache Word Recognition	* + .5	+ .64
Spache Consonant Sound Test	−	+ .66
Dorval, Wallach, and Wallach (1978)	*Tutored vs. Control Group*	
Spache Word Recognition	* + 1.6 to 1.8	−
Spache Reading Passages	−	−
CTBS	−	+ .75

*Computation based on median scores.

the tutoring were compared to similar students in the same school the previous year, to similar students in a comparison school who received the services of a full-time reading aide in their regular reading class, and to other students in the same comparison school who received neither tutoring nor the assistance of aides. At the end of the year, students took the group-administered Comprehensive Test of Basic Skills (CTBS) and were individually assessed on the Spache Word Recognition and Reading Passages scales. The various control groups did not differ from one another, so they can be pooled.

On the Spache Word Recognition Scale, the tutored students scored eight months higher than control (G.E., 2.3 vs. 1.5, respectively). Spache Reading Passages showed the tutored students to be reading at a median grade equivalent of 1.8, whereas control students were at a median of 1.6, but again a floor effect may account for this small difference. On the CTBS, tutored students scored at the 56th percentile and comparison students at the 34th percentile, for an effect size of + .75.

Programmed Tutorial Reading

Programmed Tutorial Reading is a highly structured tutoring program used with first-graders who are in the lowest quartile on standardized reading tests. The program was originally developed by Douglas Ellson at Indiana University. The tutors for the program are paid paraprofessionals, volunteers, or parents. Students are tutored 15 minutes per day as a supplement to regular classroom instruction.

The curriculum in Programmed Tutorial Reading is designed on the principles of programmed instruction, emphasizing small steps that students are expected to master with few errors. Lessons are cycled through a sequence of sight reading, comprehension, and word analysis, which is repeated many times. Tutors are trained in specific strategies to present items, reinforce students for correct responses, and route students through the materials according to their responses.

Several studies have evaluated Programmed Tutorial Reading, but only three of these have compared the program to control groups over meaningful time periods with nonretarded populations. Table 7.8 summarizes the results of these studies.

Ellson, Harris, and Barber (1968) evaluated Programmed Tutorial Reading of two durations, over a full school year. Students were assigned to one of four tutored groups: Programmed Tutorial Reading for 15 minutes per day, Programmed Tutorial Reading for 30 minutes per day, an alternative tutoring program called Directed Tutoring for 15 minutes per day, and Directed Tutoring for 30 minutes per day. Then, a matched

TABLE 7.8   Effects of Programmed Tutoring

	Effect Sizes			
	Programmed Tutoring		*Directed Tutoring*	
Measures	*15 min. vs. Control*	*30 Min. vs. Control*	*15 min. vs. Control*	*30 Min. vs. Control*
Ellson et al. (1968)				
Ginn Total Vocabulary	+.09	+.57	+.23	−.07
Ginn Total Comprehension	+.13	+.53	+.10	−.21
Ginn Total Word Analysis	−.19	+.46	+.28	−.01
Standford	+.01	+.18	+.41	−.17
Ellson et al. (1965)				
Total Ginn Score	+.33			
Total Word Analysis Score	+.36			
Word Recall Score	+.78			
McCleary (1971)				
Ginn Achievement (All Students)	+.40			
Ginn Achievement (Low achievers only)	+.37			

student was identified within the classroom of each tutored student. The students were first-graders in 20 Indianapolis schools. Most of the schools served low-income populations, but the students were selected to be representative of their schools and did not necessarily have reading problems. The Directed Tutoring program did not use the programmed materials or highly structured procedures used in Programmed Tutorial Reading, but used remedial and supplementary materials more like those typically used in classrooms or in remedial reading programs.

The results (see Table 7.8) indicate strong effects of the 30-minute Programmed Tutorial Reading Program on tests provided along with students' Ginn basals (mean ES = +.52), but effects on the standardized Stanford Achievement Test were near zero, as were overall effects of the 15-minute per day program. Small positive effects were found for the 15-minute per day Directed Tutoring program, but (oddly) effects of the 30-minute Directed Tutoring treatment were slightly negative. Another study, by Ellson, Barber, Engle, and Kampwerth (1965), compared 15 minutes per day of Programmed Tutorial Reading for a semester to an untreated control group. In this case, moderate positive effects were found on the three measures used.

The largest methodologically adequate study of Programmed Tutorial Reading was done by McCleary (1971) in Lenoir County, North Carolina. In this study, low-achieving first-graders were matched and assigned to experimental or control groups. The experimental students were tutored for the entire school year for 15 minutes per day. Positive effects on the Ginn reading test were found for the sample as a whole (ES = +.37) and for the poorest readers (ES = +.40). In addition, retentions in first grade were 55 percent lower in the tutored group than in the nontutored group. Taken together, the evaluations of Programmed Tutorial Reading suggest that the program has positive effects on student reading achievement, but the effects are smaller and less consistent than those for the programs that use certified teachers.

DISCUSSION

One-to-one tutoring of low-achieving primary-grade students is without doubt one of the most effective instructional innovations available. Across 16 separate studies of cohorts involving five different tutoring methods, effect sizes were substantially positive in nearly every case. The five tutoring programs discussed here vary enormously in curriculum, tutoring methods, duration, integration with regular classroom instruction, and other characteristics. The studies are equally diverse in populations, measures, and procedures. However, some patterns can be perceived.

First, programs that use certified teachers as tutors appeared to obtain substantially larger impacts than those that use paraprofessionals. Effect sizes for Programmed Tutorial Reading and the Wallach Tutorial Program generally fall in the range of +.20 to +.75, whereas those for the programs using certified teachers produce average effects from +.55 to +2.37 by the end of first grade. The teacher-delivered and paraprofessional-delivered models also differ in curriculum. Both the Wallach model and Programmed Tutorial Reading use highly structured, clearly described instructional materials, which in the latter program are explicitly patterned on programmed instructional methods usually designed for self-instruction. In contrast, the three teacher-administered models rely on teachers' judgment, flexibility, and knowledge of how children learn.

Only one of the programs, Success for All, is designed to integrate completely with regular classroom instruction, and this program also produces some of the largest effect sizes. However, Prevention of Learning Disabilities not only fails to integrate tutoring with classroom instruction but does not even explicitly teach reading—instead, it focuses on building the perceptual skills often lacking in children who have learning disabilities. Two of the three studies of this approach found strong positive effects on student reading.

Several studies evaluated the *cumulative* and *lasting* effects of one-to-one tutoring in the early grades. Studies of two Success for All schools (Slavin et al., 1992) found that as students continued into second and third grades, initial positive effects continued to grow. Similar cumulative effects were found for Prevention of Learning Disabilities in two studies (Silver & Hagin, 1979; Arnold et al., 1977) but not in a third (Mantzicopoulos et al., 1990). Silver and Hagin (1979) also found that students who experienced Prevention of Learning Disabilities for a full year learned more than those who had it for a semester, and Ellson and colleagues (1968) found that gains were greater when students received 30 minutes per day of Programmed Tutorial Reading than when they received only 15 minutes.

Because one-to-one tutoring (especially by a certified teacher) is expensive, the lasting effects of this approach are of great importance. Reading Recovery has been evaluated for lasting effects, and the results are positive but complex. On one hand, the raw score gains that students made on Text Reading Level in first grade have maintained through the end of third grade in two different cohorts (Pinnell, 1988; DeFord et al., 1988). On the other hand, because standard deviations of this measure increase each year, effect size estimates have diminished each year for both cohorts. A one-year follow-up of Prevention of Learning Disabilities showed consistently positive effects for the third-graders for most measures, with the exception of performance on the Gates-MacGinitie Comprehension test. The effects for reading comprehension decreased one year after the intervention.

Two of the tutorial programs, Success for All (Slavin et al., 1992) and Programmed Tutorial Reading (McCleary, 1971) documented substantial reductions in retentions as a result of first-grade tutoring, and Success for All also showed reductions in special education referrals.

It is important to note that there is no magic in the one-to-one tutoring setting itself; the form and the content of tutoring appear to matter a great deal. Ellson and associates (1968) found the Programmed Tutorial Reading model to be significantly more effective than a standard "directed tutoring" intervention, and Arnold and associates (1977) found the Prevention of Learning Disabilities (TEACH) program to be considerably more effective than "regular tutoring." Mantzicopoulos and colleagues (1990) failed to replicate the findings of the earlier studies of Prevention of Learning Disabilities, but similarly found few effects of a standard phonics-based tutoring approach. An Ohio statewide study of Reading Recovery similarly failed to find any positive effects of two alternative models of one-to-one tutoring (Pinnell et al., 1991). These findings, plus the apparent advantage of tutoring by certified teachers over tutoring by paraprofessionals, provides support for the proposition advanced earlier in this chapter that for tutoring to be maximally effective, it must not only increase the amount of time, incentive value, and appropriateness to students' needs but improve the quality of instruction.

Is Tutoring Cost Effective?

It does not come as a surprise that one-to-one tutoring of primary-grade students is effective. A more important question is whether it is effective enough to justify its considerable cost. One way to address this question is to compare tutoring to other expensive interventions. For example, experiments in Tennessee, New York City, Toronto, and Indiana have reduced class size by almost half. This is the same as hiring an additional teacher for each class, who could instead be used to provide one-to-one tutoring for 20 minutes per day to about 15 students. The best and most successful of these class size experiments, a Tennessee statewide study, found a cumulative effect of substantially reducing class size from kindergarten to third grade of about +.25 (Word et al., 1990)—less than that found in any of the tutoring models. Other studies of halving class size have found even smaller effects (see Chapter 6). The effects of having aides work in the classroom have been found to be minimal in many studies (see Scheutz, 1980); the same aides could be used as tutors using models designed for that purpose, or replaced by teachers for a greater impact.

On the other hand, it is not yet established that a heavy investment in first grade will pay off in permanent gains for at-risk students. The Reading Recovery and Prevention of Learning Disabilities results hold out some hope for lasting gains, and the cumulative effects of Success for All also show promise for maintaining initial gains. Reductions in retentions and special education referrals, seen in two of the tutoring models, have both immediate and long-term impacts on the costs of education for low achievers. Substantial savings due to reduced retentions and special education placements have been shown for Reading Recovery (Dyer, 1992) and for Success for All (Slavin et al., 1992). However, if first-grade tutoring models prove to have long-term effects, either without additional intervention (as in Reading Recovery) or with low-cost continuing intervention (as in Success for All), cost effectiveness will not be the only criterion for deciding to use these models. If it is known that large numbers of students can be successful in reading the first time they are taught, and that the success not only lasts but also builds a basis for later success, then educators and legislators may perceive an obligation to do whatever it takes to see that all students do in fact receive that which is necessary for them to succeed.

Future Research

In many ways, research on preventive tutoring models is in its infancy. Although the studies reviewed here clearly indicate a strong positive effect of well-designed tutoring models, there are many important issues to be understood.

On the programmatic side, one important set of questions concerns how much reading failure can be prevented using resources short of one-to-one instruction by certified teachers. Could one-to-two or one-to-three instruction be nearly as effective? Could forms of tutoring using paraprofessionals be devised that would be as nearly as effective as forms requiring certified teachers? Must tutoring be done daily or could it be done less frequently? How much time must be allotted to tutoring each day?

More work is clearly needed on long-term effects of tutoring, not only on achievement but also on special education referrals and need for long-term remediation—critical elements in any consideration of cost effectiveness. Also, studies of alternative approaches to tutoring are needed. Successful models range from the phonemic, rigidly prescribed Programmed Tutorial Reading to the "learning to read by reading" emphases of Reading Recovery and Success for All to the focus on specific perceptual deficits of Prevention of Learning Disabilities. In the studies, it may be that each of these types of approaches would be successful with different children, and that someday educators may know which type of program will work best with children of a given profile.

Also, in measuring the effectiveness of tutoring, more performance-based measures must be used to evaluate reading. This will help educators understand the process that occurs during tutoring rather than pre- to postmeasures on standardized tests.

A great deal of work is needed to understand *why* tutoring is effective. The rudimentary explanation offered in this chapter must be replaced by a far more sophisticated understanding of cognitive and motivational processes activated in tutoring that are not activated to the same degree (at least for at-risk children) in the regular classroom. Understanding how at-risk children learn to read in tutoring would contribute to an understanding of how at-risk children learn in general; the tutoring setting provides an ideal laboratory in which the process of learning to read can be observed as it unfolds over time.

CONCLUSIONS

Although much more information is needed about how tutoring works and how to maximize its effectiveness (and minimize its cost), it is clear from the research reviewed in this chapter that one-to-one tutoring is an effective means of preventing student reading failure. As such, preventive tutoring deserves an important place in discussions of reform in compensatory, remedial, and special education. If one knows how to ensure that students will learn to read in the early grades, one has an ethical and perhaps legal responsibility to see that they do so. Preventive tutoring is the best available possibility for providing a reliable means of abolishing illiteracy among young children who are at risk for school failure.

REFERENCES

Arnold, L. E., Barnebey, N., McManus, J., Smeltzer, D. J., Conrad, A., & Desgranges, L. (1977). Prevention of specific perceptual remediation for vulnerable first-graders. *Archives of General Psychiatry, 34,* 1279–1294.

Bausell, R., Moody, W., & Walzl, F. (1972). A factorial study of tutoring versus classroom instruction. *American Educational Research Journal, 9,* 591–597.

Bloom, B. S. (1981). *All our children learning.* New York: McGraw-Hill.

Carroll, J. B. (1963). A model for school learning. *Teachers College Record, 64,* 723–733.

Carter, L. F. (1984). The sustaining effects study of compensatory and elementary education. *Educational Researcher, 13,* 4–13.

Clay, M. M. (1985). *The early detection of reading difficulties.* Exeter, NH: Heinemann.

Cloward, R. D. (1967). Studies in tutoring. *Journal of Experimental Education, 36,* 14–25.

Council of Chief State School Officers. (1987). *Elements of a model state statute to provide educational entitlements for at-risk students.* Washington, DC: Author.

Council of Chief State School Officers. (1989). *Success for all in a new century.* Washington, DC: Author.

Day, J. D., Cordon, L. A., & Kerwin, M. L. (1989). Informal instruction and development of cognitive skills: A review and critique of research. In C. B. McCormick, G. E. Miller, & M. Pressley (Eds.), *Cognitive strategy research: From basic research to educational applications.* New York: Springer Verlag.

DeFord, D., Pinnell, G. S., Lyons, C., & Young, P. (1988). *Reading Recovery: Volume IX, Report of the follow-up studies.* Columbus, OH: Ohio State University.

Devin-Sheehan, L., Feldman, R. S., & Allen, V. L. (1976). Research on children tutoring children: A critical review. *Review of Educational Research, 46,* 355–385.

Dorval, B., Wallach, L., & Wallach, M. A. (1978). Field evaluation of a tutorial reading program emphasizing phoneme identification skills. *The Reading Teacher, 31* (7), 784–790.

Durrell, D. D., & Catterson, J. H. (1980). *Durrell analysis of reading difficulty* (3rd ed.). New York: The Psychological Corporation.

Dyer, P. (1992). Reading Recovery: A cost-effectiveness and educational-outcomes analysis. *ERS Spectrum, 10* (1), 10–19.

Edmonds, R. R. (1981). Making public schools effective. *Social Policy, 12,* 56–60.

Ellson, D. G., Barber, L., Engle, T. L., & Kampwerth, L. (1965). Programmed tutoring: A teaching aid and a research tool. *Reading Research Quarterly, 1,* 77–127.

Ellson, D. G., Harris, P., & Barber, L. (1968). A field test of programmed and directed tutoring. *Reading Research Quarterly, 3,* 307–367.

Fresko, B., & Eisenberg, T. (1983). The effect of two years of tutoring on mathematics and reading achievement. *Journal of Experimental Education, 17,* 89–100.

Glass, G., McGaw, B., & Smith, M. L. (1981). *Meta-analysis in social research.* Beverly Hills, CA: Sage.

Goodman, K., Watson, B., & Burke, B. (1987). *Reading miscue inventory* (2nd ed.) New York. Richard C. Owens.

Greenfield, P. M. (1984). A theory of the teacher in the learning activities of everyday life. In B. Rogoff & J. Lave (Eds.), *Everyday cognition: Its development in social context.* Cambridge, MA: Harvard University press.

Greenwood, C. R., Delquardi, J. C., & Hall, R. V. (1989). Longitudinal effects of classwide peer tutoring. *Journal of Educational Psychology, 81,* 371–383.

Hagin, R. A., Silver, A. A., & Beecher, R. (1978). Scanning, diagnosis, and intervention in the prevention of learning disabilities: II. Teach: Learning tasks for the prevention of learning disabilities, *Journal of Learning Disabilities, II* (7), 54–57.

Harris, P. (1974). *Programmed tutorial reading project.* (Submission to Joint Dissemination Review Panel). Washington, DC: U.S. Department of Education.

Harrison, G., & Gottfredson, C. (1986, Spring). Peer tutoring: A viable alternative to cross-age tutoring. *Contemporary Issues in Reading,* 125–131.

Huck, C. S., & Pinnell, G. S. (1986). *The Reading Recovery Project in Columbus, Ohio. Pilot Year, 1984–85.* Columbus, OH: Ohio State University.

Kennedy, M. M., Birman, B. F., & Demaline, R. E. (1986). *The effectiveness of Chapter 1 services.* Washington, DC: Office of Educational Research and Improvement, U.S. Department of Education.

Lloyd, D. N. (1978). Prediction of school failure from third grade data. *Educational and Psychological Measurement, 38,* 1193–1200.

Lyons, C., Pinnell, G. S., DeFord, D., McCarrier, A., & Schnug, J. (1989). *The Reading Recovery Project in Columbus, Ohio. Year 3: 1988–1989.* Columbus, OH: Ohio State University.

Madden, N. A., & Livermon, B. J. (1990). *Success for All beginning reading: A manual for teachers* (3rd ed.). Baltimore, MD: The Johns Hopkins University, Center for Research on Effective Schooling for Disadvantaged Students.

Madden, N. A., & Slavin, R. E. (1989). Effective pullout programs for students at risk. In R. E. Slavin, N. L. Karweit, & N. A. Madden (Eds.), *Effective programs for students at risk.* Boston: Allyn and Bacon.

Madden, N. A., Slavin, R. E., Karweit, N. L., Dolan, L. J., & Wasik, B. A. (in press). Success for All: Longitudinal effects of a restructuring program for inner-city elementary schools. *American Educational Research Journal.*

Madden, N. A., Slavin, R. E., Karweit, N. L., Dolan, L., Wasik, B. A., Shaw, A., Leighton, M., & Mainzer, K. L. (1991). *Success for All: Third year results.* Paper presented at the annual convention of the American Educational Research Association, Chicago, April.

Maheady, L., Sacca, M. K., & Harper, G. F. (1987). Classwide student tutoring teams: The effects of peer mediated instruction on the academic performance of secondary mainstreamed students. *Journal of Special Education, 21,* 107–121.

Mantzicopoulos, P., Morrison, D., Stone, E., & Setrakian, W. (1990). *Academic effects of perceptually and phonetically based intervention for vulnerable readers.* Paper presented at the American Educational Research Association, Boston.

McCleary, E. (1971). Report of results of tutorial reading project. *The Reading Teacher, 24,* 556–559.

Pinnell, G. S. (1988). *Sustained effects of a strategy-centered early intervention program in reading.* Paper presented at the annual convention of the American Educational Research Association, New Orleans, April.

Pinnell, G. S. (1989). Reading Recovery: Helping at-risk children learn to read. *Elementary School Journal, 90,* 161–182.

Pinnell, G. S., DeFord, D. E., & Lyons, C. A. (1988). *Reading Recovery: Early intervention for at-risk first graders.* Arlington, VA: Educational Research Service.

Pinnell, G. S., Lyons, C. A., DeFord, D. E., Bryk, A. S., & Seltzer, M. (1991). *Studying the effectiveness of early intervention approached for first grade children having difficulty in reading.* Columbus: Ohio State University, Martha L. King Language and Literacy Center.

Pinnell, G. S., Short, A. G., Lyons, C. A., & Young, P. (1986). *The Reading Recovery Project in Columbus, Ohio. Year 1: 1985–1986.* Columbus, OH: Ohio State University.

Polloway, E. A., Cronin, M. E., & Patton, J. R. (1986). The efficiency of group versus one-to-one instruction. *Remedial and Special Education, 7* (1), 22–30.

Scheutz, P. (1980). *The instructional effectiveness of classroom aides.* Pittsburgh, PA: University of Pittsburgh, Learning Research and Development Center.

Scruggs, T. E., & Richter, L. (1985). Tutoring learning disabled students: A critical review. *Learning Disability Quarterly, 8,* 274–286.

Shaver, J. P., & Nuhn, D. (1971). The effectiveness of tutoring underachievers in reading and writing. *Journal of Educational Research, 65,* 107–112.

Silver, A. A., & Hagin, R. A. (1979). *Prevention of Learning Disabilities.* (Submission to Joint Dissemination Review Panel). Washington, DC: U.S. Department of Education.

Silver, A. A., Hagin, R. A., & Beecher, R. (1981). A program for secondary prevention of learning disabilities: Research in academic achievement and in emotional adjustment. *Journal of Preventive Psychiatry, 1,* 77–87.

Slavin, R. E. (1986). Best-evidence synthesis: An alternative to meta-analytic and traditional reviews. *Educational Researcher, 15* (9), 5–11.

Slavin, R. E. (1987a). A theory of school and classroom organization. *Educational Psychologist, 22,* 89–108.

Slavin, R. E. (1987b). Mastery learning reconsidered. *Review of Educational Research, 57,* 175–213.

Slavin, R. E. (1987c). Ability grouping and student achievement in elementary school: A best-evidence synthesis. *Review of Educational Research, 57,* 347–350.

Slavin, R. E. (1989). Class size and student achievement: Small effects of small classes. *Educational Psychologist, 24,* 99–110.

Slavin, R. E. (1990). Ability grouping and student achievement in secondary schools: A best-evidence synthesis. *Review of Educational Research, 60,* 471–499.

Slavin, R. E., Madden, N. A., Karweit, N. L., Dolan, L., & Wasik, B. A. (1990). *Success for All: Effects of variations in duration and resources of a schoolwide elementary restructuring program.* Paper presented at the annual convention of the American Educational Research Association, Boston, April.

Slavin, R. E., Madden, N. A., Karweit, N. L., Dolan, L., & Wasik, B. A. (1992). *Success for All: A relentless approach to prevention and early intervention in elementary schools.* Arlington, VA: Educational Research Service.

Slavin, R. E., Madden, N. A., Karweit, N. L., Livermon, B. J., & Dolan, L. (1990). Success for All: First-year outcomes of a comprehensive plan for reforming urban education. *American Educational Research Journal, 27* (2), 255–278.

Slavin, R. E., & Yampolsky, R. (1991). *Success for All and the language minority student.* Paper presented at the annual convention of the American Educational Research Association, Chicago, April.

Vygotsky, L. S. (1978). *Mind in society: The development of higher psychological processes.* Cambridge, MA: Harvard University Press.

Wallach, L., Wallach, M. A., Dozier, M. G. & Kaplan, N. E. (1977). Poor children learning to read do not have trouble with auditory discrimination but do have trouble with phoneme recognition. *Journal of Educational Psychology, 69,* 36–39.

Wallach, M. A., & Wallach, L. (1976). *Teaching all children to read.* Chicago: University of Chicago Press.

Wood, D., Bruner, J. S., & Ross, G. (1976). The role of tutoring in problem-solving. *Journal of Child Psychology & Psychiatry, 17,* 89–100.

Woodcock, R. W. (1984). *Woodcock language proficiency battery.* Allen, TX: DLM.

Word, E., Johnston, J., Bain, H. P., Fulton, B. D., Zaharias, J. B., Lintz, M. N., Achilles, C. M., Folger, J., & Breda, C. (1990). *Student/Teacher Achievement Ratio (STAR): Tennessee's K–3 class size study, final report.* Nashville: Tennessee State Department of Education.

▶ 8

Success for All

A Comprehensive Approach to Prevention and Early Intervention

ROBERT E. SLAVIN   NANCY A. MADDEN
NANCY L. KARWEIT   LAWRENCE J. DOLAN
BARBARA A. WASIK

There are many individual programs and practices known to increase the chances that students will succeed in the early grades. High-quality preschool and kindergarten programs, improved curriculum and instruction in reading and other skills, and one-to-one tutoring for at-risk first-graders are all effective, at least in the short run, in increasing student performance. Some of these have also been found to help students from being retained or assigned to special education. Strategies of this kind have been discussed in the earlier chapters of this book.

If each of these strategies is known to prevent school failure, what would be the effect of integrating them in a comprehensive schoolwide program? This chapter further describes the program called Success for All, which combines research-based preschool programs, kindergarten programs, and elementary-age programs in reading, writing, and language arts with one-to-one tutoring for first graders failing in reading, family support activities, and other elements.

This chapter is adapted from R. Slavin et al., 1992. *Success for All: A Relentless Approach to Prevention and Early Intervention in Elementary Schools.* Arlington, VA: Educational Research Service.

The idea behind Success for All is to use everything known about effective instruction for students at risk to direct all aspects of school and classroom organization toward the goal of preventing academic deficits from appearing in the first place, recognizing and intensively intervening with any deficits that do appear, and providing students with a rich and full curriculum to enable them to build on their firm foundation in basic skills. The commitment of Success for All is to do whatever it takes to see that every child makes it through third grade at or near grade level in reading and other basic skills, and then goes beyond this in the later grades.

Usual practices in elementary schools are diametrically opposed to the principle of prevention and early intervention emphasized in Success for All. Most elementary schools provide a kindergarten that is adequate for most students, a first grade that is adequate for most students, and so on. Starting in first grade, a certain number of students begin to fall behind, and over the course of time these students are assigned to remedial programs (such as Chapter 1) or to special education, or are simply retained. Our society's tacit assumption is that those students who fall by the wayside are defective in some way. Perhaps they have learning disabilities, or low IQs, or poor motivation, or parents who are unsupportive of school learning, or other problems. One assumes that since most students do succeed with standard instruction in the early grades, there must be something wrong with those who do not.

Success for All is built around the assumption that every child can learn, as a practical, attainable reality. In particular, every child without organic retardation can learn to read. Some children need more help than others, and some may need different approaches than those needed by others, but one way or another, every child can make it in school.

The first requirement for the success of every child is *prevention*. This means providing excellent preschool and kindergarten programs; improving curriculum, instruction, and classroom management throughout the grades; assessing students frequently to make sure they are making adequate progress; and establishing cooperative relationships with parents so they can support students learning at home.

Top-quality curriculum and instruction from age 4 on will ensure the success of most students but not all of them. The next requirement for the success of all students is *intensive early intervention*. This means one-to-one tutoring by certified teachers for first-graders who have reading problems. It means being able to work with parents and social service agencies to be sure that all students attend school, have medical services or eyeglasses if they need them, have help with behavior problems, and so on.

The most important idea in Success for All is that the school must *relentlessly continue with every child until that child is succeeding.* If prevention is not enough, the child may need tutoring. If this is not enough, he or she may need help with behavior or attendance or eyeglasses. If this is not enough, he or she may need a different reading program. In a Success for All school, "good enough" is never good enough. The school does not merely provide services to children, it constantly assesses the results of the services it provides and keeps varying or adding services until every child is making it.

ORIGINS OF SUCCESS FOR ALL

The Success for All program began in 1986 as a response to a challenge made to a group at Johns Hopkins University by Baltimore's superintendent, Alice Pinderhughes; its school-board president, Robert Embry; and a former Maryland Secretary of Human Resources, Kalman "Buzzy" Hettleman. They asked the authors of this chapter what it would take to ensure the success of *every* child in schools serving large numbers of disadvantaged students. At the time, we (the authors) were working on a book called *Effective Programs for Students at Risk* (Slavin, Karweit, & Madden, 1989), so we were very interested in this question. After many discussions, the superintendent asked us to go to the next step, to work with Baltimore's Elementary Division to actually plan a pilot program. We met for months with a planning committee, and finally produced a plan and selected a school to serve as a site. The school was Abbottston Elementary School, an all-African-American school in which approximately 83 percent of students qualified for free lunch. In September of 1986, "Fantastic Abbottston" opened as the first Success for All school. Initially the additional costs needed to fund the program, about $400,000 per year, came from a Chapter 2 grant, but Abbottston's program is now supported entirely by Chapter 1.

The first-year results at Abbottston were very positive (see Slavin, Madden, Karweit, Livermon, & Dolan, 1990). In comparison to matched control students, Abbottston students had much higher reading scores, and retentions and special education placements were substantially reduced.

In 1988–89, Success for All was substantially expanded in Baltimore. Under funding from a private foundation, a fully funded Success for All site was established at City Springs Elementary School, the most disadvantaged school in the city. In addition, four schools began to use a version of the program that could be funded by existing Chapter 1 dollars, without the extra resources provided to Abbottston and City Springs. We also began implementation of Success for All at Francis Scott Key Elementary School, one of the poorest schools in Philadelphia, in which a majority of the students are Cambodian. Key School gave us our first experience in adapting Success for All to meet the needs of limited English-proficient students. In more recent years, Success for All has expanded to schools throughout the United States. As of this writing, the program exists in 12 states. Among the districts currently implementing the program are Montgomery, Alabama; Charleston, South Carolina; Memphis, Tennessee; Fort Wayne, Indiana; Modesto, California; Wichita Falls, Texas; and Caldwell, Idaho, in addition to Baltimore and Philadelphia.

OVERVIEW OF SUCCESS FOR ALL COMPONENTS

Success for All has somewhat different components at different sites, especially depending on the resources available to implement the program. High-resource schools have additional funds beyond usual Chapter 1 dollars, whereas low-resource schools usually just have their usual Chapter 1 allocations. The main elements of Success for All and typical differences according to levels of resources are described in the following sections (adapted from Slavin et al., 1990).

Reading Tutors

One of the most important elements of the Success for All model is the use of tutors to promote students' success in reading. One-to-one tutoring is the most effective form of instruction known (see Slavin, Karweit, & Madden, 1989; Wasik & Slavin, 1990). The tutors are certified teachers with experience teaching Chapter 1, special education, and/or primary reading. Tutors work one-on-one with students who are having difficulties keeping up with their reading groups. The tutoring occurs in 20-minute sessions taken from an hour-long social studies period. In general, tutors support students' success in the regular reading curriculum, rather than teaching different objectives. For example, the tutor will work with a student on the same story and concepts being read and taught in the regular reading class. However, tutors seek to identify learning problems and use different strategies to teach the same skills and also teach metacognitive skills beyond those taught in the classroom program (Wasik & Madden, 1991). High-resource schools have six or more tutors, moderate-resource schools have three to five tutors, and low-resource schools have two to three tutors, depending on school size, need for tutoring, and other factors.

During daily 90-minute reading periods, tutors serve as additional reading teachers to reduce class size for reading to about 15 in high-resource schools and about 20 in moderate- and low-resource schools (because they have fewer tutors to reduce class size). Reading teachers and tutors use brief forms to communicate about students' specific problems and needs and meet at regular times to coordinate their approaches with individual children.

Initial decisions about reading group placement and the need for tutoring are based on informal reading inventories that the tutors give to each child. Subsequent reading group placements and tutoring assignments are made based on curriculum-based assessments given every eight weeks, which include teacher judgments as well as more formal assessments. First-graders receive priority for tutoring, on the assumption that the primary function of the tutors is to help all students be successful in reading the first time, before they fail and become remedial readers.

Reading Program

Students in grades 1 through 3 are regrouped for reading. The students are assigned to heterogeneous, age-grouped classes with class sizes of about 25 most of the day, but during a regular 90-minute reading period they are regrouped by reading performance levels into reading classes of 15 to 20 students all at the same level. For example, a second-grade, first-semester reading class might contain first-, second-, and third-grade students all reading at the same level.

Regrouping allows teachers to teach the whole reading class without having to break the class into reading groups. This greatly reduces the time spent in seatwork and increases direct instruction time, eliminating workbooks, dittos, or other follow-up activities that have traditionally been used in classes that have multiple reading groups. The regrouping is a form of the Joplin Plan, which has been found to increase reading achievement in the elementary grades (Slavin, 1987).

Reading teachers at every grade level begin the reading time by reading children's literature to students and engaging them in a discussion of the story to enhance their understanding of the story, listening and speaking vocabulary, and knowledge of story structure. In kindergarten and first grade, the program emphasizes development of basic language skills with the use of Story Telling and Retelling (STaR), which involves the students in listening to, retelling, and dramatizing children's literature (Karweit, Coleman, Waclawiw, & Petza, 1990). Big books as well as oral and written composing activities allow students to develop concepts of print as they also develop knowledge of story structure. Peabody Language Development Kits are used to further develop receptive and expressive language.

Beginning Reading (Madden & Livermon, 1990) is usually introduced in the second semester of kindergarten. The K–1 reading program uses as its base a series of phonetically regular but meaningful and interesting mini-books developed for the program (see Slavin et al., 1992) and emphasizes repeated oral reading to partners as well as to the teacher. Letters and letter sounds are introduced in an active, engaging set of activities that begins with oral language and moves into written symbols. Individual sounds are integrated into a context of words, sentences, and stories.

Instruction is provided in story structure, specific comprehension skills, and integration of reading and writing.

When students reach the primer reading level, they use a form of Cooperative Integrated Reading and Composition (CIRC) (Stevens, Madden, Slavin, & Farnish, 1987) with the district's basal series or tradebooks. CIRC uses cooperative learning activities built around story structure, prediction, summarization, vocabulary building, decoding practice, and story-related writing. Students engage in partner reading and structured discussion of the stories or novels, and work toward mastery of the vocabulary and content of the story in teams. Story-related writing is also shared within teams. Cooperative learning both increases students' motivation and engages students in cognitive activities known to contribute to reading comprehension, such as elaboration, summarization, and rephrasing (see Slavin, 1990).

In addition to these story-related activities, teachers provide direct instruction in reading comprehension skills (such as finding the main idea and understanding figurative language), and students practice these skills in their teams. Classroom libraries of tradebooks at students' reading levels are provided for each teacher, and students read books of their choice for homework for 20 minutes each night. Home readings are shared via presentations, summaries, puppet shows, and other formats twice a week during "book club" sessions. Research on CIRC has found it to significantly increase students' reading comprehension and language skills (Stevens et al., 1987).

Beginning in the second year of program implementation, Success for All schools usually implement a writing/language arts program based primarily on cooperative learning principles (see Slavin, Madden, & Stevens, 1989/90).

Eight-Week Reading Assessments

At eight-week intervals, reading teachers assess student progress through the reading program. The results of the assessments are used to determine who is to receive tutoring, to change students' reading groups, to suggest other adaptations in students' programs, and to identify students who need other types of assistance, such as family interventions or screening for vision and hearing problems.

Preschool and Kindergarten

Most of the Success for All schools provide a half-day preschool and/or a full-day kindergarten for eligible students. The preschool and kindergarten programs focus on providing a balanced and developmentally appropriate learning experience for young children. The curriculum emphasizes the development and use of language. It provides a balance of academic readiness and nonacademic music, art, and movement activities in a series of thematic units. Readiness activities include use of the Peabody Language Development Kits and Story Telling and Retelling (STaR) in which students retell stories read by the teachers (Karweit & Coleman, 1991). Prereading activities begin during the second semester of kindergarten.

Family Support Team

One of the basic tenets of the Success for All philosophy is that parents are an essential part of the formula for success. A family support team works in each school, serving to make families feel comfortable in the school and become active supporters of their child's education as well as providing specific services (Haxby & Madden, 1991). In the high-resource schools, social workers, attendance monitors, and other staff are added to the school's usual staff. In moderate- and low-resource schools, the family support team consists of the Chapter 1 parent liaison, vice-principal (if any), counselor (if any), facilitator, and any other appropriate staff already present in the school. The family support team works to involve parents in support of their children's success in school. It contacts parents whose children are frequently absent to see what resources can be provided to assist the family in getting their children to school. Parenting education is provided for interested families. Family support staff, teachers, and parents work together to solve school behavior problems. Also, family support staff are called on to provide assistance when students seem to be working at less than their full potential because of problems at home. Families of students who are not receiving adequate sleep or nutrition, need glasses, are not attending school regularly, or are exhibiting serious behavior problems receive family support assistance.

The family support team is strongly integrated into the academic program of the school. It receives referrals from teachers and tutors regarding children who are not making adequate academic progress, and thereby constitutes an additional stage of intervention for students in need above and beyond that provided by the classroom teacher or tutor. The family support team also encourages and trains the parents to fulfill numerous volunteer roles within the school, ranging from providing a listening ear to emerging readers to helping in the school cafeteria.

Special Education

Every effort is made to deal with students' learning problems within the context of the regular classroom, as supplemented by tutors. Tutors evaluate students' strengths and weaknesses and develop strategies to teach in the most effective way. In some schools, special education teachers work as tutors and reading teachers with students identified as learning disabled as well as other students experiencing learning problems. One major goal of Success for All is to keep students with learning problems out of special education if at all possible, and to serve any students who do qualify for special education in a way that does not disrupt their regular classroom experience (see Slavin et al., 1991).

Program Facilitator

A program facilitator works at each school to oversee (with the principal) the operation of the Success for All model. High-resource schools have a full-time facilitator, whereas moderate- and low-resource schools usually have half-time facilitators. The facilitator helps plan the Success for All program, helps the principal with scheduling, and visits classes and tutoring sessions frequently to help teachers and tutors with individual problems. He or she works directly with the teachers on implementation of the curriculum, classroom management, and other issues; helps teachers and tutors deal with any behavior problems or other special problems; and coordinates the activities of the family support team with those of the instructional staff.

Teachers and Teacher Training

The teachers and tutors are regular certified teachers. They receive detailed teacher's manuals supplemented by three days of in-service at the beginning of the school year. For teachers of grades 1 through 3 and for reading tutors, these training sessions focus on implementation of the reading program, and their detailed teacher's manuals cover general teaching strategies as well as specific lessons. Preschool and kindergarten teachers and aides are trained in the use of the STaR and Peabody programs, thematic units, and other aspects of the preschool and kindergarten models. Tutors later receive an additional day of training on tutoring strategies and reading assessment.

Throughout the year, additional in-service presentations are made by the facilitators and other project staff on such topics as classroom management, instructional pace, and cooperative learning. Facilitators also organize many informal sessions to allow teachers to share problems and problem solutions, suggest changes, and discuss individual children. The staff development model used in Success for All emphasizes relatively brief initial training with extensive classroom follow-up, coaching, and group discussion.

Advisory Committee

An advisory committee composed of the building principal, program facilitator, teacher representatives, family support staff, and one or more parent representatives meets regularly to review the progress of the program and to identify and solve any problems that arise.

RESEARCH ON SUCCESS FOR ALL

As of this writing, Success for All has been annually evaluated for four years in its first Baltimore site, Abbottston Elementary School, and for three years in four additional Baltimore sites and one site in Philadelphia. Other evaluations in Memphis and rural Berlin, Maryland, have been conducted for one and two years, respectively. This chapter summarizes the findings of this research.

EVALUATION DESIGN

Matching

Success for All schools are always matched with comparison schools that are similar in the percent of the students receiving free lunch, historical achievement level, and other factors. Students from these schools are tested on the same individual reading assessments as students in the Success for All schools. Success for All students are then individually matched with a control student on standardized achievement tests scores, usually from kindergarten. The purpose for this individual matching (within matched schools) is primarily to allow us to follow individual children over time even if they are ultimately retained or end up in special education.

Measures

The main tests of reading used in Success for All are individually administered by specially trained testers, usually graduate and undergraduate education students from local colleges. The specific measures used are as follows.

Language.   Two tests of receptive and expressive language are typically individually administered to preschool and kindergarten students.

  1. Test of Language Development (TOLD; Newcomer & Hammill, 1988). Individually administered Picture Vocabulary and Sentence Imitation

Scales from the TOLD are used to assess receptive and expressive language concepts, respectively, of preschool and kindergarten students.

2. Merrill Language Screening Test (Mumm, Secord, & Dykstra, 1980). The individually administered comprehension scale from the Merrill is used to assess the ability of preschool and kindergarten students to understand complex story structure.

Reading.   Three individually administered reading scales selected from two widely used, nationally standardized reading batteries are used to assess a full range of reading skills: word attack (Woodcock Word Attack), recognition of letters and key sight words (Woodcock Letter-Word), and oral reading fluency and comprehension (Durrell Oral Reading). These scales are described below.

1. Woodcock Language Proficiency Battery (Woodcock, 1984). Two Woodcock scales, Letter-Word Identification and Word Attack, are individually administered to students in grades K through 3. The Letter-Word scale is used to assess recognition of letters and common sight words, and the Word Attack scale assesses phonetic synthesis skills.

2. Durrell Analysis of Reading Difficulty (Durrell & Catterson, 1980). The Durrell Oral Reading scale is administered to students in grades 1 through 3. Oral Reading presents a series of graded reading passages that students read aloud, followed by comprehension questions. The Durrell Silent Reading scale has also been administered in all years except 1991.

In addition to these individually administered measures, we typically obtain measures of retentions, special education placements, and attendance from school district records.

Analyses

Data have been analyzed using analyses of covariance, with pretests as covariates. Outcomes are characterized in terms of effect sizes, which are the differences between experimental and control means divided by the control group's standard deviations. All analyses use raw or standard scores; grade equivalents are reported to facilitate understanding but are not used in the analyses. For each of the analyses of reading achievement in grades 1 through 3, comparisons are made between all students at each grade level, and then separate analyses compare students who scored in the lowest 25 percent of their grades on pretests. The purpose of this low

25 percent analysis is to see the degree to which the Success for All program affects the achievement of the students who are most at risk.

Findings: Combining Effects Across Sites and Years

In order to summarize the results of the Success for All evaluations over the years, we use a method that is common in medical research (see, for example, Lilienfeld & Lilienfeld, 1980) but rare in educational research: combining the results of small-scale experiments conducted in different locations at different times into one large-scale experiment. In medicine such a procedure is called multisite clinical trials, as when patients with a particular disease entering a variety of hospitals over some period of time are given either a new drug or a placebo. If the disease is relatively rare, no one hospital's experiment would have an adequate sample to assess the drug's effects, but combining results over many hospitals over time does provide an adequate sample. In the case of Success for All, we have combined experimental-control comparisons in different schools over the years. For example, across the eight Success for All schools from which we have adequate data, 22 first-grade cohorts have experienced the program. By using the cohort as the unit of analysis, we can ask and answer many questions that would be difficult to answer looking only at schools in a given year.

We call this method a *multisite replicated experiment* design. Pooling effects across many experiments is, of course, a common procedure in meta-analysis (Glass, McGaw, & Smith, 1981), but there is a key difference between a meta-analysis and a multisite replicated experiment. Meta-analysis has been criticized for "combining apples and oranges," putting together the results of experiments that differ in treatments, measures, and many other features (see, for example, Slavin, 1984). In multisite replicated experiments, similar treatments, measures, and experimental designs are used in all sites, so results can be more confidently pooled.

In the comparisons presented in the following sections, results are combined across schools and years to answer important questions about the effects of Success for All on student reading achievement. The original data for these analyses are taken from the annual reports on Success for All in Baltimore (Madden et al., in press), Philadelphia (Slavin & Yampolsky, 1991), Berlin, Maryland (Slavin & Madden, 1991), and Memphis (Ross & Smith, 1991). In these comparisons, effect sizes are averaged across all individually administered reading measures (Woodcock & Durrell) for each cohort (a particular grade level within a particular school). A student is only considered to have had the Success for All treatment if he or she entered the program in first grade or earlier, so only such students are included in combined analyses. As a result, there are a total of 22 first-grade cohorts, 14 second-grade cohorts, and 7 third-grade cohorts across the eight Success for

All schools: Abbottston (four years of implementation), four additional Baltimore schools (three years), plus one school each in Philadelphia (three years), Berlin, Maryland (two years), and Memphis (one year). The situation of Philadelphia's Francis Scott Key Elementary is unique, because all analyses separated Asian and non-Asian students. In this school, effects for Asian and non-Asian students were averaged, but no separate analyses for students in the lowest 25 percent of their classes were possible. For this reason, the number of cohorts for the low 25 percent analysis were 19 first grades, 12 second grades, and 6 third grades.

Effects of Success for All Across Cohorts

The effects of Success for All on the reading achievement of all students who have experienced the program since first grade or earlier are shown in Figure 8.1. The figure shows that, in grade-equivalent terms, the difference

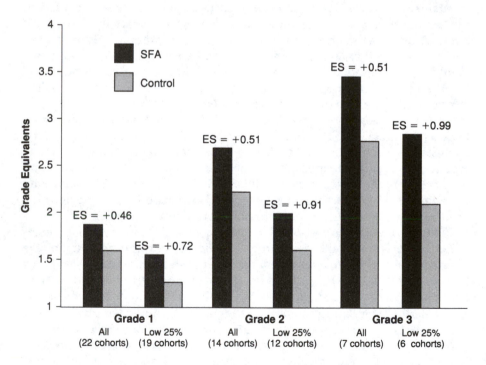

FIGURE 8.1   Baltimore Success for All Schools: Average Grade Equivalents and Effect Sizes (All Years)

Note: Includes all students in all years of program implementation who were in Success for All or control schools since first grade.

between Success for All and control schools increases from first to second to third grade. Success for All students outperform their matched control groups by almost three months in first grade, almost five months in second grade, and almost seven months in third grade. Because standard deviations also increase each year, the differences in effect size terms are essentially stable, rising only from +.46 in first grade to +.51 in third. For the lowest 25 percent of students, effect sizes as well as grade-equivalent differences rise in successive grades. First-grade differences average almost three months (ES = +.72); second-grade differences four months (ES = +.90); and third-grade differences, more than seven months (ES = +.99). This pattern of rising grade-equivalent differences and mostly stable effect sizes means that students in Success for All not only end the first grade in good shape but continue to build their advantage over their control counterparts. This contrasts with programs that apply one-time treatments. For example, Reading Recovery (Pinnell, 1989), a first-grade tutoring model, produces impressive effects as of the end of first grade, with an average effect size on their Text Reading Level measure of +.75 (see Chapter 6). In raw score terms this difference is maintained in second and third grades but, because standard deviations also increase the differences in effect sizes, declined to +.38 in second grade and +.20 in third grade.

Do Effects Grow in Successive Years of Implementation?

The data from successive years of program implementation allow one to ask whether the effects of Success for All at a given grade level grow from year to year. Evidence on this question is summarized in Figure 8.2. The figure shows effect sizes for first- and second-graders according to the number of years their school has implemented Success for All. A clear increasing trend can be seen. For example, Success for All first-graders in the first year of implementation exceed their control counterparts by an effect size of +.32. The next class of first-graders (second implementation year) exceeds its control group by +.46. Data for years 3 and 4 are combined, since only Abbottston Elementary has a fourth year of implementation. These first-grade cohorts exceed their controls by 67 percent of a standard deviation. Similar patterns are seen for low achievers and for second-graders.

There are two likely explanations for the patterns seen in Figure 8.2. One is that the schools simply get better with practice. Success for All involves so many changes that getting all the changes implemented to a high degree of quality takes more than a year. Early implementation

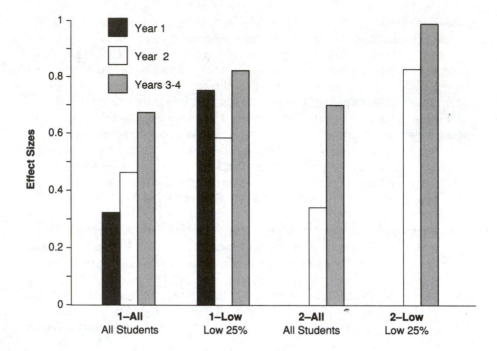

FIGURE 8.2   Growth in Reading Effects in Successive Years of Implementation, All Success for All Schools

Note: Includes all students who were in Success for All or control schools since first grade.

Source: Adapted from R. Slavin et al., 1992. *Success for All: A Relentless Approach to Prevention and Early Intervention in Elementary Schools.* Arlington, VA: Educational Research Service.

problems were particularly serious in the three Baltimore City Chapter 1 (only) schools, which (due to late notice about funding) did not get under way until November of their first year and did not fully implement such key program elements as family support until the second year.

The second likely explanation for the increasing effects of Success for All is that in each successive year of implementation students have had one more year in the program before first grade. For example, the students in the first first-grade cohort started in Success for All in first grade. Those in the second year started in kindergarten, and those in the third year started in prekindergarten. The increasing program effects seen in the first and second grades may be evidence of lasting effects of the Success for All early childhood programs. This possibility is explored in the following section.

Effects of Prekindergarten
and Kindergarten Programs

The effects of the prekindergarten and kindergarten programs in Success for All are difficult to assess in many ways. Measurement of the immediate outcomes is made problematic by the difficulty of assessing 4- and 5-year-olds, and long-term impacts are confounded with other aspects of the Success for All model. However, there are several different lenses that can focus on the evaluation of the Success for All prekindergarten and kindergarten models.

Immediate (end-of-year) effects of the Success for All prekindergarten have been compared to those of control students in matched schools who have also attended prekindergarten. These comparisons have involved only the five Baltimore schools because the others have not had prekindergarten. Combining across all measures used (described earlier in this chapter) across seven cohorts, the Success for All prekindergartens exceeded their control groups by 35 percent of a standard deviation. Kindergarten effects have been assessed in 19 cohorts, including the Baltimore sites, Philadelphia, and Memphis. The mean effect size across these assessments is +.45.

Thus it does appear that the immediate effects of the Success for All prekindergarten and kindergarten programs are positive. The best (though indirect) indication of the long-term effects of these programs is the steadily increasing reading performance of successive first-grade cohorts noted earlier. As students begin to enter first grade with experience in the Success for All kindergarten in the second year of implementation and the prekindergarten and kindergarten in the third year, their reading performance is consistently increasing.

Does Success for All Produce Success for All?

Success for All does not yet ensure success for every student. On the Durrell Oral Reading test as of spring of 1991, 15.7 percent of Success for All students were still performing at least one year below grade level, and 3.9 percent were two years behind (recall that this includes all students who would have ordinarily been assigned to special education). However, the situation in the control schools is far worse. In these schools, 38.0 percent of third-graders were reading one or more years below grade level, and 11.7 percent at least two years below. At the other end of the distribution, 18.1 percent of Success for All third-graders performed at least a year above grade level (GE = 4.9 or more) and 5 percent were two or more years above. The corresponding percentages for the control group were 12.1 and 1.9 percent (see Figure 8.3).

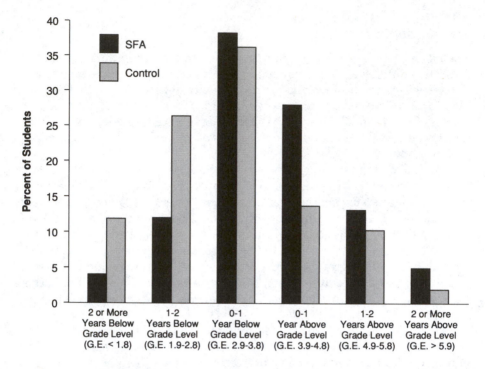

FIGURE 8.3   Distrubution of Grade-Equivalent Scores on the Durrell Oral Reading Test, Third Grades in Baltimore Success for All Schools (1991)

Will Success for All ultimately bring all children to grade level in reading? Given the program's commitment to avoiding retention and special education and the fact that most Success for All schools are in very disadvantaged neighborhoods, it seems unlikely that the program will truly ensure grade-level performance for every single child. However, the program does substantially reduce the number of children performing below level, and this effect is increasing with each successive year of implementation. Most of the current third-graders began Success for All in first grade in its first year of implementation. In later years, as students have had the benefit of the Success for All preschool and kindergarten programs, the proportion of low achievers should be reduced still further; this is already happening to a substantial degree in the first and second grades (recall Figure 8.2).

Does Money Matter?

The various Success for All schools vary considerably in levels of resources and staff. Baltimore's Abbottston and City Springs Elementary Schools began with $400,000 in addition to their usual Chapter 1 allotments,

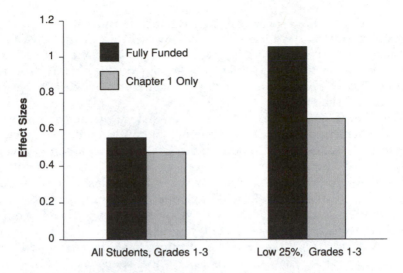

FIGURE 8.4 Differences in Reading Effects Between Fully Funded and Chapter 1-Only Schools, Baltimore City

Note: Includes all students who were in Success for All or control schools since first grade.

Source: Adapted from R. Slavin et al., 1992. *Success for All: A Relentless Approach to Prevention and Early Intervention in Elementary Schools.* Arlington, VA: Educational Research Service.

whereas the three Baltimore Chapter 1 schools received only a half-time facilitator, materials and training, a total of about $40,000 beyond their usual Chapter 1 resources.* Additional funding for schools in Philadelphia, Memphis, and Berlin fell between these extremes.

Because many other factors differentiated Baltimore and non-Baltimore sites, the best comparison on the impact of different resources is that between the two high-funded and three low-funded Baltimore schools. This comparison is shown in Figure 8.4. Combining across grades 1 through 3 and all implementation years, Figure 8.4 shows that money did not make a substantial difference for students in general. The mean effect size was +.55 for high-funded schools, and +.47 for low-funded ones. However, the difference for the most at-risk students was profound. For these students, the effect size was +1.04 for high-funded schools and +.63 for low-funded.

Other data lend support to the conclusion that the high-funded schools make much more of a difference for at-risk students than do low-funded

---

*It is interesting to note that due to changes in Baltimore's Chapter 1 program, funding for all five schools is now similar. However, the data presented here were collected at a time when there were important funding differences.

schools. Retentions are near zero for Abbottston and City Springs, but although retentions have been substantially reduced in the low-funded schools, some students are still being retained in two of the three schools. Special education data also show that Abbottston Elementary has been able to reduce to near zero its placements of students in special education for learning disabilities.

What these data mean is that it is possible to greatly improve the average achievement of inner-city students without spending significantly more money, but instead reallocating the Chapter 1 funds schools would have received anyway. The effects seen in the low-funded schools are extraordinary; for example, an effect size of +.47 is almost twice that found for reducing class size from 25 to 15 for four years in the Tennessee class size studies (see Chapter 6). However, to approach the goal of success for *every* child is much more expensive. What high-funded schools have (and low-funded ones lack) is a high ratio of tutors to students and additional family support staff. These additional personnel spend most of their time working with small numbers of children. They make a profound difference with these children, but since the most at-risk students are a small proportion of all students, their gains make only a small difference in the school's means. However, while the additional expenses required to ensure success for the most difficult children are substantial, these are the children who will ultimately cost the school system a far larger amount in special education, retentions, and other costs. For this reason, the program effects for the lowest achievers have major consequences for the cost effectiveness of Success for All.

Retentions

It is a policy of the Success for All program to avoid retaining students except under the most extreme circumstances, especially in fully funded schools. This is not to say that every child meets usual district standards for promotion at the end of each year. However, the program's philosophy holds that if students are having academic problems, they should continue to receive tutoring, instruction appropriate to their needs, family support services, and other interventions rather than repeating a grade. The result of this policy (plus the objectively higher student achievement) has been a dramatic reduction in retentions in all schools.

The reductions in retentions at all five Baltimore Success for All schools are shown in Figure 8.5. The figure shows that retentions quickly fell to near zero in the fully funded schools (Abbottston and City Springs) but declined more slowly in the Chapter 1-only schools. The cumulative effect of the different retention policies are dramatic. In the control schools, 31 percent of students who should be in fourth grade have instead been

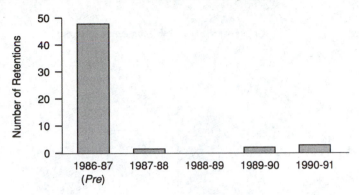

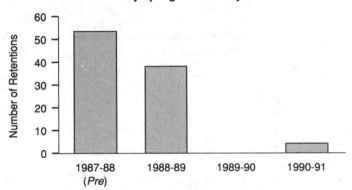

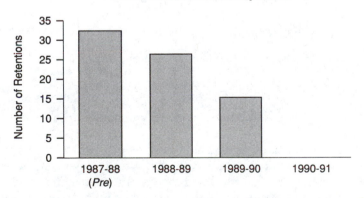

Continued

FIGURE 8.5 Retentions in Baltimore Success for All Schools

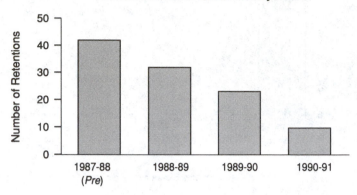

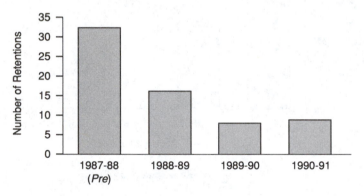

FIGURE 8.5 *Continued*

Source: Adapted from R. Slavin et al., 1992. *Success for All: A Relentless Approach to Prevention and Early Intervention in Elementary Schools.* Arlington, VA: Educational Research Service.

retained at least once. At Abbottston, the corresponding figure is 4 percent (two students).

Reversing long-standing retention policies was difficult for many Success for All schools, but over time, the school staffs have come to enthusiastically support the policy of passing marginal students and continuing to provide them with tutoring and other assistance rather than failing them. These students usually do catch up in the following year, and although they are still below grade level in performance, they do far better than their counterparts in the control group who were retained. At an annual per-pupil instructional cost of more than $4,000, an additional year of instruction for retained students is an expensive form of remediation. The same amount of money can buy about 52 weeks of daily 20-minute tutoring sessions (more than most children need)—a far more effective and humane intervention than having a student spend another year in the same grade.

Special Education

A major goal of the Success for All program is to keep students with learning problems out of special education if at all possible. When a child is having serious learning problems in a Success for All school, the staff exhausts all other possibilities before beginning the formal referral process that may lead to special education. Only after tutoring, family interventions, adjustments in curricular approaches, and other interventions have been tried is a child considered for special education, and even at the referral stage every effort is made to find solutions other than special education for students who have IQs above 70.

Like many states, Maryland uses a system of special education levels. Level 1 refers to consultation but no direct service, Level 2 to special education services up to one hour per day, Level 3 to special education services one to three hours per day, and Level 4 is a self-contained program in a regular school. Level 1 is rarely used, and Level 2 usually means services for speech. The main focus of Success for All is on reducing assignments to Levels 3 and 4, which are the typical placements for students who are considered to be learning disabled or educable mentally retarded.

Table 8.1 shows the results of Success for All's emphasis on early intervention and alternatives to special education. The table shows only students who have been in the schools since first grade and who live in the schools' attendance zone (since students are sometimes sent to special education programs outside of their normal attendance zones). At Abbottston, not a single fourth-grader who had begun the program in first grade was in special education. Among third-graders, control students were almost 50 percent more likely to be assigned to level 3 or 4 special education than were Success for All students. However, there were no differences among second-graders. Since special education placements are usually cumulative (few students ever leave special education), it is likely that the differences seen in the later grades have not yet appeared by second grade.

In Baltimore, reducing special education placements is only one among many objectives of Success for All, but there is one implementation outside of Baltimore in which reducing special education placements was a major goal. The Maryland State Department of Education's Special Education Division provided seed money for an evaluation of Success for All in a

TABLE 8.1 Cumulative Percentage of Students Assigned to Special Education in Success for All and Control Schools

	Success for All						Control				
		Level			%			Level			%
School	Total	2	3	4	3–4	School	Total	2	3	4	3–4
Grade 4											
Abbottston	32	0	0	0	0.0	A	38	0	5	2	18.4
						B	48	0	3	3	12.5
						C	45	3	1	2	6.6
						D	46	1	0	4	8.7
						E	43	0	1	3	9.3
Total	32	0	0	0	0.0	Total	220	4	10	14	10.9
Grade 3											
Abbottston	44	1	1	0	2.3	A	59	2	5	2	11.9
City Springs	50	2	1	4	10.0	B	55	0	0	4	7.3
Dallas Nicholas	31	0	0	0	0.0	C	54	1	2	1	5.6
Harriet Tubman	34	2	1	0	2.9	D	60	2	2	0	3.3
Dr. Bernard Harris	51	0	1	1	3.9	E	53	4	1	1	3.8
Total	210	5	4	5	4.3	Total	281	9	10	7	6.0
Grade 2											
Abbottston	37	1	0	0	0.0	A	77	4	3	3	7.8
City Springs	46	3	0	2	4.3	B	67	0	0	3	4.5
Dallas Nicholas	42	1	0	2	4.8	C	53	2	0	0	0.0
Harriet Tubman	56	0	3	1	5.4	D	75	2	1	2	4.0
Dr. Bernard Harris	60	3	2	1	5.0	E	69	2	1	1	2.9
Total	241	8	5	5	4.1	Total	341	8	5	9	4.1

Note: Data are for students who live in the school's attendance zone and have been in the school since first grade.

Source: Adapted from R. Slavin et al., 1992. *Success for All: A Relentless Approach to Prevention and Early Intervention in Elementary Schools.* Arlington, VA: Educational Research Service.

rural Maryland district trying to reduce its high special education placement rate. Buckingham Elementary School in Berlin, Maryland (on Maryland's eastern shore) began implementing Success for All in the 1989–90 school year. In the year before the program began, 12 students in grades K through 3 were assigned to special education for learning disabilities. In 1989–90, this was reduced by 75 percent, to only 3 students; in 1990–91, only 2 students in grades K through 3 were identified as learning disabled. Of 11 students in self-contained special education programs in September of 1989, all have been mainstreamed to levels 2 or 3 (see Slavin & Madden, 1991).

Are reductions in special education placements a consequence of reduced need for special services or of a policy of serving students in different ways? The answer is some of both. The main reason that students are identified as learning disabled is that they are reading far below grade level (Norman & Zigmond, 1980). Two years below level in third grade is a traditional criterion for referral. Recall that only 3.9 percent of all third-graders in all Success for All schools (including those who would ordinarily have been assigned to special education) are reading at this low level. In contrast, 11.7 percent of control third-graders are reading two or more years below grade level (a grade equivalent of 1.8 or less).

Attendance

Figure 8.6 shows changes in attendance at all Baltimore Success for All schools since the program began. Attendance was very poor for elementary schools but has improved at all schools, especially at the two fully funded schools (Abbottston and City Springs), which have additional staff for this purpose.

EARLY INTERVENTION WITH LANGUAGE-MINORITY CHILDREN: SUCCESS FOR ALL IN PHILADELPHIA

The fundamental assumption behind Success for All is that given appropriate instruction backed up by tutoring, family support services, and other early interventions, virtually all children can be successful in the primary grades (and beyond). This assumption makes sense for children who may be from impoverished homes but whose native language is English. It is equally sensible when children come from homes in which a language other than English is spoken, but the language of instruction is the same as the language of the home, as in bilingual programs. Research generally supports bilingual education for students with limited English proficiency (LEP) (e.g., Willig, 1985; Wong-Fillmore & Valadez, 1985). Yet there are

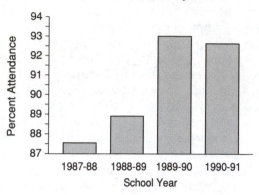

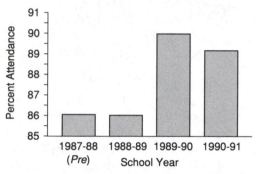

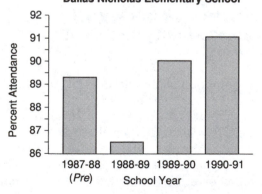

FIGURE 8.6 Attendance in Baltimore Success for All Schools

Dr. Bernard Harris Elementary School

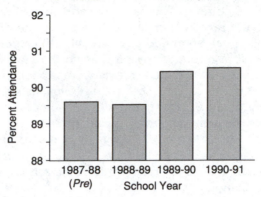

Harriet Tubman Elementary School

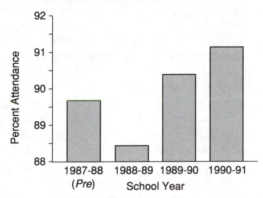

FIGURE 8.6 *Continued*

Source: Adapted from R. Slavin et al., 1992.
Success for All: A Relentless Approach to Prevention and Early Intervention in Elementary Schools.
Arlington, VA: Educational Research Service.

many circumstances in which students with limited English proficiency must be taught in English, such as when there are too few children in a school who speak a particular language to permit a bilingual program or when there are no teachers available who speak the students' languages. In such situations, students are typically taught in English, with instruction in English as a second language (ESL) given as a supplement. Is it possible to ensure the success of all children when many are learning English at the same time as they are learning reading and other skills?

We are studying this question in our first implementation of Success for All outside of Baltimore. This is at Philadelphia's Francis Scott Key Elementary School. Francis Scott Key is located in one of Philadelphia's most disadvantaged neighborhoods. Nearly all of its students qualify for free lunch. When it began in Success for All in the 1988–89 school year, approximately 50 percent of Key's students were of Southeast Asian background, particularly Cambodian. The remainder of the school was evenly divided between African-American and white students. As of the 1991–92 school year, approximately 62 percent of all students are of Asian background. The Asian students typically arrive in kindergarten speaking little or no English; in most cases, their mothers also do not speak English. One Cambodian-speaking aide is the only adult in the school who speaks the students' primary language.

Adaptations of Success for All for Limited English Proficient Students

Key School uses an ESL approach with its LEP students. That is, students are assigned to ESL teachers for varying periods of time each day depending on their English skills. In most ways the Success for All program used at Key is the same as that used in monolingual schools elsewhere. However, several adaptations are made to meet the needs of LEP students.

One important adaptation is the use of fifth-graders to tutor kindergarten students (unfortunately, Key does not have a preschool program). All kindergartners are tutored, but the Cambodian children are tutored by bilingual Cambodian fifth-graders, who help them transition from Cambodian to English. The tutors read and translate English books and, later in the year, listen to the kindergartners read from their Beginning Reading books and other materials. By the end of the year, the conversations between tutors and tutees are primarily in English, with only occasional Cambodian explanations when a child is experiencing difficulties. The kindergarten program in Success for All always emphasizes language development, and the Cambodian students participate in Peabody, STaR, and other activities along with their non-LEP classmates.

The ESL program at Key is closely tied to the Success for All reading program. ESL teachers teach a reading class and then serve as tutors for LEP children. During separate ESL instruction, the ESL teachers go over the content being taught in Beginning Reading or Beyond the Basics to make sure that all students are understanding the material. The program's philosophy is that in an ESL program, success will be defined in terms of performance in English on the school's curriculum (see Garcia, 1991), especially its reading curriculum. As a result, the ESL teacher's most important task, especially in grades 1 and up, is to see that students learn the English they will need to succeed.

Findings

Figure 8.7 shows the results at Francis Scott Key for both Asian and non-Asian students on the three individually administered reading measures in grades 1 through 3. As is clear from the figure, Asian students at Key are performing far better than Asian students in the control school at every grade level (see Slavin & Yampolsky, 1991). The mean difference in grade equivalents between Success for All and control Asian students is five months in first grade (ES = +1.24), 1.2 years in second grade (ES = +1.85), and eight months in third grade (ES = +.64). All differences on all measures are statistically significant (p < .05 or less). In addition, the Asian students performed significantly better on a measure of English language proficiency in grades K through 2.

Results for non-Asians, also shown in Figure 8.7, are mostly like those

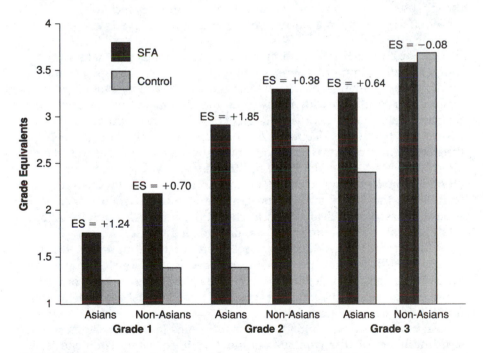

FIGURE 8.7 Francis Scott Key Elementary (Philadelphia) Average Grade Equivalents and Effect Sizes for Asian and Non-Asian Students

found in assessments elsewhere. First-graders average 5.5 months ahead of control students in first grade (ES = +.70) and six months in second grade (ES = +.38). However, no differences were found in third grade.

CONCLUSION

The evidence summarized in this chapter shows that Success for All has impacts on a variety of indicators. It substantially increases reading achievement, especially for students who are most at risk. It substantially reduces retentions and special education placements for learning disabilities. It increases attendance. The Philadelphia study of Success for All shows that the program can have substantial effects on the reading performance and language proficiency of students with limited English proficiency. Not only are the effects of Success for All large but they increase with each year students spend in the program and with each successive year of implementation. Most of the program's effects on reading achievement for students in general can be achieved for little or no money beyond the Chapter 1 funds ordinarily available in high-poverty schools, but much larger effects for the most at-risk students can be achieved with enhanced funding.

Although much is known about the effectiveness of Success for All, much is still unknown. There is some evidence that the preschool and kindergarten elements of Success for All are effective, but longer-term evaluations of schools with and without these elements are needed. Information is also needed on the degree to which each program element contributes to the overall effects. A three-semester evaluation of the Beginning Reading program without other program elements did find positive effects (see Madden et al., 1990), but this study involved only two experimental and two control schools. The contributions made by the tutors, the facilitators, the family support program, and other elements need to be separately assessed. Evaluations of the Success for All writing/language arts and mathematics programs are also needed.

Of particular importance is assessment of the long-term effects of Success for All beyond the elementary years. The rationale for any early intervention program depends on the idea that investing in young students will pay off in the long run, yet it will take at least a decade to really understand the long-term impacts.

Success for All was initially designed for use in urban schools serving large numbers of disadvantaged students whose native language is English. Yet as time goes on, we are also evaluating the program in different settings, including rural schools, schools serving many students with limited English proficiency, and schools whose primary interest is in reducing

special education placements. We have early evidence concerning each of these but will be studying them in more detail. In particular, we are developing a Spanish version of the program for use in bilingual programs and are modifying the program to focus even more on diverting students from special education (see Slavin et al., 1991).

In addition to further understanding the effects of Success for All in various settings, we need to further understand strategies for disseminating the model, studying our training procedures, the long-term role of the facilitator, processes for collaboration, and other key program elements.

Research on Success for All suggests that by combining many of the programs and practices identified as effective in the research summarized in the earlier chapters of this book, substantial and lasting changes in students' school success can be brought about. We do not claim that every element of Success for All is the best possible solution to the problems of high-poverty elementary schools. We are constantly learning about our own program and modifying it to meet local needs or to improve it at all sites. There are also quite different programs that have been successful in achieving similar ends, such as Reading Recovery (Pinnell, 1989) and James Comer's (1988) program. There are many plausible ways to solve the same problems, and different programs are appropriate to different circumstances. What is important is that we never lose sight of the goal of school reform to enhance the achievement of *all* students, and that we constantly assess our own programs and stick with the students, the teachers, the administrators, and the programs themselves until we are sure that every child is learning.

REFERENCES

Comer, J. (1988). Educating poor minority children. *Scientific American, 259,* 42–48.

Durrell, D., & Catterson, J. (1980). *Durrell Analysis of Reading Difficulty.* New York: The Psychological Corporation.

Garcia, E. E. (1991). Bilingualism, second language acquisition, and the education of Chicano language minority students. In R. R. Valencia (Ed.), *Chicano school failure and success: Research and policy agendas for the 1990's.* New York: Falmer Press.

Glass, G. V., McGaw, B., & Smith, M. L. (1981). *Meta-analysis in social research.* Beverly Hills, CA: Sage.

Haxby, B., & Madden, N. A. (1991). *Success for All family support manual.* Baltimore, MD: Johns Hopkins University, Center for Research on Effective Schooling for Disadvantaged Students.

Karweit, N. L., & Coleman, M. A. (1991). *Early childhood programs in Success for All.* Paper presented at the annual convention of the American Educational Research Association, Chicago, April.

Karweit, N. L., Coleman, M. A., Waclawiw, I., & Petza, R. (1990). *Story Telling and Retelling (STaR): Teacher's manual.* Baltimore, MD: Johns Hopkins University, Center for Research on Effective Schooling for Disadvantaged Students.

Lilienfeld, A. M., & Lilienfeld, D. E. (1980). *Foundations of epidemiology* (2nd ed.). New York: Oxford University Press.

Madden, N. A., & Livermon, B. J. (1990). *Success for All beginning reading: A manual for teachers* (3rd rev. ed.). Baltimore, MD: The Johns Hopkins University, Center for Research on Effective Schooling for Disadvantaged Students.

Madden, N. A., Slavin, R. E., Karweit, N. L., Dolan, L., & Wasik, B. A. (1990). *Success for All: Effects of variations in duration and resources of a schoolwide elementary restructuring program.* Paper presented at the annual convention of the American Education Research Association, Boston, April.

Madden, N. A., Slavin, R. E., Karweit, N. L., Dolan, L. J., & Wasik, B. A. (1993). Longitudinal effects of a restructuring program for inner-city elementary schools. *American Educational Research Journal.*

Mumm, M., Secord, W., & Dykstra, K. (1980). *Merrill Language Screening Test.* New York: The Psychological Corporation.

Newcomer, P. L., & Hammill, D. D. (1988). *Test of language development—2.* Austin, TX: Pro-Ed.

Norman, C., & Zigmond, N. (1980). Characteristics of children labeled and served as learning disabled in school systems affiliated with Child Service and Demonstration centers. *Journal of Learning Disabilities, 13,* 542–547.

Pinnell, G. S. (1989). Reading Recovery: Helping at-risk children learn to read. *Elementary School Journal, 90,* 161–182.

Ross, S. M., & Smith, L. J. (1991). *Final report: 1991 Success for All program in Memphis.* Memphis: Memphis State University, Center for Research in Educational Policy.

Slavin, R. E. (1984). Meta-analysis in education: How has it been used? *Educational Researcher, 13* (8), 6–15, 24–27.

Slavin, R. E. (1987). Ability grouping and student achievement in elementary schools: A best-evidence synthesis. *Review of Educational Research, 57,* 293–336.

Slavin, R. E. (1990). *Cooperative learning: Theory, research, and practice.* Englewood Cliffs, NJ: Prentice Hall.

Slavin, R. E., Karweit, N. L., & Madden, N. A. (Eds.) (1989). *Effective programs for students at risk.* Boston: Allyn and Bacon.

Slavin, R. E., & Madden, N. A. (1991). *Success for All at Buckingham Elementary: Second year evaluation.* Baltimore, MD: Center for Research on Effective Schooling for Disadvantaged Students.

Slavin, R. E., Madden, N. A., Karweit, N. L., Dolan, L., & Wasik, B. A. (1992). *Success for All: A relentless approach to prevention and early intervention in elementary schools.* Arlington, VA: Educational Research Service.

Slavin, R. E., Madden, N. A., Karweit, N. L., Dolan, L., Wasik, B. A., Shaw, A., Mainzer, K. L., & Haxby, B. (1991). Neverstreaming: Prevention and early intervention as alternatives to special education. *Journal of Learning Disabilities, 24,* 373–378.

Slavin, R. E., Madden, N. A., Karweit, N. L., Livermon, B. J., & Dolan, L. (1990). Success for All: First-year outcomes of a comprehensive plan for reforming urban education. *American Educational Research Journal, 27,* 255–278.

Slavin, R. E., Madden, N. A., & Stevens, R. J. (1989/90). Cooperative learning models for the 3 R's. *Educational Leadership, 47* (4), 22–28.

Slavin, R. E., & Yampolsky, R. (1991). *Effects of Success for All on students with limited English proficiency: A three-year evaluation.* Baltimore, MD: Johns Hopkins University, Center for Research on Effective Schooling for Disadvantaged Students.

Stevens, R. J., Madden, N. A., Slavin, R. E., & Farnish, A. M. (1987). Cooperative Integrated Reading and Composition: Two field experiments. *Reading Research Quarterly, 22,* 433–454.

Stevens, R. J., & Shaw, A. H. (1990). *Listening comprehension.* Baltimore, MD: Johns Hopkins University, Center for Research on Effective Schooling for Disadvantaged Students.

Wasik, B. A., & Madden, N. A. (1991). *Success for All tutoring manual.* Baltimore, MD: Johns Hopkins University, Center for Research on Effective Schooling for Disadvantaged Students.

Wasik, B. A., & Slavin, R. E. (1990). *Preventing early reading failure with one-to-one tutoring: A best-evidence synthesis.* Paper presented at the annual convention of the American Educational Research Association, Boston, April.

Willig, A. C. (1985). A meta-analysis of selected studies on the effectiveness of bilingual education. *Review of Educational Research, 55,* 269–317.

Wong-Fillmore, L., & Valadez, C. (1986). Teaching bilingual learners. In M. C. Wittrock (Ed.), *Handbook of research on teaching* (3rd ed.). New York: Macmillan.

Woodcock, R. W. (1984). *Woodcock Language Proficiency Battery.* Allen, TX: DLM.

9

Preventing Early School Failure

Implications for Policy and Practice

ROBERT E. SLAVIN

Once upon a time there was a town that was having a serious health problem. Approximately 30 percent of the children in the town were coming down with typhoid and other diseases because of contaminated drinking water. The town council allocated millions to medical care for the typhoid victims, yet some of them died or were permanently disabled. One day, an engineer proposed to the town council that they install a water treatment plant, which would prevent virtually all cases of the disease. "Ridiculous!" fumed the mayor. "We can't afford it!" The engineer pointed out that they were already paying millions for treatment of a preventable disease. "But if we bought a water treatment plant," the mayor responded, "how could we afford to treat the children who already have the disease?" "Besides," added a councilman, "most of our children don't get the disease. The money we spend now is targeted to exactly the children who need it!" After a brief debate, the town council rejected the engineer's suggestion.*

*Adapted from Slavin, Madden, Karweit, Dolan, and Wasik, 1991.

The town council's decision in this parable is, of course, a foolish one. From a purely economic point of view, the costs of providing medical services to large numbers of children over a long time were greater than the cost of the water treatment plant. What is more important, children were being permanently damaged by a preventable disease.

In education, there are policies that are all too much like those of the foolish town council. A substantial number of children fail to learn to read adequately in the early grades. Many are retained, assigned to special education, or maintained for many years in remedial programs. The financial costs of providing long-term remedial services after a student has already failed are staggering, but even more tragic are the consequences for individual children who discover so early that they are failing in what is for them their full-time job.

Despite some improvements and a growing acceptance of the idea that prevention and early intervention are preferable to remediation, the overwhelming emphasis of programs (and funding) for at-risk students remains on remediation. The unspoken assumption behind policies favoring remediation and retention over prevention and early intervention is that there are substantial numbers of students who, due to low IQs, impoverished family backgrounds, or other factors, are unlikely to be able to keep up with their classmates and will therefore need long-term supportive services to keep them from falling further behind. Perhaps if early school failure were in fact unavoidable for the many students who now fail, there might be a rationale for continuing with the policies educators now follow.

The evidence presented in this book unequivocally undermines the proposition that school failure is inevitable for any but the most retarded children. Further, the programs and practices that, either alone or in combination, have the strongest evidence of effectiveness for preventing school failure for virtually all students are currently available and replicable. None of them is exotic or radical. At the policy level, one can choose to eradicate school failure or one can choose to allow it to continue. It is irresponsible to pretend that there are no choices.

Although it is known that prevention and early intervention can prevent school failure, it is also known that different approaches to prevention and early intervention have very different effects. Some common approaches appear to have no benefits at all, while others appear to have short-lived effects.

This chapter has two primary purposes. One is to summarize the evidence presented in the earlier chapters concerning "what works" in prevention and early intervention. The second is to discuss the meaning of these findings for educational policy and practice, in particular for compensatory education, special education, and school reform in general.

PREVENTING EARLY SCHOOL FAILURE: WHAT WORKS?

Throughout this book we have attempted to apply a consistent set of standards to the many programs and practices we have reviewed. Whenever possible we have expressed the effects of each in terms of effect size (proportion of a standard deviation separating experimental and control groups). Making comparisons of effects across different measures, populations, age levels, time periods, and other factors is an inexact and often flawed procedure, and we have tried to avoid oversimplified numerical summaries of complex experiments. Our conclusions, summarized below, are based on the quality, consistency, and breadth of the evidence relating each policy or practice to immediate and lasting effects on student outcomes, especially reading performance, retentions, placements in special education, and other key indicators.

Birth to Three Years: Interventions

It is clear from Chapter 2 that both child-centered and family-centered interventions with at-risk children can make a substantial and, in many cases, lasting difference in their IQ scores. The child-based interventions are ones in which infants and toddlers are placed in stimulating, developmentally appropriate settings for some portion of the day. Family-centered interventions provide parents with training and materials to help them stimulate their children's cognitive development, to help them with discipline and health problems, and to help them with their own vocational and home management skills.

The IQ effects of the programs for children from birth to age 3 were mostly seen immediately after the interventions were implemented, but in a few cases longer-lasting effects were found. The extremely intensive Milwaukee Project (Garber, 1988), which provided 35 hours per week of infant stimulation—including one-on-one interaction with trained caregivers followed by high-quality preschool, parent training, and vocational skills training—found the largest long-lasting effects. At age 10, the children (of mildly retarded mothers) had IQs like those of low-risk children, and they were substantially higher than those of a randomly selected control group of at-risk children (ES = +1.77).

The studies of interventions for children from birth to age 3 have rarely studied effects on indicators of actual school success, such as reading performance, retentions, or special education placements, but they have demonstrated that IQ is not a fixed attribute of children; it can be modified by changing the child's environment at home and/or in special center-based programs (see Ramey & Campbell, 1984). It apparently takes intensive intervention over a period of several years to produce *lasting* effects on measures of cognitive functioning, but even the least intensive models, which often produced strong immediate effects, may be valuable starting points for an integrated combination of age-appropriate preventive approaches over the child's early years.

Preschool

Chapter 3 discussed research on the long-term effects of preschool on early school success. In comparison to similar children who do not attend preschool, those who do attend preschool have been found to be higher in IQ and language proficiency scores immediately following the preschool experience, although follow-up assessments typically find that these gains do not last beyond the early elementary years at most. In addition, there is little evidence to indicate that preschool experience has any effect on elementary reading performance. The most important lasting benefits of preschool are on other variables. Several studies have found lasting effects of preschool experience on retentions and placements in special education. Very long-term impacts of preschool on dropouts, delinquency, and other behaviors have also been found (Berrueta-Clement et al., 1984). It may be that the effects of preschool on outcomes for teenagers are due to the shorter-term effects on retentions and special education placements in the elementary grades. Retentions and special education placements in elementary school have been found to be strongly related to high school dropout (Lloyd, 1978).

Attendance at a high-quality preschool program can have long-term benefits for children, but it is equally clear that in itself preschool experience is not enough to prevent early school failure, particularly because preschool effects have not been evident on students' reading performance. Preschool experiences for 4-year-olds should be part of a comprehensive approach to prevention and early intervention, but a one-year program, whatever its quality, cannot be expected to solve all the problems of at-risk children. Prekindergarten programs implemented as part of comprehensive programs for children from birth to age 5 or in connection with changes in the early elementary grades are much more likely than one-year programs to have lasting achievement effects.

Kindergarten

Since the great majority of children now attend kindergarten or other structured programs for 5-year-olds, the main questions about kindergarten in recent years have focused on full-day versus half-day programs and on effects of particular instructional models for kindergarten. Research comparing full- and half-day programs, summarized in Chapter 4, generally found positive effects of full-day programs on end-of-year measures of reading readiness, language, and other objectives. However, the few studies that have examined full-day kindergarten effects have failed to find evidence of maintenance even at the end of first grade.

Several specific kindergarten models were found to be effective on end-of-kindergarten assessments. Among these were Alphaphonics, Astra's Magic Math, MECCA, TALK, and MARC. These are all structured, sequenced approaches to building prereading and language skills felt to be important predictors of success in first grade. However, of these, only Alphaphonics presented evidence of long-term effects on student reading performance. IBM's Writing to Read computer program had small positive effects on end-of-kindergarten measures, but longitudinal studies have failed to show any carryover to first- or second-grade reading.

Retention, Developmental Kindergarten, and Transitional First Grades

Many schools attempt in one form or another to identify young children who are at risk for school failure and give them an additional year before second grade to catch up with grade-level expectations. Students who perform poorly in kindergarten or first grade may simply be retained and recycled through the same grade. Alternatively, students who appear to be developmentally immature may be assigned to a two-year developmental kindergarten or junior kindergarten sequence before entering first grade. Many schools have a transitional first grade or "pre-first" program designed to provide a year between kindergarten and first grade for children who appear to be at risk.

Interpreting studies of retention and early extra-year programs is difficult. Among other problems, it is unclear whether the appropriate comparison group should be similar children of the *same age* who were promoted or similar children in the *same grade* as the one in which students were retained. That is, should a student who attended first grade twice be compared to second-graders (his or her original classmates) or first-graders (his or her new classmates)?

Studies that have compared students who experienced an extra year before second grade (reviewed in Chapter 5) have generally found that these students appear to gain on achievement tests in comparison to their same-grade classmates but not in comparison to their agemates. Further, any positive effects of extra-year programs seen in the year following the retention or program participation consistently wash out in later years. Clearly, the experience of spending another year in school before second grade has no long-term benefits. In contrast, studies of students who have been retained before third grade find that, controlling for their achievement, such students are far more likely than similar nonretained students to drop out of school (Lloyd, 1978).

Class Size and Instructional Aides

A popular policy in recent years has been to reduce class size markedly in the early elementary grades. Because it is so politically popular and straightforward (albeit expensive) to implement, class size reduction should in a sense be the standard against which all similarly expensive innovations should be judged.

Decades of research on class size have established that small reductions in class size (e.g., from 25 to 20) have few, if any, effects on student achievement. However, research has held out the possibility that larger reductions (e.g., from 25 to 15) may have educationally meaningful impacts. Chapter 6 evaluated this evidence.

The largest and best-controlled study ever done on this question was a recent statewide evaluation in Tennessee (Word et al., 1990) in which students were randomly assigned to classes of 15 with no aide, 25 with an aide, or 25 with no aide in kindergarten and then maintained in the same configurations through the third grade. This study found moderate effects (ES = +.25) in favor of the small classes as of the third grade. A year after the study, this difference had fallen to a mean of +.13 (Nye et al., 1991). Other statewide studies of class size reduction in the first grade in South Carolina (Johnson & Garcia-Quintana, 1978) and Indiana (Farr, Quilling, Bessel, & Johnson, 1987) found even smaller effects of substantial reductions in class size.

The Tennessee class size study also evaluated the effects of providing instructional aides to classes of 25 in grades K through 3. The effects of the aides were near zero in all years. This is consistent with the conclusions of an earlier review by Schuetz (1980). However, evidence reviewed in Chapter 6 did find that aides could be effective in providing one-to-one tutoring to at-risk first-graders.

Reducing class size may be a part of an overall strategy for getting students off to a good start in school, but it is clearly not an adequate intervention in itself.

Nongraded Primaries and Other School Organization Issues

Chapter 6 also discussed research on the nongraded primary, in which students are flexibly regrouped according to skill levels across grade lines and proceed through a hierarchy of skills at their own paces. This was an innovation of the 1950s and 1960s that is currently making a comeback in the 1990s.

Research from the first wave of implementation of the nongraded primary support the use of simple forms of this strategy but not complex ones. Simple forms are ones in which students are regrouped across grade lines for instruction (especially in reading and mathematics) and are taught in groups. In their very simplest versions, this strategy is essentially identical to the Joplin Plan, cross-grade grouping for reading only (see Slavin, 1987). These simple nongraded programs primarily have the effect of allowing teachers to accommodate instruction to individual needs without requiring students to do a great deal of seatwork (as is customary in traditional reading groups, for example). In contrast, complex forms of the nongraded primary that made extensive use of individualized instruction, learning stations, and open space were not generally effective in increasing student achievement (Gutiérrez & Slavin, 1992).

Chapter 6 also reviewed research on ability grouping in the early elementary grades. The evidence on this practice clearly fails to support ability grouped class assignment (e.g., high, middle, and low first-grade classes). Research on the use of reading groups within the class is too scant for any conclusions, but the positive effects of the Joplin Plan, which usually does not use within-class reading groups, suggests that reading grouping may not be an optimal solution to accommodating student heterogeneity in reading skill in the early grades.

One-to-One Tutoring

Of all the strategies reviewed in this book, the most effective by far for preventing early reading failure are approaches incorporating one-to-one tutoring of at-risk first-graders. Chapter 7 focuses on five specific tutoring models. One of these, the tutoring model used in Success for All is primarily discussed in Chapter 8. In addition to Success for All, Reading Recovery (Pinnell, 1989), and Prevention of Learning Disabilities (Silver & Hagin, 1990) are programs that use certified teachers as tutors; the Wallach Tutorial Program (Wallach & Wallach, 1976) and Programmed Tutorial Reading (Ellson, Barber, Engle, & Kempwerth, 1965) use paraprofessionals, and are correspondingly much more prescribed and scripted.

The immediate reading outcomes for all forms of tutoring are very positive, but the largest and longest-lasting effects have been found for the three programs that use teachers rather than aides as tutors. Reading Recovery is a highly structured model requiring a year of training and feedback. It emphasizes direct teaching of metacognitive strategies, "learning to read by reading," teaching of phonics in the context of students' reading, and integration of reading and writing. Two follow-up studies of this program have found that strong positive effects seen at the end of first grade do maintain into second and third grades, but due to increasing standard deviations in each successive grade, effect sizes diminish. Effects on reducing retentions were found in second grade in one study, but these effects had mostly washed out by third grade.

Prevention of Learning Disabilities focuses on remediating specific perceptual deficits as well as improving reading skill, and usually operates for two school years (Reading Recovery never goes beyond first grade). Reading effects of this program were substantial in two of three studies at the end of the program, and in one follow-up study remained very large as of the end of third grade. The tutoring component of Success for All resembles that of Reading Recovery in that it emphasizes "learning to read by reading" and teaching of metacognitive strategies, but it is different from both Reading Recovery and Prevention of Learning Disabilities in that it is closely coordinated with the regular classroom instruction in reading (see Chapter 8).

Success for All tutoring is given to at-risk students until they are performing adequately, and may therefore continue into second grade in some cases. However, most students who receive any tutoring remain in tutoring for one semester in first grade. The Success for All program includes many components in addition to tutoring, such as improvements in curriculum and instruction from preschool to grade 5 and a family support program, so the unique effects of tutoring cannot be separated out. However, reading effects for the lowest-achievement quarter of students (who receive the most tutoring services) have been substantial in several evaluations and have maintained through the third grade in every case. In addition, substantial reductions in retentions and special education placements have been found.

Success for All

Each of the strategies presented in Chapters 2 through 7 has focused on one slice of the at-risk child's life: birth to age 3, 4 (preschool), 5 (kindergarten), and 6 to 7 (first and second grades). While the birth to age 3 and preschool programs have often integrated services to children with services to parents, the programs for older youngsters have tended to focus only on academics and, in most cases, only one aspect of the academic program such as class size, length of day, grouping, or tutoring in reading.

How much could school failure be prevented if at-risk children were provided with a coordinated set of interventions over the years designed to prevent learning problems from developing in the first place and intervening intensively and effectively when they do occur? This is the question posed in research on Success for All, summarized in Chapter 8.

The idea behind Success for All is to provide children with whatever programs and resources they need to succeed throughout their elementary years. The emphasis is on prevention and early intervention. Prevention includes the provision of high-quality preschool and/or full-day kindergarten programs; research-based curriculum and instructional methods in all grades, preschool to grade 5; reduced class size and nongraded organization in reading; building positive relationships and involvement with parents; as well as other elements. Early intervention includes one-to-one tutoring in reading from certified teachers for students who are beginning to fall behind in first grade; family support programs to solve any problems of truancy, behavior, or emotional difficulties; and health or social service problems. In essence, Success for All combines the most effective interventions identified in the earlier chapters of this book and adds to them extensive staff development in curriculum and instruction and a school organizational plan flexibly using resources to ensure student success, to provide whatever it takes to see that students read, stay out of special education, and are promoted each year.

Research on Success for All (Slavin et al., 1992) has found substantial positive effects on the reading performance of all students in grades 1 through 3, and on reductions in retentions and special education placements. The lasting effects of Success for All into third grade are the largest of any of the strategies reviewed in this book, but they cannot be interpreted as maintenance assessments, as the program continues through the elementary grades. However, with few exceptions, the program beyond the first grade consists of improved curriculum and instruction, staff development, and family support services, not continued tutoring.

INTEGRATING SERVICES ACROSS THE YEARS

There is a consistent pattern seen across most of the programs and practices reviewed in this book. Whatever their nature, preventive programs tend to have their greatest impacts on variables closely aligned with the intervention and in the years immediately following the intervention period. The long-term research on effects of preschool on dropout and related variables is one exception to this, but on measures of IQ, reading, special education placements, and retention, preschool effects were like those of other time-limited interventions. The positive effects seen on these variables were strongest immediately after the program and then faded over time.

Some might take the observation that effects of early interventions often fade in later years as an indication that early intervention is ultimately futile. Yet such a conclusion would be too broad. What research on early intervention suggests is that there is no "magic bullet"—no program that, administered for one or two years, will ensure the success of at-risk children throughout their school careers and beyond. However, it is equally clear that there are key developmental hurdles that children must successfully negotiate in their first decade of life and that *it is known how to ensure that virtually all of them do so.*

The first hurdle, for children from birth to age 5, is development of the cognitive, linguistic, social, and psychological basis on which later success depends. Second, by the end of first grade, students should be well on the way to reading. Each year afterward, students need to make adequate progress in basic and advanced skills, at least enough to avoid any need for remedial or special education and to be promoted each year.

Research on programs for children from birth to age 3, on preschool, and on kindergarten shows that educators know how to deliver to first-grade children with good language skills, cognitive skills, and self-concepts, no matter what their family backgrounds or personal characteristics may be. Research on tutoring, instruction, curriculum, and organization of early grades education shows that educators know how to deliver to third-grade students who can read, regardless of their family and personal backgrounds. This book focused on early interventions, but it is important to note that there are many programs and practices with strong evidence of effectiveness for at-risk students throughout the grades (see Slavin, Karweit, & Madden, 1989). Rather than expecting short-term interventions to have long-term effects, at-risk children must be provided with the services they need at a particular age or developmental stage.

Does this mean that intensive (and therefore expensive) "preventive" services must be provided to at-risk students forever? For a very small proportion of students, a portion of those now served in special education, perhaps this is so. But for the great majority of students, including nearly all of those currently served in compensatory education programs and most of those now called "learning disabled," we believe that *intensive* intervention will only be needed for a brief period, primarily one-to-one tutoring in first grade. After these students are well launched in reading, they still need high-quality instruction and other services in the later elementary grades to continue to build on their strong base. Improving instruction by means of implementing research-based curriculum and instructional methods, top-quality professional development, and improved school organization is relatively inexpensive.

If a cook puts a high flame under a stew, brings it to a boil, and then turns it off, the stew will not cook. If the cook puts a stew on simmer without first bringing it to a boil, the stew will not cook. Only by bringing the stew to a boil and then simmering will the stew cook. By the same token, intensive early intervention for at-risk children with no follow-up in improved instruction is unlikely to produce lasting gains, and mild interventions over extended periods may also fail to bring low achievers into the educational mainstream. Yet intensive early intervention followed by long-term (inexpensive) improvements in instruction, curriculum, and other services can produce substantial and lasting gains.

The best evidence for this perspective comes from research on Success for All. This program usually begins with 4-year-olds, giving them high-quality preschool and kindergarten experiences. These are enough for many children, but for those who have serious reading problems, the program provides one-to-one tutoring, primarily in first grade. After that, improvements in curriculum and instruction, plus long-term family support services, are intended to maintain and build on the substantial gains students make in tutoring. The program's findings have shown the effectiveness of this approach; not only do at-risk students perform far better than matched control students at the end of first grade but their advantage continues to grow in second, third, and fourth grades. This is not to say that the particular elements implemented in Success for All are all optimal or essential. Other preschool or kindergarten models, reading models, or tutoring models could be more effective, and outcomes for the most at-risk children could probably be enhanced by intervening before age 4. What is important here is only one demonstration of the idea that linking prevention, early intervention, and continuing instructional improvement can prevent school failure for nearly all students.

How Many Students Can Succeed and at What Cost?

The research summarized in this book shows is that virtually every child can succeed in the early grades *in principle*. The number who will succeed in fact depends on the resources schools are willing to devote to ensuring success for all and to the willingness to reconfigure the resources already devoted to remedial and special education and related services.

We have evidence (particularly from the Success for All research) to suggest that it is possible to ensure the school success of the majority of disadvantaged, at-risk students using the local and Chapter 1 funds already allocated to these schools in different ways (primarily to improve curriculum, instruction, and classroom management in the regular classroom). However, to ensure the success of all at-risk students takes a greater investment. There is a large category of students who would fail to learn to read without intervention, but succeed with good preschool and kindergarten experiences, improved reading curriculum and instruction, perhaps brief tutoring at a critical juncture, eyeglasses, family support, or other relatively inexpensive assistance. A much smaller group of students might require extended tutoring, more intensive family services, and so on. A smaller group still would need intensive intervention before preschool as well as improved early childhood education, tutoring, and other services to succeed in school. One could imagine that any child who is not seriously retarded could succeed in school if he or she had some combination of the intensive services for children from birth to age 3 used in the Milwaukee Project, the high-quality preschool programs used in the Perry Preschool model, the tutoring provided by Reading Recovery or other models, and the improvements in curriculum, instruction, family support, and other services (along with tutoring) provided throughout the elementary grades by Success for All. Yet the cost for ensuring the success of these extremely at-risk children would, of course, be enormous.

Figure 9.1 illustrates the choice that policy makers must face. The costs of ensuring the success of at-risk children are assumed to increase

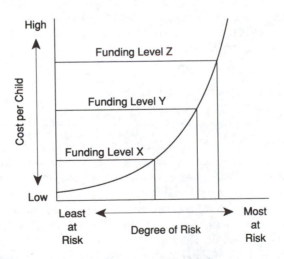

FIGURE 9.1 Theoretical Relationship Between Children's Degree of Risk and Costs of Ensuring School Success

exponentially as the degree of risk increases. By making wise use of limited funds (funding level X), one could probably ensure the success of most at-risk students. Ensuring success for each additional child beyond this costs an increasing amount per child. At a much higher cost (funding level Z), one could ensure the success of almost every child.

From a simplistic conception of cost effectiveness, one might conclude that funding level X (low funding for good programs) provides the greatest good to the greatest number at the lowest cost. Yet even in the most cold-hearted economic analysis, such a conclusion would be false. A multirisk child (such as a child from an impoverished and disorganized home with low IQ and poor behavior) will, without effective intervention, cost schools and society an enormous amount. Even in the mid-term, excess costs in special or remedial education over the elementary years are themselves staggering. This leaves aside the likely long-term costs of dropout, delinquency, early pregnancy, and so on (see Barnett & Escobar, 1977). The key issue for at-risk students is not *if* additional costs will be necessary but *when* they should be provided. By every standard of evidence, logic, and compassion, dollars used preventively make more sense than the same dollars used remedially.

Nothing in this discussion should be interpreted as suggesting that dollars can magically be turned into success. This book has noted many types of investments that have failed to make any marked impact on achievement. Money does not ensure success, but the programs that *do* ensure success cost money. The task of research on early intervention is to identify means of bringing about desired outcomes as effectively and efficiently as possible in order to present policy makers with realistic alternatives to current practice.

IMPLICATIONS OF SUCCESS FOR ALL FOR COMPENSATORY EDUCATION*

Once upon a time, there was a train company experiencing a high rate of accidents. The company appointed a commission to look into the matter, and the commission issued a report noting its major finding, which was that when accidents occurred, damage was primarily sustained to the last car in the train. As a result of this finding, the company established a policy requiring that before each train left the station, the last car was to be uncoupled! (Slavin, 1991).

All too often in its 25-year history, compensatory education has primarily pursued a "last car" strategy in providing for the needs of low-achieving students. The attention and resources of Chapter 1 and its

---

*Portions of this section are adapted from Slavin, 1991. © 1991, Phi Delta Kappan, Inc.

predecessor, Title I, have mostly gone into identifying and remediating the damage sustained by individual children. Yet the fault lies not in the children but in the system that failed to prevent the damage in the first place, just as the damage to the last car was due to the train system and had nothing to do with the last car in itself.

There are new winds of change in discussions of Chapter 1. The 1988 Hawkins-Stafford bill reauthorizing Chapter 1 introduced new flexibility in use of Chapter 1 funds and shifted the focus of Chapter 1 monitoring toward an insistence on outcomes for children. The bill also made it easier for schools serving highly impoverished populations to use their funds for all children, not just identified low achievers. Further, significant increases in Chapter 1 funding create new opportunities. Its 1992–93 annual budget of $6.7 billion represents an increase of $2.4 billion (56 percent) over its 1987–88 level. The popularity of Chapter 1 is at an all-time high; its 1988 reauthorization passed both houses of Congress nearly unanimously. However, all of these changes create only the possibility of significant reform. They do not guarantee that reform will actually take place, much less that students will actually benefit.

In their first 25 years, Chapter 1 and Title 1 have made an important contribution to the education of low-achieving disadvantaged students. The Sustaining Effects Study of the 1970s found that Chapter 1 students learned more than other "needy" children, but did not close their substantial gap with "non-needy" students (Carter, 1984). Perhaps the best indication of the contribution made by Chapter 1 is indirect; the slow but steady reduction in the achievement gap between African-American and Hispanic students and white students is often attributed to an effect of Chapter 1/Title I (e.g., Carroll, 1987). Yet it is always possible to make a good program better.

Chapter 1 can be much more than it is today. It can be an engine of change in the education of disadvantaged children. It can ensure the basic skills of virtually all children; in essence, it can help this nation's schools put a floor under the achievement expectations for all nonretarded children so that all children will have the basic skills necessary to profit from regular classroom instruction. It can help schools toward teaching of a full and appropriate curriculum for all students, but particularly for those who by virtue of being "at risk" too often receive a narrow curriculum emphasizing isolated skills. It can make the education of disadvantaged and at-risk students a top priority for all schools.

Preventing Early Reading Failure

Perhaps the most important objective of compensatory education must be to ensure that children are successful in reading the first time they are taught, and never become remedial readers. The importance of reading success in the early grades is apparent to anyone who works with at-risk students. As has been noted at many points in this book, the consequences of failing to learn to read in the early grades are severe. For example, disadvantaged students who have failed a grade and are reading below grade level are extremely unlikely to graduate from high school. Chapter 1 itself has few effects beyond the third grade (Kennedy, Birman, & Demaline, 1986), which suggests the difficulties inherent in intervening too late. Retentions and special education referrals are usually based on early reading deficits.

Almost all children, regardless of social class or other factors, enter first grade full of enthusiasm, motivation, and self-confidence, fully expecting to succeed in school (see, for example, Entwistle & Hayduk, 1981). By the end of first grade, many of these students have already discovered that their initial high expectations were not justified, and have begun to see school as punishing and demeaning. Trying to remediate reading failure later on is very difficult, because by then students who have failed are likely to be unmotivated, to have poor self-concepts as learners, to be anxious about reading, and to hate it. Reform is needed at all levels of education, but no goal of reform is as important as seeing that all children start off their school careers with success, confidence, and a firm foundation in reading.

The evidence presented in this book indicates that reading failure in the early grades is fundamentally preventable. The outcomes summarized in Chapters 7 and 8 show that well-structured programs incorporating one-to-one tutoring can greatly reduce reading failures. The findings of the Success for All studies in particular show that a coordinated combination of preschool, kindergarten, early reading and family support approaches can virtually eliminate reading failure even among the most disadvantaged and at-risk students. This and other evidence suggest that reading failure is preventable for nearly all children, even a substantial portion of those who are typically categorized as learning disabled.

If reading failure *can* be prevented, it *must* be prevented. Chapter 1 is the logical program to take the lead in giving schools serving disadvantaged students the resources and programs necessary to see that all children learn to read.

Enhancing Prevention and Regular Classroom Instruction

One of the most fundamental principles of Chapter 1/Title I has been that compensatory funds must be focused on the lowest-achieving students in qualifying schools. In principle, this makes sense, in that it avoids spreading Chapter 1 resources too thinly to do low achievers any good. But in practice, this requirement has led to many problems, including a lack of consistency or coordination between regular and Chapter 1 instruction, disruption of children's regular classroom instruction, labeling of students who receive services, and unclear responsibility for children's progress (Allington & Johnston, 1989; Stein, Leinhardt & Bickel, 1989).

It is time to recognize that the best way to prevent students from falling behind is to provide them with preventive services in preschool and kindergarten and top-quality instruction in their regular classrooms. A substantial portion of Chapter 1 funds (say, 20 percent) should be set aside for staff development and adoption of programs known to be effective by teachers in Chapter 1 schools. For example, by hiring one less aide, schools could instead devote up to $20,000 per year to staff development—a huge investment in terms of what schools typically spend but a small one in terms of what Chapter 1 schools receive. No one could argue that the educational impact of one aide could approach that of faithful and intelligent implementation of effective curricula and instructional practices in regular classrooms throughout the school; research on the achievement effects of instructional aides found that they make little or no measurable difference in achievement (see Chapter 6).

For this amount of money, a school could pay for extensive in-service, in-class follow-up by trained "circuit riders" and release time for teachers to observe each other's classes and to meet to compare notes, as well as purchase needed materials and books. The achievement benefits of effective classroom instruction all day would far outweigh the potential benefits of remedial service.

Success for All provides one demonstration of how a schoolwide emphasis on staff development and adoption of effective practices could be implemented under Chapter 1 funding and could greatly affect the learning of all students. Even schools with no extra resources were able to make a substantial difference in student reading achievement (see Chapter 8) by using research-based approaches in a comprehensive schoolwide plan. Chapter 1 must help create a situation in which eligible schools are able to select from among a set of programs known to be effective and are then able to use Chapter 1 funds to obtain the in-service, follow-up, and materials needed to ensure top-quality implementation of whatever methods the schools have chosen.

To bring about a situation in which schools can choose from among effective programs, several initiatives are needed. Chapter 1 should be funding development and evaluation of promising practices, including second-party evaluations of programs that already exist. It should also be funding research on processes of disseminating effective practices to individual schools. It should be helping establish training centers around the country able to help schools implement effective practices. It should be examining its funding and accountability requirements to see that they support, rather than inhibit, schools from using Chapter 1 funds to improve their overall instructional practices.

Chapter 1 should not only be a staff development program—there is still a need for service targeted to individual children (for example, to provide tutoring to first-graders having difficulty in reading) and for funding of preschool and full-day kindergarten programs for poor children. However, without a major investment in staff development, Chapter 1 services will always be shoveling against the tide, trying to patch up individual children's deficits without being able to affect the setting in which Chapter 1 students spend the great majority of their day—the regular classroom. Under current regulations, schools can use a small portion of their Chapter 1 dollars for staff development, but this rarely goes into the kind of training, follow-up, and assessment needed to effectively implement validated programs. One-day workshops with no follow-up are far more typical.

The obvious objection to devoting substantial resources to prevention and staff development is that students not eligible for Chapter 1 would benefit from Chapter 1 dollars at least as much as those who are eligible. This objection can be answered in three ways. First, Chapter 1 accountability procedures should continue to focus entirely on the achievement of Chapter 1-eligible students, so schools implementing programs for all students have to make certain that they are making a difference with low achievers (see Slavin & Madden, 1991). Second, to withhold effective and cost-effective programs from eligible students because noneligible students might benefit is perverse; it is like withholding funds intended for water treatment to instead serve individual children with typhoid (recall the parable that opens this chapter). Third, research finds that regardless of their own personal characteristics, poor students in schools with large numbers of poor children achieve less well than equally poor students in less disadvantaged schools (Kennedy, Jung, & Orland, 1986). There is a case to be made that students in schools serving disadvantaged students deserve assistance even if they are not low achievers themselves. Educators should be particularly concerned about poor and minority students who may be doing well enough to avoid Chapter 1 identification but are still not achieving their full potential. Such children may not need direct service, but there is certainly a strong rationale for federal assistance to improve the quality of their regular classroom instruction.

Chapter 1 is extremely important to the most vulnerable children. For more than 25 years it has focused attention and resources on low-achieving students in disadvantaged schools. Yet Chapter 1 can be much more than it is today. It can become proactive in preventing learning problems rather than only reactive in remediating problems that are already serious. It can ensure literacy for every child; it can become a major force in bringing effective programs into schools serving disadvantaged students; and it can reward schools for doing a good job with at-risk students.

IMPLICATIONS FOR SPECIAL EDUCATION POLICY*

For more than 20 years, the most important debates in special education research and policy have revolved around the practice of mainstreaming, particularly mainstreaming students who have mild academic handicaps, such as those identified as learning disabled. From early on, most researchers and policy makers have favored mainstreaming students who are academically disabled to the maximum extent possible (e.g., Leinhardt & Pallay, 1982; Madden & Slavin, 1983), and the passage of PL 94-142 in 1975 put the federal government squarely behind this effort. Since that time, students with academic disabilities have certainly spent more time in general education classes than they did before, but the number of students identified for special education services has risen dramatically. Since 1975, the proportion of students categorized as learning disabled has risen more than 250 percent, whereas the category of educable mental retardation has diminished only slightly (Office of Special Education and Rehabilitative Services, 1989).

Despite the increase in mainstreaming, significant proportions of both special and general education teachers have never been comfortable with the practice. At the school level, holding mainstreaming in place is often like holding together two positively charged magnets; it can be done, but only if external pressure is consistently applied. General education teachers are quite naturally concerned about the difficulty of teaching extremely heterogeneous classes, and special education teachers, seeing themselves as better trained to work with academically disabled students and more concerned about them, are often reluctant to send their students into what they may perceive as an inappropriate environment.

Solutions to the problems of mainstreaming children with academic disabilities have generally been built around attempts to improve the capacity of the general classroom teacher to accommodate the needs of a heterogeneous classroom. For example, forms of individualized instruction (e.g., Slavin, 1984; Wang & Birch, 1984), cooperative and peer-mediated instruction (e.g., Jenkins, Jewell, Leceister, Jenkins, & Troutner, 1990;

*This section is adapted from "Neverstreaming: Prevention and Early Intervention as an Alternative to Special Education" by R. Slavin, N. Madden, N. Karweit, L. Dolan, B. Wasik, A. Shaw, K. Mainzer, & B. Haxby, 1991, *Journal of Learning Disabilities*, 24, pp. 373–378. Copyright 1991 by PRO-ED, Inc. By permission.

Slavin, Stevens, & Madden, 1988), and teacher consultation models (e.g., Idol-Maestas, 1981) are based on the idea that to fully integrate students with academic disabilities, teachers need new programs and skills.

Improving the capacity of the general education classroom to meet diverse needs is an essential part of a comprehensive strategy to serve academically handicapped students, but it is not enough. The problem is that once a child is academically disabled (or significantly behind his or her peers for any reason), neither mainstreaming nor special or remedial education are likely to bring the child up to age-appropriate achievement norms. From a school organization perspective, the low achievement of the academically disabled child puts a strain on the school (and the child himself or herself) that is likely to last throughout the child's school career. Mainstreaming may be the best alternative for most children who have academic disabilities, but if so, it is only the least unappealing of many unappealing options.

A far better approach is to intervene early in children's school careers to ensure that they never fall behind in the first place. An approach emphasizing prevention and early, intensive, and untiring intervention to bring student performance within normal limits might be called "neverstreaming" because its intention is to see that nearly all children remain in the mainstream by intervening to prevent the academic difficulties that would lead them to be identified for separate special education services (Slavin et al., 1991).

Success One Year at a Time

One key concept underlying neverstreaming is that instructional programs must help students start with success and then maintain that success at each critical stage of development. First, all students should arrive in kindergarten with adequate mental and physical development. This requires investments in prenatal and infant and toddler health care, parent training, early stimulation programs for at-risk toddlers, effective preschool programs, and so on. The next critical juncture is assurance that all students leave first grade well on their way to success in reading and other critical skills. This requires effective kindergarten and first-grade instruction and curriculum, family support programs to ensure parental support of the school's goals, and one-to-one tutoring or other intensive interventions for students who are having difficulties in reading. As students move into second and third grades and beyond, this would mean continuing to improve regular classroom instruction, to monitor student progress, and to intervene intensively as often as necessary to maintain at-risk students at a performance level at which they can fully profit from the same instruction given to students who were never at risk.

The idea of neverstreaming is to organize school and nonschool resources and programs to relentlessly and systematically prevent students from becoming academically handicapped from their first day of school (or earlier) to their last (or later). Rather than just trying to adapt instruction to student heterogeneity, neverstreaming attacks the original problem at its source, attempting to remove the low end of the performance distribution by preventing whatever deficits can be prevented, intensively intervening to identify and remediate any remaining deficits, and maintaining interventions to keep at-risk students from sliding back as they proceed through the grades.

Is Neverstreaming Feasible?

For neverstreaming to be a viable concept, one must have confidence that prevention and early intervention can in fact bring the great majority of at-risk students to an acceptable level of academic performance and prevent unnecessary special education referrals. The research summarized in this book on programs for students at risk of academic difficulties have shown the potential of prevention and early intervention to keep students in the early grades from starting the process of falling behind that often ultimately results in assignment to special education. In particular, there is a growing body of evidence to suggest that reading failure is fundamentally preventable for a very large proportion of at-risk students. Reading failure is a key element of the profile of most students identified as learning disabled (Norman & Zigmond, 1980).

In particular, the findings of the Milwaukee Project (Chapter 2) and of high-quality preschool programs (Chapter 3), of tutoring programs (Chapter 7), and of Success for All (Chapter 8) illustrate the potential of prevention and early intervention to keep students from falling far behind their agemates, to keep them from failing, and to keep them from being assigned to special education for learning disabilities. Most of the schools in which these preventive strategies were evaluated serve very disadvantaged student populations; many experience problems with truancy, inadequate health care, parental poverty, drug involvement, and other problems that are unusual even among urban schools. Yet in these schools, students are performing at or near national norms, and even the lowest achievers are well on their way to reading, are being promoted, and are staying out of special education. More typical schools without many of these challenges should be able to ensure that virtually all nonretarded students are successful in reading as well as in other basic skills and can therefore stay out of separate special education programs.

How Many Students Can Be Neverstreamed?

It is too early to say precisely what proportion of the students now identified as having academic handicaps can be neverstreamed, which is to say prevented from ever having learning deficits serious enough to warrant special education. It may be that as educators' knowledge and experience grow, it will become possible to avoid separate special education for the great majority of students currently categorized as learning disabled, (about 4.8 percent of all students ages 3 to 21; Office of Special Education and Rehabilitative Services, 1989) plus some proportion of those identified as mildly mentally retarded and behaviorally handicapped. For example, more than 80 percent of at-risk students in Reading Recovery are successfully discontinued and then continue reading adequately through the upper elementary grades (see Chapter 7). Looking at data from three to four years of implementation of Success for All, it is clear that even the very lowest achieving third-graders are reading at a level that would allow them to participate successfully in regular classroom instruction. Less than 4 percent of Success for All third-graders scored two years below grade level, one-third the proportion in the control schools. Although 16 percent of Success for All students were at least a year below level, 38 percent of control students scored this poorly. With continuing improvements in curriculum and instruction through the fifth grade, these third-graders should all complete their elementary years with an adequate basis in reading, and this should greatly increase their chances of success in the secondary grades. There is no reason to believe that similar strategies in mathematics, spelling, writing, and other subjects would not have similar impacts, particularly to the degree that success in these areas depends on reading skills.

The number of students who can be neverstreamed is not only dependent on the effectiveness of prevention and early intervention but also on the degree to which general education can become better able to accommodate student differences. For example, use of cooperative learning, individualized instruction, and other strategies can also increase the ability of classroom teachers to meet individual needs (see Slavin, Stevens, & Madden, 1988). In one sense, the idea of neverstreaming is to work from two sides at the same time—making the classroom better able to accommodate individual differences and reducing the severity of deficits in the first place to make accommodation of differences much easier.

The Role of Special Education in a Neverstreamed World

Obviously, there will always be students who will continue to need top-quality special education services, such as those who are retarded or severely emotionally disturbed, as well as those with physical, speech, or language deficits and those with severe learning disabilities. In a neverstreamed school, traditionally configured special education services would still be provided to these students, with an emphasis on prevention and early intervention and on providing services in the least restrictive environment. One effect of neverstreaming should be to allow special education to return to its focus on more severely impaired students—those truly in need of *special* services as distinct from enhancements to general education. Special education also has a key role to play in providing consultation to classroom teachers on such issues as adapting instruction to accommodate diverse needs and learning styles, improving classroom management, and assessing students. For example, even students who are reading well may have learning and behavior problems that classroom teachers may need help to accommodate. Special education consultants might include among their responsibilities working with individual children for brief periods to learn how to succeed with them and then returning them to their teachers and tutors.

If neverstreaming were to become institutionalized on a broad scale, it would create a need for a new category of teachers—professional tutors. Effective tutoring is not simply a matter of putting one teacher with one student; there are several studies of tutoring that have found unsystematic forms of tutoring to have few effects on learning (see Chapter 7). The education and supervision of tutors might take place under the auspices of special education, particularly as states and districts are moving toward funding formulas that allow special education personnel and funds to be used for prevention as well as for services to students who already have individualized educational plans.

Unresolved Issues

Clearly, there is much one needs to know to maximize the degree to which students at risk can be successfully neverstreamed. Educators need to experiment with alternative models of early prevention, early childhood education, beginning instruction in reading and other basic skills, tutoring, family support, in-service, and school change to find ever more effective strategies in each of these areas and to find optimal mixes of elements. One particular question of great importance is whether tutoring in reading and other basic skills is enough to keep all nonretarded students from falling behind, or whether instruction specific to neurological deficits needs to be provided for some students, either preventively or in the later grades.

At the policy level, many other issues must be resolved. First, a consensus must be reached that investments in early education will pay off in the long run. Second, a willingness to devote funds to prevention must be instilled. This implies that there must be a willingness at the policy level to increase funds for early education for some period of time, because it would be irresponsible to strip funds away from remedial services for students already in the system to concentrate them on prevention and early intervention for younger students. In addition, regulatory changes allowing more flexible uses of special education, Chapter 1, and other categorical funds are necessary. The Success for All program has substantially benefited from the new flexibility in Chapter 1 regulations introduced in the 1988 Hawkins-Stafford bill, but this flexibility is mostly limited to schools serving very disadvantaged populations.

At the moment, neverstreaming should be seen as a goal rather than a well-developed policy. However, if this goal is to be realized, educators need to focus their energies on research, development, evaluation, and demonstration to move toward a day when students with learning disabilities and other students at risk of academic handicaps can confidently expect what neither mainstreaming nor special education can guarantee them today—not only services but success.

CONCLUSION

Early school failure can be prevented for nearly every child. The knowledge that this is a practical and attainable reality must have consequences for this country's policies toward at-risk students. If educators know how to prevent school failure and do not take advantage of this knowledge, then the blame lies with the educators, not the children who fail or their parents or their communities. If we, as a society, decide to make school failure a thing of the past, we can do so. The choice is there to be made.

After deciding that the problem of early school failure must be solved, however, then society must implement strategies that are both effective and cost effective. The purpose of this book is to describe the current state of the art and to compare alternative approaches in terms of their likely impacts on children. Like all scientific conclusions, the ones presented here are tentative; future evidence may make some of them obsolete. Yet it would be irresponsible to wait to act until all the evidence is in. More than enough is now known to make informed decisions about building programs to help all children become successful students.

REFERENCES

Allington, R. L., & Johnston, P. (1989). Coordination, collaboration, and consistency: The redesign of compensatory and special education interventions. In R. E. Slavin, N. L. Karweit, & N. A. Madden (Eds.), *Effective programs for students at risk.* Boston: Allyn and Bacon.

Barnett, W. S., & Escobar, C. M. (1977). The economics of early educational intervention: A review. *Review of Educational Research, 57,* 387–414.

Berrueta-Clement, J. R., Schweinhart, L. J., Barnett, W. S., Epstein, A. S., & Weikart, D. P. (1984). *Changed lives.* Ypsilanti, MI: High/Scope.

Carroll, J. B. (1987). The national assessments in reading: Are we misreading the findings? *Phi Delta Kappan, 68,* 424–428.

Carter, L. F. (1984). The sustaining effects study of compensatory and elementary education. *Educational Researcher, 13* (7), 4–13.

Ellson, D. G., Barber, L., Engle, T. L., & Kempwerth, L. (1965). Programmed tutoring: A teaching aid and a research tool. *Reading Research Quarterly, 1,* 77–127.

Entwisle, D., & Hayduk, L. (1981). Academic expectations and the school achievement of young children. *Sociology of Education, 54,* 34–50.

Farr, B., Quilling, M., Bessel, R., & Johnson, W. (1987). *Evaluation of PRIME TIME: 1986–1987. Final report.* Indianapolis: Advanced Technology.

Garber, H. L. (1988). *The Milwaukee Project: Preventing mental retardation in children at risk.* Washington, DC.: American Association on Mental Retardation.

Gutiérrez, R., & Slavin, R. E. (1992). Achievement effects of the nongraded elementary school: A best-evidence synthesis. *Review of Educational Research, 62,* 333–376.

Idol-Maestas, L. (1981). A teacher training model: The resource/consulting teacher. *Behavioral Disorders, 6,* 108–121.

Jenkins, J. R., Jewell, M., Leceister, N., Jenkins, L., & Troutner, N. (1990). *Development of a school building model for educating handicapped and at risk students in general education classes.* Paper presented at the annual convention of the American Educational Research Association, Boston, April.

Johnson, L. M., & Garcia-Quintana, R. A. (1978). *South Carolina first grade pilot project 1976–77: The effects of class size on reading and mathematics achievement.* Columbia, SC: South Carolina Department of Education.

Kennedy, M. M., Birman, B. E., & Demaline, R. E. (1986). *The effectiveness of Chapter 1 services.* Washington, DC: Office of Education Research and Improvement, U.S. Department of Education.

Kennedy, M. M., Jung, R. K., & Orland, M. E. (1986). *Poverty, achievement, and the distribution of compensatory education services.* Washington, DC: Office of Educational Research and Improvement, U.S. Department of Education.

Leinhardt, G., & Pallay, A. (1982). Restrictive educational settings: Exile or haven? *Review of Educational Research, 52,* 557–578.

Lloyd, D. N. (1978). Prediction of school failure from third-grade data. *Educational and Psychological Measurement, 38,* 1193–1200.

Madden, N. A., & Slavin, R. E. (1983). Mainstreaming students with mild academic handicaps: Academic and social outcomes. *Review of Educational Research, 53,* 519–569.

Norman, C., & Zigmond, N. (1980). Characteristics of children labeled and served as learning disabled in school systems affiliated with Child Service and Demonstration centers. *Journal of Learning Disabilities, 13,* 542–547.

Nye, B. A., Zaharias, J. B., Fulton, B. D., Achilles, C. M., & Hooper, R. (1991). *The lasting benefits study: A continuing analysis of the effect of small class size in kindergarten through third grade on student achievement test scores in subsequent grade levels.* Nashville, TN: Tennessee State University.

Office of Special Education and Rehabilitative Services. (1989). *Annual report to congress on the implementation of the Handicapped Act.* Washington, DC: U.S. Department of Education.

Pinnell, G. S. (1989). Reading Recovery: Helping at-risk children learn to read. *Elementary School Journal, 90,* 161–182.

Ramey, C. T., & Campbell, F. A. (1984). Preventive education for high-risk children: Cognitive consequences of the Carolina Abecedarian Project. *American Journal of Mental Deficiency, 88,* 515–523.

Schuetz, P. (1980). *The instructional effectiveness of classroom aides.* Pittsburgh, PA: University of Pittsburgh, Learning Research and Development Center.

Silver, A. A., & Hagin, R. A. (1990). *Disorders of learning in childhood.* New York: Wiley.

Slavin, R. E. (1984). Team assisted individualization: Cooperative learning and individualized instruction in the mainstreamed classroom. *Remedial and Special Education, 5* (6), 33–42.

Slavin, R. E. (1987). Ability grouping and student achievement in elementary schools: A best-evidence synthesis. *Review of Educational Research, 57,* 293–336.

Slavin, R. E. (1991). Chapter 1: A vision for the next quarter-century. *Phi Delta Kappan, 72* (8), 586–592.

Slavin, R. E. (1994). School and classroom organization in beginning reading: Class size, aides, and instructional grouping. In R. E. Slavin, N. L. Karweit, B. A. Wasik, & N. A. Madden (Eds.), *Preventing early reading failure: Research on effective strategies.* Boston: Allyn and Bacon.

Slavin, R. E., Karweit, N. L., & Madden, N. A. (Eds.) (1989). *Effective programs for students at risk.* Boston: Allyn and Bacon.

Slavin, R. E., & Madden, N. A. (1991). Modifying Chapter 1 program improvement guidelines to reward appropriate practices. *Educational Evaluation and Policy Analysis, 13,* 369–379.

Slavin, R. E., Madden, N. A., Karweit, N. L., Dolan, L. J., & Wasik, B. A. (1991). Success for All: Ending reading failure from the beginning. *Language Arts, 68,* 47–52.

Slavin, R. E., Madden, N. A., Karweit, N. L., Dolan, L., & Wasik, B. A. (1992). *Success for All: A relentless approach to prevention and early intervention in elementary schools.* Arlington, VA: Educational Research Service.

Slavin, R. E., Madden, N. A., Karweit, N. L., Dolan, L., Wasik, B. A., Shaw, A., Mainzer, K. L., & Haxby, B. (1991). Neverstreaming: Prevention and early intervention as alternatives to special education. *Journal of Learning Disabilities, 24*, 373–378.

Slavin, R. E., Stevens, R. J., & Madden, N. A. (1988). Accommodating student diversity in reading and writing instruction: A cooperative learning approach. *Remedial and Special Education, 9*, 60–66.

Stein, M. K., Leinhardt, G., & Bickel, W. (1989). Instructional issues for teaching students at risk. In R. E. Slavin, N. L. Karweit, & N. A. Madden (Eds.), *Effective programs for students at risk.* Boston: Allyn and Bacon.

Wallach, M. A., & Wallach, L. (1976). *Teaching all children to read.* Chicago: University of Chicago Press.

Wang, M. C., & Birch, J. W. (1984). Comparison of a full-time mainstreaming program and a resource room approach. *Exceptional Children, 51*, 33–40.

Word, E., Johnston, J., Bain, H. P., Fulton, B. D., Zaharias, J. B., Lintz, M. N., Achilles, C. M., Folger, J., & Breda, C. (1990). *Student/Teacher Achievement Ratio (STaR): Tennessee's K–3 class size study, final report.* Nashville: Tennessee State Department of Education.

Index

Date Due

APR 2 8 2000			
JUN 2 2 2000			
NOV 2 6 '00			
MAR 1 3 2001			
AUG 2 7 2002			

PRINTED IN U.S.A.   CAT. NO. 24 161   BRO DART